JUMP AT HOME
GRADE
3

NEW EDITION

ALSO BY JOHN MIGHTON

The Myth of Ability

The End of Ignorance

JUMP MATH SERIES

JUMP at Home Grade 1

JUMP at Home Grade 2

JUMP at Home Grade 3

JUMP at Home Grade 4

JUMP at Home Grade 5

JUMP at Home Grade 6

JUMP at Home Grade 7

JUMP at Home Grade 8

JUMP AT HOME

GRADE 3

NEW EDITION

Worksheets for the JUMP Math Program

JOHN MIGHTON

ANANSI

First published in 2004 by House of Anansi Press Inc.

Revised edition published in 2010 by
House of Anansi Press Inc.
110 Spadina Avenue, Suite 801
Toronto, ON, M5V 2K4
Tel. 416-363-4343
Fax 416-363-1017
www.houseofanansi.com

Distributed in Canada by   Distributed in the United States by
HarperCollins Canada Ltd.   Publishers Group West
1995 Markham Road   1700 Fourth Street
Scarborough, ON, M1B 5M8   Berkeley, CA 94710
Toll free tel. 1-800-387-0117   Toll free tel. 1-800-788-3123

House of Anansi Press is committed to protecting our natural environment. As part of our efforts, this book is printed on Ancient Forest Friendly paper that contains 100% recycled fibres (40% post-consumer waste and 60% pre-consumer waste) and is processed chlorine-free.

Some of the material in this book has previously been published by JUMP Math.

Every reasonable effort has been made to contact the holders of copyright for materials reproduced in this work. The publishers will gladly receive information that will enable them to rectify any inadvertent errors or omissions in subsequent editions.

16 15 14 13 12   2 3 4 5 6

Library and Archives Canada Cataloguing in Publication

Cataloguing data available from Library and Archives Canada

Library of Congress Control Number: 2010924086

Acknowledgements

Authors – Dr. John Mighton (Ph.D. Mathematics, Ashoka Fellow, Fellow of the Fields Institute for Research in Mathematical Sciences), Dr. Sindi Sabourin (Ph.D. Mathematics, BEd), and Dr. Anna Klebanov (Ph.D. Mathematics)
Consultant – Jennifer Wyatt (M.A. Candidate, B.Ed.)
Contributors – Betony Main, Lisa Hines, and Sheila Mooney
Layout – Katie Baldwin, Rita Camacho, Tony Chen, Lyubava Fartushenko, and Pam Lostracco

This book, like the JUMP program itself, is made possible by the efforts of the volunteers and staff of JUMP Math.

Canada Council   Conseil des Arts   **ONTARIO ARTS COUNCIL**
for the Arts   du Canada   **CONSEIL DES ARTS DE L'ONTARIO**

We acknowledge for their financial support of our publishing program the Canada Council for the Arts, the Ontario Arts Council, and the Government of Canada through the Canada Book Fund.

Printed and bound in Canada

Contents

Unit 3: Measurement 1

Unit 4: Logic and Systematic Search 1

Unit 5: Patterns & Algebra 2

Unit 6: Number Sense 2

Introduction: About JUMP Math

There is a prevalent myth in our society that people are born with mathematical talent, and others simply do not have the ability to succeed. Recent discoveries in cognitive science are challenging this myth of ability. The brain is not hard-wired, but continues to change and develop throughout life. Steady, incremental learning can result in the emergence of new abilities.

The carefully designed mathematics in the JUMP Math program provide the necessary skills and knowledge to give your child the joy of success in mathematics. Through step-by-step learning, students celebrate success with every question, thereby increasing achievement and reducing math anxiety.

John Mighton: Founder of JUMP Math

"Nine years ago I was looking for a way to give something back to my local community. It occurred to me that I should try to help kids who needed help with math. Mathematicians don't always make the best teachers because mathematics has become obvious to them; they can have trouble seeing why their students are having trouble. But because I had struggled with math myself, I wasn't inclined to blame my students if they couldn't move forward."
— John Mighton, *The End of Ignorance*

JUMP Math, a national charity dedicated to improving mathematical literacy, was founded by John Mighton, a mathematician, bestselling author, and award-winning playwright. The organization grew out of John's work with a core group of volunteers in a "tutoring club"; their goal was to meet the needs of the most challenged students from local schools. Over the next three years John developed the early material — simple handouts for the tutors to use during their one-on-one teaching sessions with individual students. This period was one of experimentation in developing the JUMP Math method. Eventually, John began to work in local inner-city schools, by placing tutors in the classrooms. This led to the next period of innovation: using the JUMP Math method on small groups of students.

Teachers responded enthusiastically to the success they saw in their students and wanted to adapt the method for classroom use. In response, the needs of the teachers for curriculum-based resources were met by the development of workbooks. These started out as a series of three remedial books with limited accompanying teacher materials, released in fall 2003. The effectiveness of these workbooks led quickly to the development of grade-specific, curriculum-based workbooks. The grade-specific books were first released in 2004. Around that time, the power of teacher networks in creating learning communities was beginning to take shape.

Inspired by the work he has done with thousands of students over the past twenty years, John has systematically developed an approach to teaching mathematics that is based on fostering brain plasticity and emergent intelligence, and on the idea that children have more potential in mathematics than is generally believed. Linking new research in cognitive science to his extensive observations of students, John calls for a re-examination of the assumptions that underlie current methods of teaching mathematics.

JUMP Math, as a program and as an organization, developed in response to the needs of the students, teachers, schools, and communities where John and the volunteers were working. Recognizing the potential of all students to succeed in mathematics, and to succeed in school, was the motivation that John needed to dedicate more than ten years of his life developing a mathematics program that achieved his vision.

JUMP Math: An Innovative Approach

In only ten years, JUMP Math has gone from John's kitchen table to a thriving organization reaching more than 50,000 students with high-quality learning resources and training for 2,000 teachers. It continues to work with community organizations to reach struggling students through homework clubs and after-school programs. Through the generous support of our sponsors, JUMP Math donates resources to classrooms and homework clubs across Canada. The organization has also inspired thousands of community volunteers and teachers to donate their time as tutors, mentors, and trainers.

JUMP Math is unique; it builds on the belief that every child can be successful at mathematics by

- Promoting positive learning environments and building confidence through praise and encouragement;
- Maintaining a balanced approach to mathematics by concurrently addressing conceptual and procedural learning;
- Achieving understanding and mastery by breaking mathematics down into small sequential steps;
- Keeping all students engaged and attentive by "raising the bar" incrementally; and,
- Guiding students strategically to explore and discover the beauty of mathematics.

JUMP Math recognizes the importance of reducing math anxiety. Research in psychology has shown that our brains are extremely fallible: our working memories are poor, we are easily overwhelmed by too much new information, and we require a good deal of practice to consolidate skills and concepts. These mental challenges are compounded when we are anxious. The JUMP approach has been shown to reduce math anxiety significantly.

JUMP Math scaffolds mathematical concepts rigorously and completely. The materials were designed by a team of mathematicians and educators who have a deep understanding of and a love for mathematics. Concepts are introduced in rigorous steps, and prerequisite skills are included in the lesson. Breaking down concepts and skills into steps is often necessary even with the more able students. Math is a subject in which a gifted student can become a struggling student almost overnight, because mathematical knowledge is cumulative.

Consistent with emerging brain research, JUMP Math provides materials and methods that minimize differences between students, allowing teachers, tutors, and parents to more effectively improve student performance in mathematics. Today, parents have access to this unique innovation in mathematics learning with the revised JUMP at Home books.

JUMP Math at Home

JUMP at Home has been developed by mathematicians and educators to complement the mathematics curriculum that your child learns at school. Each grade covers core skills and knowledge to help your child succeed in mathematics. The program focuses on building number sense, pattern recognition, and foundations for algebra.

JUMP at Home is designed to boost every student's confidence, skills, and knowledge. Struggling students will benefit from practice in small steps, while good students will be provided with new ways to understand concepts that will help them enjoy mathematics even more and to exceed their own expectations.

JUMP Math in Schools

JUMP Math also publishes full curriculum-based resources — including student workbooks, teacher guides with daily lesson plans, and blackline masters — that cover all of the Ontario and the Western Canada mathematics curriculum. For more information, please visit the JUMP Math website, www.jumpmath.org, to find out how to order.

Evidence that JUMP Math Works

JUMP Math is a leader in promoting third-party research about its work. A recent study by researchers at the Ontario Institute for Studies in Education (OISE), the University of Toronto, and Simon Fraser University found that in JUMP Math classrooms conceptual understanding improved significantly for weaker students. In Lambeth, England, researchers reported that after using JUMP Math for one year, 69 percent of students who were two years behind were assessed at grade level.

Cognitive scientists from The Hospital for Sick Children in Toronto recently conducted a randomized-controlled study of the effectiveness of the JUMP math program. Studies of such scientific rigour remain relatively rare in mathematics education research in North America. The results showed that students who received JUMP instruction outperformed students who received the methods of instruction their teachers would normally use, on well-established measures of math achievement.

Using JUMP at Home

"In the twenty years that I have been teaching mathematics to children, I have never met an educator who would say that students who lack confidence in their intellectual or academic abilities are likely to do well in school. JUMP Math has been carefully designed to boost confidence. It has proven to be an extremely effective approach for convincing even the most challenged student that they can do well in mathematics."
— John Mighton

Helping your child discover the joy of mathematics can be fun and productive. You are not the teacher but the tutor. When having fun with mathematics, remember the JUMP Math T.U.T.O.R. principles:

Take responsibility for learning:
If your child doesn't understand a concept, it can always be clarified further or explained differently. As the adult, you are responsible for helping your child understand. If they don't get it, don't get frustrated — get creative!

Use positive reinforcement:
Children like to be rewarded when they succeed. Praise and encouragement build excitement and foster an appetite for learning. The more confidence a student has, the more likely they are to be engaged.

Take small steps:
In mathematics, it is always possible to make something easier. Always use the JUMP Math worksheets to break down the question into a series of small steps. Practice, practice, practice!

Only indicate correct answers:
Your child's confidence can be shaken by a lack of success. Place checkmarks for correct answers, then revisit questions that your child is having difficulty with. Never use Xs!

Raise the bar:
When your child has mastered a particular concept, challenge them by posing a question that is slightly more difficult. As your child meets these small challenges, you will see their focus and excitement increase.

And remember: if your child is falling behind, teach the number facts! It is a serious mistake to think that students who don't know their number facts can always get by in mathematics using a calculator or other aids. Students can certainly perform operations on a calculator, but they cannot begin to solve problems if they lack a sense of numbers. Students need to be able to see patterns in numbers, and to make estimates and predictions about numbers, in order to have any success in mathematics. We have put together some fun activities to help you and your child get ready for mathematics!

Counting Backwards

In mathematics, it is important for your child to learn how to count backwards. Many children find counting backwards much more difficult than counting forwards. Here are some things you can do to help your child learn and practice this skill.

Keep Score . . . Backwards!

Count backwards every time you make a catch or hit a ball when you play games such as ping-pong or catch. Start at 5, 10, or 20, and play until you reach 0. Did someone drop or miss the ball? Don't start counting back from the last number — add 3 first! For example, if someone misses the ball at 11, start counting back again from 14. (Your child knows how to add 3, so let him/her do it!)

Count Down the Time

Next time you use a timer around the house (e.g., to microwave popcorn), tell your child how you know when the time is almost up. Watch and chant the last 10 or 20 seconds of the countdown together.

Play Plus or Minus 1

(Game adapted from *Card Games for Smart Kids* by Dr. Margie Golick.)

You will need one deck of cards. Start by removing all of the face cards (King, Queen, Jack) from the deck.

Goal: To place all 40 cards into a new pile
To play:

1. Put the deck face down and turn over the top card. What number is it? Start a new pile with this card.
2. Turn over the next card. What number is it? If it is **1 more or 1 less** than the last card, add it to the pile. Otherwise, put it in another pile (the discard pile).
3. Keep turning cards over and putting them in the appropriate piles until the deck runs out. Then repeat with the cards in the discard pile (and start a new discard pile).
4. Keep playing with the cards in the discard pile. Eventually, you will have placed all the cards into the new pile (and you win!) or you will have some cards left over.

Variation:

Play Plus or Minus 2: Cards go into the new pile if they are **2 more or 2 less** than the last card drawn.

Wait or Go?

Some pedestrian traffic signals include a countdown. If you see such a signal, point out to your child when the countdown starts. Have your child watch the countdown and count backwards with it. Discuss how the countdown helps pedestrians cross the street safely. How do the lights change when the number reaches 0? How does knowing that 9 is far from 0, but 2 is close to 0 help you decide if you have enough time to cross the street or if you should wait?

Sorting

In mathematics, it is important for your child to learn how to sort things into groups. Here are some things you can do together to help your child practice sorting.

Sort laundry

Ask your child to help you sort the laundry into different groups, such as
*   shirts, pants, socks
*   dark clothes, light clothes
*   your clothes, my clothes

Discuss with your child how all of the items in a group are the same and how the groups differ. Can your child think of another way to sort the laundry?

Sort Grocery Items

Ask your child to help you sort grocery items into groups, such as
*   dairy products, meat products, other
*   things we store in the fridge, things we don't store in the fridge
*   things we eat, things we don't eat (e.g., tissues, cat litter, soap)

You can also sort by shape or colour. Can your child think of another way to sort the items?

Sort Cutlery

Ask your child to sort cutlery before putting it away. What groups did your child create? Ask your child to explain why he/she sorted the items that way.

Sort Toys, Books, and Games

Ask your child to sort toys, books, and games before putting them away. If your child's toys are already sorted (e.g., books in a bookcase, games in a box), ask your child to describe how they are sorted. Which items are grouped together? How many groups are there?

How Are Items Sorted?

Look for examples of sorting everywhere you go: at the grocery store, in the library, in stores and shops. Discuss how the items on a shelf or in an aisle are sorted and why they might be sorted that way. For example,

- shoes in a shoe store are often sorted first by age and gender (men, women, kids) and then by type (dress shoes, running shoes, boots, and so on);
- flowers in a flower shop are sorted by type (carnations, lilies, roses) and then sometimes by colour; and
- books at the library or in a bookstore are sorted by subject and by age (fiction, cookbooks, children's books, and so on)

Length

In mathematics, your child needs to learn about length. Comparing lengths is something we all do in daily life. Here are some ways you can compare lengths together at home.

Compare Lengths Directly — Socks

Ask your child to help you sort and match socks after washing. Demonstrate comparing two socks of different lengths by lining up the heel-to-toe parts side by side. Ask: Which one is longer? Which one do you think is mine? Sort the remaining socks into two piles, long and short. (This activity will work best if you have many pairs of plain, unpatterned socks or at least two different sizes of the same pattern.) You can finish sorting and matching the socks together. Once you have sorted them by size, match them by colour and pattern.

Compare Lengths Directly and Indirectly — Hands and Feet

Ask your child: Whose hand is bigger — yours or mine? How can we check? Hold your hand up to your child's to compare them. Then compare the length of your hands to the length of your mittens or gloves. Ask: Will my hand fit in your mitten? Will your hand fit in mine? Repeat for feet and socks/shoes.

Now ask: What's longer — your foot or my hand? How can we check? Before comparing them directly, compare your child's shoe or sock to your glove. Ask: Which one is longer? Your child might want to revise his/her answer to the first question. Now line your hand up with your child's foot to compare the lengths directly.

Here's another way to compare the lengths of your hands and feet indirectly: Trace your child's foot onto paper and ask your child to trace your hand onto paper. Cut the two tracings out and place them one on top of the other.

Compare and Order Lengths

Ask relatives or friends who live far away to trace one hand or paint a handprint onto paper and mail it to you. Compare their hands to yours and your child's. Order the hands from longest to shortest. Who has the longest hand? Who has the shortest hand? With older children, use a ruler and measure directly.

Basic Operations

In mathematics, your child needs to know addition, subtraction, and skip counting forwards (e.g., 5, 10, 15, . . .) and backwards (e.g., 10, 8, 6, . . .). If you have stairs in your home, the games below can help your child master these concepts.

To begin, attach numbers to each step, starting with 1 on the first (bottom) step and going up. (Higher numbers are thus higher in space.) Put a 0 on the floor before the first step. You will also need dice for each game.

Games for 1 Player

- **Adding on Stairs.** Model finding $5 + 3$: Stand on the step marked 5 and go up 3 steps. Give children a die to roll. If the first roll is 5, they move up 5 steps and say $0 + 5 = 5$. If the second roll is 4, they move up 4 steps and say $5 + 4 = 9$. Play continues until children reach the top of the stairs. At the end, children will have to roll the exact number needed to land on the top step.
- **Subtracting on Stairs.** Play as above, but start on the top step and move down, e.g., $8 - 3 = 5$.
- **Skip Counting by 2s on Stairs.** Children walk up the steps, one at a time, and say every number that their left (or right) foot lands on. Children should start at 0, and take the number of steps determined by the roll of a die. If they roll a 5, they take 5 steps and say either "1, 3, 5" or "0, 2, 4." The goal is to get to the top of the stairs.
- **Skip Counting Back by 2s on Stairs.** Play as above, but start at the top step and move down.

A Cooperative Game for 2–4 Players

This game combines addition and subtraction. Note that players do not play against each other, but instead work as a team. Parents and children can play together.

- **Adding or Subtracting on Stairs.** Players start on predetermined steps (e.g., 0, 5, 10, and 20). Each player rolls the die in turn and moves accordingly. Players can choose whether to move up (add) or down (subtract), but there can never be more than one player on a step at any time, and players cannot move to the bottom (1) or top step once play has begun. Players say the addition or subtraction sentence corresponding to their move (e.g., $8 - 2 = 6$) and try to make as many moves as possible as a team before they get stuck. Play again and try to improve. A supervising or participating adult (or older child) can keep track of how many moves were made.

Telling the Time

In mathematics, your child is learning how to tell time. Your child knows that the "short hand" on a clock is called the hour hand. Because it is longer than the hour hand, we call the minute hand "the long hand."

In class, children often talk about what they do when the hour hand is pointing at different numbers. For example; when the hour hand points at the 10, we go outside for recess. When the hour hand points at the 3, we know that school is almost over.

Here are some ways you can talk about time at home. You will need an analogue clock (a clock with hands).

What Would You Be Doing If . . .

At different times on the weekend, ask your child what he or she would be doing if this were a school day. Emphasize the position of the hour hand each time.

Where Is the Short Hand? What Will We Do?

Ask your child where the short hand is pointing at different times during the day, such as at mealtimes or other regularly scheduled activities (e.g., lessons, visits to friends or family). Then do the reverse: Point out the position of the short hand and ask your child to identify the activity. If you eat supper around 6 p.m., you might say: The short hand is close to the 6. What will we be doing soon?

It's Time For . . .

Identify events that happen at the same time every day or week. For example, if your child has a favourite television show, point out where the short hand is when the show starts. Ask: Is the show on at the same time every day? Every Saturday? How could we check? (Check that channel every day at the same time for a week and record the answers in a chart.)

Changes in Time

Investigate natural events that change predictably over time. Record the times of the events daily or weekly for a few weeks (or more!). Then look for patterns. For example:

- What time does it get dark outside?
- How do shadows change? Find a landmark or familiar object near your home that is sometimes in the shade and sometimes in the light. What time does it come into or out of the shade?

"Children will never fulfill their extraordinary potential until we remember how it felt to have so much potential ourselves. There was nothing we weren't inspired to look at or hold, or that we weren't determined to find out how to do. Open the door to the world of mathematics so your child can pass through." — John Mighton

Mental Math Skills: Addition and Subtraction

PARENT:

If your child doesn't know their addition and subtraction facts, teach them to add and subtract using their fingers by the methods taught below. You should also reinforce basic facts using drills, games and flash cards. There are mental math strategies that make addition and subtraction easier: Some effective strategies are taught in the next section. (Until your child knows all their facts, allow them to add and subtract on their fingers when necessary.)

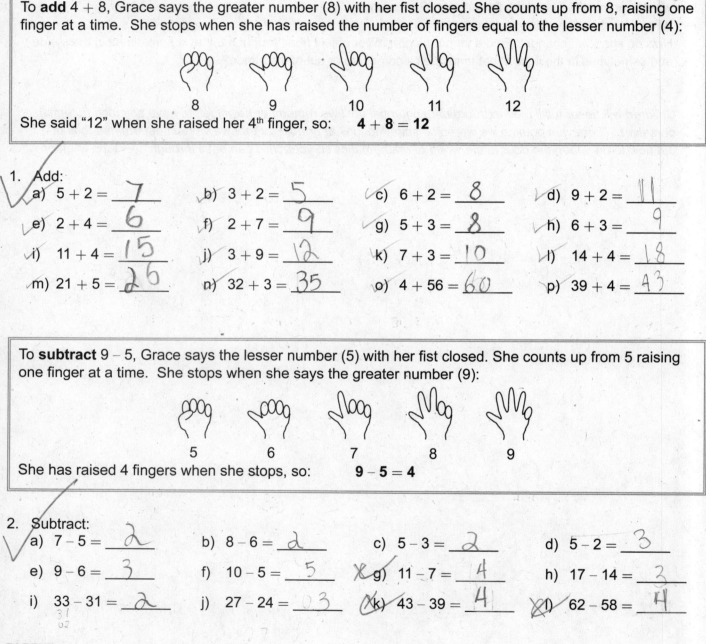

To **add** $4 + 8$, Grace says the greater number (8) with her fist closed. She counts up from 8, raising one finger at a time. She stops when she has raised the number of fingers equal to the lesser number (4):

| 8 | 9 | 10 | 11 | 12 |

She said "12" when she raised her 4th finger, so: $4 + 8 = 12$

1. Add:
   a) $5 + 2 = 7$ b) $3 + 2 = 5$ c) $6 + 2 = 8$ d) $9 + 2 = 11$

   e) $2 + 4 = 6$ f) $2 + 7 = 9$ g) $5 + 3 = 8$ h) $6 + 3 = 9$

   i) $11 + 4 = 15$ j) $3 + 9 = 12$ k) $7 + 3 = 10$ l) $14 + 4 = 18$

   m) $21 + 5 = 26$ n) $32 + 3 = 35$ o) $4 + 56 = 60$ p) $39 + 4 = 43$

To **subtract** $9 - 5$, Grace says the lesser number (5) with her fist closed. She counts up from 5 raising one finger at a time. She stops when she says the greater number (9):

| 5 | 6 | 7 | 8 | 9 |

She has raised 4 fingers when she stops, so: $9 - 5 = 4$

2. Subtract:
   a) $7 - 5 = 2$ b) $8 - 6 = 2$ c) $5 - 3 = 2$ d) $5 - 2 = 3$

   e) $9 - 6 = 3$ f) $10 - 5 = 5$ g) $11 - 7 = 4$ h) $17 - 14 = 3$

   i) $33 - 31 = 2$ j) $27 - 24 = 03$ k) $43 - 39 = 4$ l) $62 - 58 = 4$

PARENT:

To prepare for the next section (Mental Math), teach your child to add 1 to any number mentally (by counting forward by 1 in their head) and to subtract 1 from any number (by counting backward by 1).

Mental Math Skills: Addition and Subtraction *(continued)*

PARENT: Children who don't know how to add, subtract, or estimate readily are at a great disadvantage in mathematics. Children who have trouble memorizing addition and subtraction facts can still learn to mentally add and subtract numbers in a short time if they are given daily practice in a few basic skills.

SKILL 1 – Adding 2 to an Even Number   2, 4, 6, 8, 10

This skill has been broken down into a number of sub-skills. After teaching each sub-skill, you should give your child a short diagnostic quiz to verify that they have learned the skill. I have included sample quizzes for Skills 1 to 4.

i) *Naming the next one-digit even number:*

Numbers that have ones digit 0, 2, 4, 6, or 8 are called the *even numbers*. Using drills or games, teach your child to say the sequence of one-digit even numbers without hesitation. Ask them to imagine the sequence going on in a circle so that the next number after 8 is 0 (0, 2, 4, 6, 8, 0, 2, 4, 6, 8, . . .). Then play the following game: name a number in the sequence and ask your child to give the next number in the sequence. Don't move on until they have mastered the game.

ii) *Naming the next greatest two-digit even number:*

Case 1 – Numbers that end in 0, 2, 4, or 6
Write an even two-digit number that ends in 0, 2, 4, or 6 on a piece of paper. Ask your child to name the next greatest even number. They should recognize that if a number ends in 0, then the next even number ends in 2; if it ends in 2, then the next even number ends in 4, etc. For instance, the number 54 has ones digit 4, so the next greatest even number will have ones digit 6.

> **QUIZ**
>
> Name the next greatest even number:
>
> a) 52 : 54   b) 64 : 66   c) 36 : 38   d) 22 : 24   e) 80 : 82

Case 2 – Numbers that end in 8
Write the number 58 on a piece of paper. Ask your child to name the next greatest even number. Remind them that even numbers must end in 0, 2, 4, 6, or 8. But 50, 52, 54, and 56 are all less than 58, so the next greatest even number is 60. Your child should see that an even number ending in 8 is always followed by an even number ending in 0 (with a tens digit that is one higher).

> **QUIZ**
>
> Name the next greatest even number:
>
> a) 58 : 60   b) 68 : 70   c) 38 : 40   d) 48 : 50   e) 78 : 80

iii) *Adding 2 to an even number:*

Point out to your child that adding 2 to any even number is equivalent to finding the next even number: e.g., $46 + 2 = 48$, $48 + 2 = 50$, etc. Knowing this, your child can easily add 2 to any even number.

Mental Math Skills: Addition and Subtraction *(continued)*

> **QUIZ**
> Add:
> a) $26 + 2 = 28$ b) $82 + 2 = 84$ c) $40 + 2 = 42$ d) $58 + 2 = 60$ e) $34 + 2 = 36$

SKILL 2 – Subtracting 2 from an Even Number

i) *Finding the preceding one-digit even number:*

Name a one-digit even number and ask your child to give the preceding number in the sequence. For instance, the number that comes before 4 is 2, and the number that comes before 0 is 8. (Remember: the sequence is circular.)

ii) *Finding the preceding two-digit even number:*

Case 1 – Numbers that end in 2, 4, 6, or 8
Write a two-digit number that ends in 2, 4, 6, or 8 on a piece of paper. Ask your child to name the preceding even number. They should recognize that if a number ends in 2, then the preceding even number ends in 0; if it ends in 4, then the preceding even number ends in 2, etc. For instance, the number 78 has ones digit 8, so the preceding even number has ones digit 6.

> **QUIZ**
> Name the preceding even number:
> a) 48 : 46   b) 26 : 24   c) 34 : 32   d) 62 : 60   e) 78 : 76

Case 2 – Numbers that end in 0
Write the number 80 on a piece of paper and ask your child to name the preceding even number. They should recognize that if an even number ends in 0, then the preceding even number ends in 8 (but the ones digit is one less). So the even number that comes before 80 is 78.

> **QUIZ**
> Name the preceding even number:
> a) 40 : 38   b) 60 : 58   c) 80 : 78   d) 50 : 48   e) 30 : 28

ii) *Subtracting 2 from an even number:*

Point out to your child that subtracting 2 from any even number is equivalent to finding the preceding even number: e.g., $48 - 2 = 46$, $46 - 2 = 44$, etc.

> **QUIZ**
> Subtract:
> a) $58 - 2 = 56$ b) $24 - 2 = 22$ c) $36 - 2 = 34$ d) $42 - 2 = 40$ e) $60 - 2 = 58$

Mental Math Skills: Addition and Subtraction *(continued)*

SKILL 3 – Adding 2 to an Odd Number

i) *Naming the next one-digit odd number:*

Numbers that have ones digit 1, 3, 5, 7, or 9 are called *odd numbers*. Using drills or games, teach your child to say the sequence of one-digit odd numbers without hesitation. Ask them to imagine the sequence going on in a circle so that the next number after 9 is 1 (1, 3, 5, 7, 9, 1, 3, 5, 7, 9, . . .). Then play the following game: name a number in the sequence and ask your child to give the next number in the sequence. Don't move on until they have mastered the game.

ii) *Naming the next greatest two-digit odd number:*

Case 1 – Numbers that end in 1, 3, 5, or 7
Write an odd two-digit number that ends in 1, 3, 5, or 7 on a piece of paper. Ask your child to name the next greatest odd number. They should recognize that if a number ends in 1, then the next odd number ends in 3; if it ends in 3 then the next odd number ends in 5, etc. For instance, the number 35 has ones digit 5, so the next greatest odd number will have ones digit 7.

> **QUIZ** Name the next greatest odd number:
>
> a) 51 : _____   b) 65 : _____   c) 37 : _____   d) 23 : _____   e) 87 : _____

Case 2 – Numbers that end in 9
Write the number 59 on a piece of paper. Ask your child to name the next greatest odd number. Remind them that odd numbers must end in 1, 3, 5, 7, or 9. But 51, 53, 55, and 57 are all less than 59. The next greatest odd number is 61. Your child should see that an odd number ending in 9 is always followed by an odd number ending in 1 (with a tens digit that is one higher).

> **QUIZ** Name the next greatest odd number:
>
> a) 59 : _____   b) 69 : _____   c) 39 : _____   d) 49 : _____   e) 79 : _____

iii) *Adding 2 to an odd number:*

Point out to your child that adding 2 to any odd number is equivalent to finding the next odd number: e.g., $47 + 2 = 49$, $49 + 2 = 51$, etc. Knowing this, your child can easily add 2 to any odd number.

> **QUIZ** Add:
>
> a) $27 + 2 =$ ___   b) $83 + 2 =$ ___   c) $41 + 2 =$ ___   d) $59 + 2 =$ ___   e) $35 + 2 =$ ___

       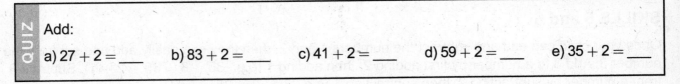 **Introduction**

Mental Math Skills: Addition and Subtraction (continued)

SKILL 4 – Subtracting 2 from an Odd Number

i)   *Finding the preceding one-digit odd number:*

Name a one-digit odd number and ask your child to give the preceding number in the sequence. For instance, the number that comes before 3 is 1, and the number that comes before 1 is 9. (Remember: the sequence is circular.)

ii)   *Finding the preceding two-digit odd number:*

Case 1 – Numbers that end in 3, 5, 7, or 9
Write a two-digit number that ends in 3, 5, 7, or 9 on a piece of paper. Ask your child to name the preceding odd number. They should recognize that if a number ends in 3, then the preceding odd number ends in 1; if it ends in 5, then the preceding odd number ends in 3, etc. For instance, the number 79 has ones digit 9, so the preceding odd number has ones digit 7.

> **QUIZ**
>
> Name the preceding odd number:
>
> a) 49 : _____   b) 27 : _____   c) 35 : _____   d) 63 : _____   e) 79 : _____

Case 2 – Numbers that end in 1
Write the number 81 on a piece of paper and ask your child to name the preceding odd number. They should recognize that if an odd number ends in 1, then the preceding odd number ends in 9 (but the ones digit is one less). So the odd number that comes before 81 is 79.

> **QUIZ**
>
> Name the preceding odd number:
>
> a) 41 : _____   b) 61 : _____   c) 81 : _____   d) 51 : _____   e) 31 : _____

iii)   *Subtracting 2 from an odd number:*

Point out to your child that subtracting 2 from any odd number is equivalent to finding the preceding odd number: e.g., $49 - 2 = 47$, $47 - 2 = 45$, etc.

> **QUIZ**
>
> Subtract:
>
> a) $59 - 2 = $ ___   b) $25 - 2 = $ ___   c) $37 - 2 = $ ___   d) $43 - 2 = $ ___   e) $61 - 2 = $ ___

SKILLS 5 and 6

Once your child can add and subtract the numbers 1 and 2, then they can easily add and subtract the number 3: Add 3 to a number by first adding 2, then adding 1 (e.g., $35 + 3 = 35 + 2 + 1$). Subtract 3 from a number by subtracting 2, then subtracting 1 (e.g., $35 - 3 = 35 - 2 - 1$).

Mental Math Skills: Addition and Subtraction *(continued)*

PARENT: All of the addition and subtraction tricks you teach your child should be reinforced with drills, flashcards, and tests. Eventually they should memorize their addition and subtraction facts and shouldn't have to rely on the mental math tricks. One of the greatest gifts you can give your child is to teach them their number facts.

SKILLS 7 and 8

Add 4 to a number by adding 2 twice (e.g., $51 + 4 = 51 + 2 + 2$). Subtract 4 from a number by subtracting 2 twice (e.g., $51 - 4 = 51 - 2 - 2$).

SKILLS 9 and 10

Add 5 to a number by adding 4 then 1. Subtract 5 by subtracting 4 then 1.

SKILL 11

Your child can add pairs of identical numbers by doubling (e.g., $6 + 6 = 2 \times 6$). They should either memorize the 2 times table or they should double numbers by counting on their fingers by 2s.

Add a pair of numbers that differ by 1 by rewriting the larger number as 1 plus the smaller number (then use doubling to find the sum): e.g., $6 + 7 = 6 + 6 + 1 = 12 + 1 = 13$; $7 + 8 = 7 + 7 + 1 = 14 + 1 = 15$.

SKILLS 12, 13, and 14

Add a one-digit number to 10 by simply replacing the zero in 10 with the one-digit number: e.g., $10 + 7 = 17$.

Add 10 to any two-digit number by simply increasing the tens digit of the two-digit number by 1: e.g., $53 + 10 = 63$.

Add a pair of two-digit numbers (with no carrying) by adding the ones digits of the numbers and then adding the tens digits: e.g., $23 + 64 = 87$.

SKILLS 15 and 16

To add 9 to a one-digit number, subtract 1 from the number and then add 10: e.g., $9 + 6 = 10 + 5 = 15$; $9 + 7 = 10 + 6 = 16$. (Essentially, your child simply has to subtract 1 from the number and then stick a 1 in front of the result.)

To add 8 to a one-digit number, subtract 2 from the number and add 10: e.g., $8 + 6 = 10 + 4 = 14$; $8 + 7 = 10 + 5 = 15$.

SKILLS 17 and 18

To subtract a pair of multiples of ten, simply subtract the tens digits and add a zero for the ones digit: e.g., $70 - 50 = 20$.

To subtract a pair of two-digit numbers (without carrying or regrouping), subtract the ones digit from the ones digit and the tens digit from the tens digit: e.g., $57 - 34 = 23$.

Introduction

Mental Math — Further Strategies

Further Mental Math Strategies

1. Your child should be able to explain how to use the strategies of "rounding the subtrahend (i.e., the number you are subtracting) up to the nearest multiple of ten."

Examples:

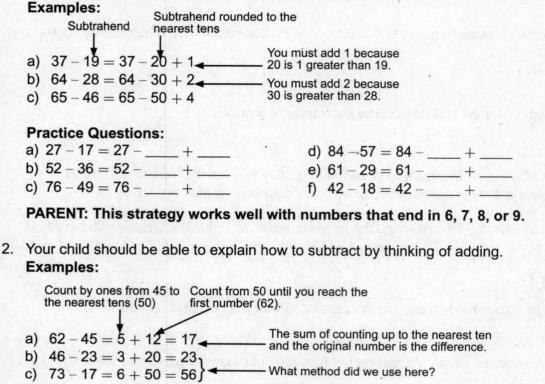

a) $37 - 19 = 37 - 20 + 1$ — You must add 1 because 20 is 1 greater than 19.

b) $64 - 28 = 64 - 30 + 2$ — You must add 2 because 30 is greater than 28.

c) $65 - 46 = 65 - 50 + 4$

Practice Questions:

a) $27 - 17 = 27 - \underline{\quad} + \underline{\quad}$

b) $52 - 36 = 52 - \underline{\quad} + \underline{\quad}$

c) $76 - 49 = 76 - \underline{\quad} + \underline{\quad}$

d) $84 - 57 = 84 - \underline{\quad} + \underline{\quad}$

e) $61 - 29 = 61 - \underline{\quad} + \underline{\quad}$

f) $42 - 18 = 42 - \underline{\quad} + \underline{\quad}$

PARENT: This strategy works well with numbers that end in 6, 7, 8, or 9.

2. Your child should be able to explain how to subtract by thinking of adding.

Examples:

Count by ones from 45 to the nearest tens (50)   Count from 50 until you reach the first number (62).

a) $62 - 45 = 5 + 12 = 17$ — The sum of counting up to the nearest ten and the original number is the difference.

b) $46 - 23 = 3 + 20 = 23$

c) $73 - 17 = 6 + 50 = 56$ — What method did we use here?

Practice Questions:

a) $88 - 36 = \underline{\quad} + \underline{\quad} = \underline{\quad}$

b) $58 - 21 = \underline{\quad} + \underline{\quad} = \underline{\quad}$

c) $43 - 17 = \underline{\quad} + \underline{\quad} = \underline{\quad}$

d) $74 - 28 = \underline{\quad} + \underline{\quad} = \underline{\quad}$

e) $93 - 64 = \underline{\quad} + \underline{\quad} = \underline{\quad}$

f) $82 - 71 = \underline{\quad} + \underline{\quad} = \underline{\quad}$

3. Your child should be able to explain how to "use doubles."

Examples:

Minuend

If you add the subtrahend to itself, and the sum is equal to the minuend, then the subtrahend is the same as the difference.

a) $12 - 6 = 6$ $6 + 6 = 12$ — Same value as minuend

b) $8 - 4 = 4$

Subtrahend plus itself

Practice Questions:

a) $6 - 3 = \underline{\quad}$

b) $10 - 5 = \underline{\quad}$

c) $14 - 7 = \underline{\quad}$

d) $18 - 9 = \underline{\quad}$

e) $16 - 8 = \underline{\quad}$

f) $20 - 10 = \underline{\quad}$

Mental Math Exercises

PARENT: Teaching the material on these Mental Math worksheets may take several lessons. Your child will need more practice than is provided on these pages. These pages are intended as a test to be given when you are certain your child has learned the materials fully.

PARENT: Teach skills 1, 2, 3, and 4 as outlined on pages xvii–xx before you allow your child to answer Questions 1 through 12:

1. Name the <u>even</u> number that comes <u>after</u> the number. Answer in the blank provided:

    a) 32 _____   b) 46 _____   c) 14 _____   d) 92 _____   e) 56 _____

    f) 30 _____   g) 84 _____   h) 60 _____   i) 72 _____   j) 24 _____

2. Name the <u>even</u> number that comes <u>after</u> the number:

    a) 28 _____   b) 18 _____   c) 78 _____   d) 38 _____   e) 68 _____

3. Add:
    REMEMBER: Adding 2 to an even number is the same as finding the next even number.

    a) $42 + 2 =$ _____   b) $76 + 2 =$ _____   c) $28 + 2 =$ _____   d) $16 + 2 =$ _____

    e) $68 + 2 =$ _____   f) $12 + 2 =$ _____   g) $36 + 2 =$ _____   h) $90 + 2 =$ _____

    i) $70 + 2 =$ _____   j) $24 + 2 =$ _____   k) $66 + 2 =$ _____   l) $52 + 2 =$ _____

4. Name the <u>even</u> number that comes <u>before</u> the number:

    a) **38** _____   b) **42** _____   c) **56** _____   d) **72** _____   e) **98** _____

    f) **48** _____   g) **16** _____   h) **22** _____   i) **66** _____   j) **14** _____

5. Name the <u>even</u> number that comes <u>before</u> the number:

    a) **30** _____   b) **70** _____   c) **60** _____   d) **10** _____   e) **80** _____

6. Subtract:
    REMEMBER: Subtracting 2 from an even number is the same as finding the preceding even number.

    a) $46 - 2 =$ _____   b) $86 - 2 =$ _____   c) $90 - 2 =$ _____   d) $14 - 2 =$ _____

    e) $54 - 2 =$ _____   f) $72 - 2 =$ _____   g) $12 - 2 =$ _____   h) $56 - 2 =$ _____

    i) $32 - 2 =$ _____   j) $40 - 2 =$ _____   k) $60 - 2 =$ _____   l) $26 - 2 =$ _____

7. Name the <u>odd</u> number that comes <u>after</u> the number:

    a) 37 _____   b) 51 _____   c) 63 _____   d) 75 _____   e) 17 _____

    f) 61 _____   g) 43 _____   h) 81 _____   i) 23 _____   j) 95 _____

8. Name the <u>odd</u> number that comes <u>after</u> the number:

    a) 69 _____   b) 29 _____   c) 9 _____   d) 79 _____   e) 59 _____

Mental Math Exercises *(continued)*

9. Add:
   REMEMBER: Adding 2 to an odd number is the same as finding the next odd number.

   a) $25 + 2 =$ _____   b) $31 + 2 =$ _____   c) $47 + 2 =$ _____   d) $33 + 2 =$ _____

   e) $39 + 2 =$ _____   f) $91 + 2 =$ _____   g) $5 + 2 =$ _____   h) $89 + 2 =$ _____

   i) $11 + 2 =$ _____   j) $65 + 2 =$ _____   k) $29 + 2 =$ _____   l) $17 + 2 =$ _____

10. Name the <u>odd</u> number that comes <u>before</u> the number:

    a) **39** _____   b) **43** _____   c) **57** _____   d) **17** _____   e) **99** _____

    f) **13** _____   g) **85** _____   h) **79** _____   i) **65** _____   j) **77** _____

11. Name the <u>odd</u> number that comes <u>before</u> the number:

    a) **21** _____   b) **41** _____   c) **11** _____   d) **91** _____   e) **51** _____

12. Subtract:
    REMEMBER: Subtracting 2 from an odd number is the same as finding the preceding odd number.

    a) $47 - 2 =$ _____   b) $85 - 2 =$ _____   c) $91 - 2 =$ _____   d) $15 - 2 =$ _____

    e) $51 - 2 =$ _____   f) $73 - 2 =$ _____   g) $11 - 2 =$ _____   h) $59 - 2 =$ _____

    i) $31 - 2 =$ _____   j) $43 - 2 =$ _____   k) $7 - 2 =$ _____   l) $25 - 2 =$ _____

PARENT: Teach skills 5 and 6 as outlined on page xx before you allow your child to answer Questions 13 and 14.

13. Add 3 to the number by adding 2, then adding 1 (e.g., $35 + 3 = 35 + 2 + 1$):

    a) $23 + 3 =$ _____   b) $36 + 3 =$ _____   c) $29 + 3 =$ _____   d) $16 + 3 =$ _____

    e) $67 + 3 =$ _____   f) $12 + 3 =$ _____   g) $35 + 3 =$ _____   h) $90 + 3 =$ _____

    i) $78 + 3 =$ _____   j) $24 + 3 =$ _____   k) $6 + 3 =$ _____   l) $59 + 3 =$ _____

14. Subtract 3 from the number by subtracting 2, then subtracting 1 (e.g., $35 - 3 = 35 - 2 - 1$):

    a) $46 - 3 =$ _____   b) $87 - 3 =$ _____   c) $99 - 3 =$ _____   d) $14 - 3 =$ _____

    e) $8 - 3 =$ _____   f) $72 - 3 =$ _____   g) $12 - 3 =$ _____   h) $57 - 3 =$ _____

    i) $32 - 3 =$ _____   j) $40 - 3 =$ _____   k) $60 - 3 =$ _____   l) $28 - 3 =$ _____

15. Fred has 49 stamps. He gives 2 stamps away. How many stamps does he have left?

16. There are 25 minnows in a tank. Alice adds 3 more to the tank. How many minnows are now in the tank?

Mental Math Exercises *(continued)*

PARENT: Teach skills 7 and 8 as outlined on page xxi.

17. Add 4 to the number by adding 2 twice (e.g., $51 + 4 = 51 + 2 + 2$):

   a) $42 + 4 =$ _____
   b) $76 + 4 =$ _____
   c) $27 + 4 =$ _____
   d) $17 + 4 =$ _____

   e) $68 + 4 =$ _____
   f) $11 + 4 =$ _____
   g) $35 + 4 =$ _____
   h) $8 + 4 =$ _____

   i) $72 + 4 =$ _____
   j) $23 + 4 =$ _____
   k) $60 + 4 =$ _____
   l) $59 + 4 =$ _____

18. Subtract 4 from the number by subtracting 2 twice (e.g., $26 - 4 = 26 - 2 - 2$):

   a) $46 - 4 =$ _____
   b) $86 - 4 =$ _____
   c) $91 - 4 =$ _____
   d) $15 - 4 =$ _____

   e) $53 - 4 =$ _____
   f) $9 - 4 =$ _____
   g) $13 - 4 =$ _____
   h) $57 - 4 =$ _____

   i) $40 - 4 =$ _____
   j) $88 - 4 =$ _____
   k) $69 - 4 =$ _____
   l) $31 - 4 =$ _____

PARENT: Teach skills 9 and 10 as outlined on page xxi.

19. Add 5 to the number by adding 4, then adding 1 (or add 2 twice, then add 1):

   a) $84 + 5 =$ _____
   b) $27 + 5 =$ _____
   c) $31 + 5 =$ _____
   d) $44 + 5 =$ _____

   e) $63 + 5 =$ _____
   f) $92 + 5 =$ _____
   g) $14 + 5 =$ _____
   h) $16 + 5 =$ _____

   i) $9 + 5 =$ _____
   j) $81 + 5 =$ _____
   k) $51 + 5 =$ _____
   l) $28 + 5 =$ _____

20. Subtract 5 from the number by subtracting 4, then subtracting 1 (or subtract 2 twice, then subtract 1):

   a) $48 - 5 =$ _____
   b) $86 - 5 =$ _____
   c) $55 - 5 =$ _____
   d) $69 - 5 =$ _____

   e) $30 - 5 =$ _____
   f) $13 - 5 =$ _____
   g) $92 - 5 =$ _____
   h) $77 - 5 =$ _____

   i) $45 - 5 =$ _____
   j) $24 - 5 =$ _____
   k) $91 - 5 =$ _____
   l) $8 - 5 =$ _____

PARENT: Teach skill 11 as outlined on page xxi.

21. Add:

   a) $6 + 6 =$ _____
   b) $7 + 7 =$ _____
   c) $8 + 8 =$ _____

   d) $5 + 5 =$ _____
   e) $4 + 4 =$ _____
   f) $9 + 9 =$ _____

22. Add by thinking of the larger number as a sum of two smaller numbers. The first one is done for you:

   a) $6 + 7 = 6 + 6 + 1$
   b) $7 + 8 =$ _____
   c) $6 + 8 =$ _____

   d) $4 + 5 =$ _____
   e) $5 + 7 =$ _____
   f) $8 + 9 =$ _____

Mental Math Exercises *(continued)*

PARENT: Teach skills 12, 13, and 14 as outlined on page xxi.

23. a) $10 + 3 =$ _____   b) $10 + 7 =$ _____   c) $5 + 10 =$ _____   d) $10 + 1 =$ _____
   e) $9 + 10 =$ _____   f) $10 + 4 =$ _____   g) $10 + 8 =$ _____   h) $10 + 2 =$ _____

24. a) $10 + 20 =$ _____   b) $40 + 10 =$ _____   c) $10 + 80 =$ _____   d) $10 + 50 =$ _____
   e) $30 + 10 =$ _____   f) $10 + 60 =$ _____   g) $10 + 10 =$ _____   h) $70 + 10 =$ _____

25. a) $10 + 25 =$ _____   b) $10 + 67 =$ _____   c) $10 + 31 =$ _____   d) $10 + 82 =$ _____
   e) $10 + 43 =$ _____   f) $10 + 51 =$ _____   g) $10 + 68 =$ _____   h) $10 + 21 =$ _____
   i) $10 + 11 =$ _____   j) $10 + 19 =$ _____   k) $10 + 44 =$ _____   l) $10 + 88 =$ _____

26. a) $20 + 30 =$ _____   b) $40 + 20 =$ _____   c) $30 + 30 =$ _____   d) $50 + 30 =$ _____
   e) $20 + 50 =$ _____   f) $40 + 40 =$ _____   g) $50 + 40 =$ _____   h) $40 + 30 =$ _____
   i) $60 + 30 =$ _____   j) $20 + 60 =$ _____   k) $20 + 70 =$ _____   l) $60 + 40 =$ _____

27. a) $20 + 23 =$ _____   b) $32 + 24 =$ _____   c) $51 + 12 =$ _____   d) $12 + 67 =$ _____
   e) $83 + 14 =$ _____   f) $65 + 24 =$ _____   g) $41 + 43 =$ _____   h) $70 + 27 =$ _____
   i) $31 + 61 =$ _____   j) $54 + 33 =$ _____   k) $28 + 31 =$ _____   l) $42 + 55 =$ _____

PARENT: Teach skills 15 and 16 as outlined on page xxi.

28. a) $9 + 3 =$ _____   b) $9 + 7 =$ _____   c) $6 + 9 =$ _____   d) $4 + 9 =$ _____
   e) $9 + 9 =$ _____   f) $5 + 9 =$ _____   g) $9 + 2 =$ _____   h) $9 + 8 =$ _____

29. a) $8 + 2 =$ _____   b) $8 + 6 =$ _____   c) $8 + 7 =$ _____   d) $4 + 8 =$ _____
   e) $5 + 8 =$ _____   f) $8 + 3 =$ _____   g) $9 + 8 =$ _____   h) $8 + 8 =$ _____

PARENT: Teach skills 17 and 18 as outlined on page xxi.

30. a) $40 - 10 =$ _____   b) $50 - 10 =$ _____   c) $70 - 10 =$ _____   d) $20 - 10 =$ _____
   e) $40 - 20 =$ _____   f) $60 - 30 =$ _____   g) $40 - 30 =$ _____   h) $60 - 50 =$ _____

31. a) $57 - 34 =$ _____   b) $43 - 12 =$ _____   c) $62 - 21 =$ _____   d) $59 - 36 =$ _____
   e) $87 - 63 =$ _____   f) $95 - 62 =$ _____   g) $35 - 10 =$ _____   h) $17 - 8 =$ _____

Mental Math (Advanced)

<u>Multiples of Ten</u>

NOTE: In the exercises below, you will learn several ways to use multiples of ten in mental addition or subtraction.

> **I** $542 + 214 = 542 + 200 + 10 + 4 = 742 + 10 + 4 = 752 + 4 = 756$
>
> $827 - 314 = 827 - 300 - 10 - 4 = 527 - 10 - 4 = 517 - 4 = 713$
>
>   Sometimes you will need to carry:
>
> $545 + 172 = 545 + 100 + 70 + 2 = 645 + 70 + 2 = 715 + 2 = 717$

1. Warm up:

    a) $536 + 100 =$ _____   b) $816 + 10 =$ c) $124 + 5 =$ ____   d) $540 + 200 =$ ____

    e) $234 + 30 =$ ___   f) $345 + 300 =$ g) $236 - 30 =$ ____   h) $442 - 20 =$ ____

    i) $970 - 70 =$ ____   j) $542 - 400 =$ k) $160 + 50 =$ ____   l) $756 + 40 =$ ____

2. Write the second number in expanded form and add or subtract one digit at a time. The first one is done for you:

    a) $564 + 215 =$ _____$564 + 200 + 10 + 5$_____ $=$ ___779___

    b) $445 + 343 =$ _____ $=$ _____

    c) $234 + 214 =$ _____ $=$ _____

3. Add or subtract mentally (one digit at a time):

    a) $547 + 312 =$ _____   b) $578 - 314 =$ _____   c) $845 - 454 =$ _____

> **II**   If one of the numbers you are adding or subtracting is close to a number that is a multiple of ten, add the multiple of ten and then add or subtract an adjustment factor:
>
> $645 + 99 = 645 + 100 - 1 = 745 - 1 = 744$
>
> $856 + 42 = 856 + 40 + 2 = 896 + 2 = 898$

> **III**   Sometimes in subtraction it helps to think of a multiple of ten as a sum of 1 and a number consisting entirely of 9s (e.g., $100 = 1 + 99$; $1000 = 1 + 999$). You never have to borrow or exchange when you are subtracting from a number consisting entirely of 9s.
>
> $100 - 43 = 1 + 99 - 43 = 1 + 56 = 57$ ⟵   *Do the subtraction, using 99 instead of 100, and then add 1 to your answer.*
>
> $1000 - 543 = 1 + 999 - 543 = 1 + 456 = 457$

4. Use the tricks you've just learned:

    a) $845 + 91 =$ _____   b) $456 + 298 =$ _____   c) $100 - 84 =$ _____   d) $1000 - 846 =$ _____

Mental Math Game: Modified Go Fish

PURPOSE:

If children know the pairs of one-digit numbers that add up to particular **target numbers**, they will be able to mentally break sums into easier sums.

EXAMPLE:

As it is easy to add any one-digit number to 10, you can add a sum more readily if you can decompose numbers in the sum into pairs that add to ten. For example:

$$7 + 5 = 7 + 3 + 2 = 10 + 2 = 12$$

These numbers add to 10.

To help children remember pairs of numbers that add up to a given target number, I developed a variation of "Go Fish" that I have found very effective.

THE GAME:

Pick any target number and remove all the cards with value greater than or equal to the target number out of the deck. In what follows, I will assume that the target number is 10, so you would take all the tens and face cards out of the deck (aces count as one).

The dealer gives each player six cards. If a player has any pairs of cards that add to 10, they are allowed to place these pairs on the table before play begins.

Player 1 selects one of the cards in their hand and asks Player 2 for a card that adds to 10 with the chosen card. For instance, if Player 1's chosen card is a 3, they may ask Player 2 for a 7.

If Player 2 has the requested card, Player 1 takes it and lays it down along with the card from their hand. Player 1 may then ask for another card. If Player 2 does not have the requested card, they say, "Go fish," and Player 1 must pick up a card from the top of the deck. (If this card adds to 10 with a card in Player 1's hand, they may lay down the pair right away.) It is then Player 2's turn to ask for a card.

Play ends when one player lays down all of their cards. Players receive 4 points for laying down all of their cards first and 1 point for each pair they have laid down.

PARENT: If your child is having difficulty, I would recommend that you start with pairs of numbers that add to 5. Take all cards with value greater than 4 out of the deck. Each player should be dealt only four cards to start with.

I have worked with several children who have had a great deal of trouble sorting their cards and finding pairs that add to a target number. I have found that the following exercise helps:

Give your child only three cards, two of which add to the target number. Ask them to find the pair that adds to the target number. After your child has mastered this step with three cards, repeat the exercise with four cards, then five cards, and so on.

PARENT: You can also give your child a list of the pairs that add to the target number. As your child gets used to the game, gradually remove pairs from the list so that they learn the pairs by memory.

Hundreds Charts

1	2	3	4	5	6	7	8	9	10
11	12	13	14	15	16	17	18	19	20
21	22	23	24	25	26	27	28	29	30
31	32	33	34	35	36	37	38	39	40
41	42	43	44	45	46	47	48	49	50
51	52	53	54	55	56	57	58	59	60
61	62	63	64	65	66	67	68	69	70
71	72	73	74	75	76	77	78	79	80
81	82	83	84	85	86	87	88	89	90
91	92	93	94	95	96	97	98	99	100

1	2	3	4	5	6	7	8	9	10
11	12	13	14	15	16	17	18	19	20
21	22	23	24	25	26	27	28	29	30
31	32	33	34	35	36	37	38	39	40
41	42	43	44	45	46	47	48	49	50
51	52	53	54	55	56	57	58	59	60
61	62	63	64	65	66	67	68	69	70
71	72	73	74	75	76	77	78	79	80
81	82	83	84	85	86	87	88	89	90
91	92	93	94	95	96	97	98	99	100

1	2	3	4	5	6	7	8	9	10
11	12	13	14	15	16	17	18	19	20
21	22	23	24	25	26	27	28	29	30
31	32	33	34	35	36	37	38	39	40
41	42	43	44	45	46	47	48	49	50
51	52	53	54	55	56	57	58	59	60
61	62	63	64	65	66	67	68	69	70
71	72	73	74	75	76	77	78	79	80
81	82	83	84	85	86	87	88	89	90
91	92	93	94	95	96	97	98	99	100

1	2	3	4	5	6	7	8	9	10
11	12	13	14	15	16	17	18	19	20
21	22	23	24	25	26	27	28	29	30
31	32	33	34	35	36	37	38	39	40
41	42	43	44	45	46	47	48	49	50
51	52	53	54	55	56	57	58	59	60
61	62	63	64	65	66	67	68	69	70
71	72	73	74	75	76	77	78	79	80
81	82	83	84	85	86	87	88	89	90
91	92	93	94	95	96	97	98	99	100

How to Learn Your Times Tables in 5 Days

PARENT:

Trying to do math without knowing your times tables is like trying to play the piano without knowing the location of the notes on the keyboard. Your child will have difficulty seeing patterns in sequences and charts, solving proportions, finding equivalent fractions, decimals and percents, solving problems etc. if they don't know their tables.

Using the method below, you can teach your child their tables in a week or so. (If you set aside five or ten minutes a day to work with them, the pay-off will be enormous.) There is really no reason for your child not to know their tables!

DAY 1: Counting by 2s, 3s, 4s, and 5s

If you have completed the JUMP Fractions unit you should already know how to count and multiply by 2s, 3s, 4s, and 5s. If you do not know how to count by these numbers you should memorize the hands:

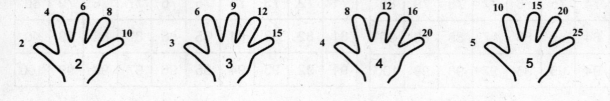

If you know how to count by 2s, 3s, 4s, and 5s, then you can multiply by any combination of these numbers. For instance, to find the product of 3×2, count by 2s until you have raised 3 fingers:

$3 \times 2 =$

DAY 2: The 9 Times Table

The numbers you say when you count by 9s are called the **multiples** of 9 (0 is also a multiple of 9). The first ten multiples of 9 (after 0) are 9, 18, 27, 36, 45, 54, 63, 72, 81, and 90. What happens when you add the digits of any of these multiples of 9 (such as $1 + 8$ or $6 + 3$)? The sum is always 9!

Here is another useful fact about the 9 times table: Multiply 9 by any number between 1 and 10 and look at the tens digit of the product. The tens digit is always one less than the number you multiplied by:

$9 \times 4 = 36$

3 is one less than 4

$9 \times 8 = 72$

7 is one less than 8

$9 \times 2 = 18$

1 is one less than 2

You can find the product of 9 and any number by using the two facts given above. For example, to find 9×7, follow these steps:

Step 1: $9 \times 7 =$ __ __

Subtract 1 from the number
you are multiplying by 9: **7 − 1 = 6**

$9 \times 7 =$ __ __

Now you know the tens digit
of the product.

How to Learn Your Times Tables in 5 Days *(continued)*

Step 2: $9 \times 7 = \underline{6}\ \underline{}$ $9 \times 7 = \underline{6}\ \underline{3}$

These two digits add to 9.   So the missing digit is $9 - 6 = \mathbf{3}$
(You can do the subtraction on your fingers if necesary.)

Practise these two steps for all of the products of 9: 9×2, 9×3, 9×4, and so on.

DAY 3: The 8 Times Table

There are two patterns in the digits of the 8 times table. Knowing these patterns will help you remember how to count by 8s.

Step 1: You can find the ones digit of the first five multiples of 8, by starting at 8 and counting backwards by 2s.

8
6
4
2
0

Step 2: You can find the tens digit of the first five multiples of 8, by starting at 0 and counting up by 1s.

08
16
24
32
40

(Of course you do not need to write the 0 in front of the 8 for the product 1×8.)

Step 3: You can find the ones digit of the next five multiples of 8 by repeating step 1.

8
6
4
2
0

Step 4: You can find the remaining tens digits by starting at 4 and counting by 1s.

48
56
64
72
80

Practise writing the multiples of 8 (up to 80) until you have memorized the complete list. Knowing the patterns in the digits of the multiples of 8 will help you memorize the list very quickly. Then you will know how to multiply by 8.

$8 \times 6 = 48$

Count by 8 until you have 6 fingers up: 8, 16, 24, 32, 40, 48.

How to Learn Your Times Tables in 5 Days *(continued)*

DAY 4: The 6 Times Table

If you have learned the 8 and 9 times tables, then you already know 6×9 and 6×8.

And if you know how to multiply by 5 up to 5×5, then you also know how to multiply by 6 up to 6×5! That is because you can always calculate 6 times a number by calculating 5 times the number and then adding the number itself to the result. The pictures below show how this works for 6×4:

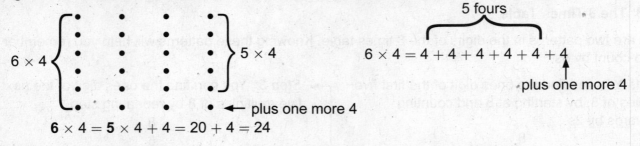

$$6 \times 4 = 5 \times 4 + 4 = 20 + 4 = 24$$

Similarly: $6 \times 2 = 5 \times 2 + 2$; $6 \times 3 = 5 \times 3 + 3$; $6 \times 5 = 5 \times 5 + 5$.

Knowing this, you only need to memorize 2 facts:

$$6 \times 6 = 36 \qquad 6 \times 7 = 42$$

Or, if you know 6×5, you can find 6×6 by calculating $6 \times 5 + 5$.

DAY 5: The 7 Times Table

If you have learned the 6, 8, and 9 times tables, then you already know 6×7, 8×7, and 9×7.

And since you also already know $1 \times 7 = 7$, you only need to memorize 5 facts:

$$2 \times 7 = 14 \qquad 3 \times 7 = 21 \qquad 4 \times 7 = 28 \qquad 5 \times 7 = 35 \qquad 7 \times 7 = 49$$

If you are able to memorize your own phone number, then you can easily memorize these 5 facts!

NOTE: You can use doubling to help you learn the facts above: 4 is double 2, so 4×7 (28) is double 2×7 (14); 6 is double 3, so 6×7 (42) is double 3×7 (21).

Try this test every day until you have learned your times tables.

1. $3 \times 5 =$ _____	2. $8 \times 4 =$ _____	3. $9 \times 3 =$ _____	4. $4 \times 5 =$ _____
5. $2 \times 3 =$ _____	6. $4 \times 2 =$ _____	7. $8 \times 1 =$ _____	8. $6 \times 6 =$ _____
9. $9 \times 7 =$ _____	10. $7 \times 7 =$ _____	11. $5 \times 8 =$ _____	12. $2 \times 6 =$ _____
13. $6 \times 4 =$ _____	14. $7 \times 3 =$ _____	15. $4 \times 9 =$ _____	16. $2 \times 9 =$ _____
17. $9 \times 9 =$ _____	18. $3 \times 4 =$ _____	19. $6 \times 8 =$ _____	20. $7 \times 5 =$ _____
21. $9 \times 5 =$ _____	22. $5 \times 6 =$ _____	23. $6 \times 3 =$ _____	24. $7 \times 1 =$ _____
25. $8 \times 3 =$ _____	26. $9 \times 6 =$ _____	27. $4 \times 7 =$ _____	28. $3 \times 3 =$ _____
29. $8 \times 7 =$ _____	30. $1 \times 5 =$ _____	31. $7 \times 6 =$ _____	32. $2 \times 8 =$ _____

Base Ten Blocks

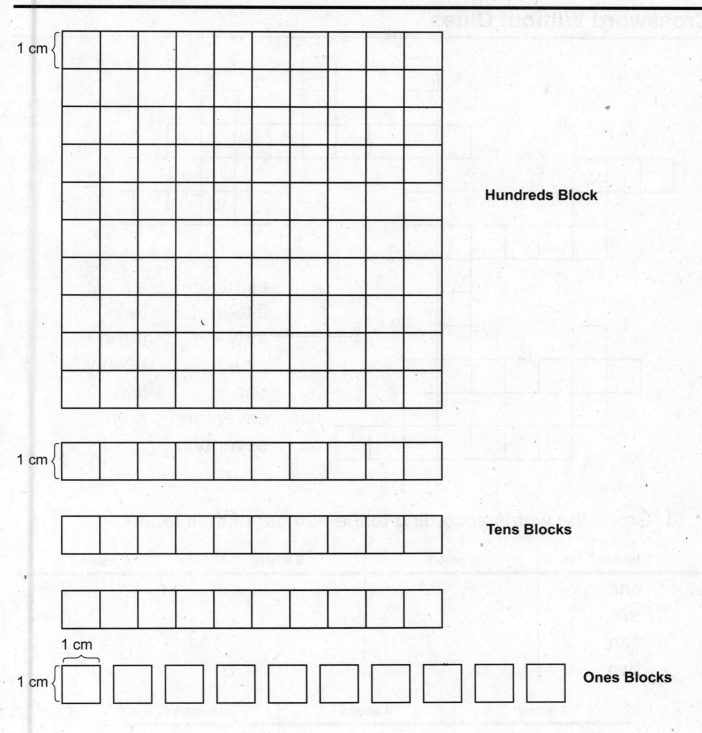

1 cm — Hundreds Block

1 cm — Tens Blocks

1 cm

1 cm — Ones Blocks

No unauthorized copying

Crossword Without Clues

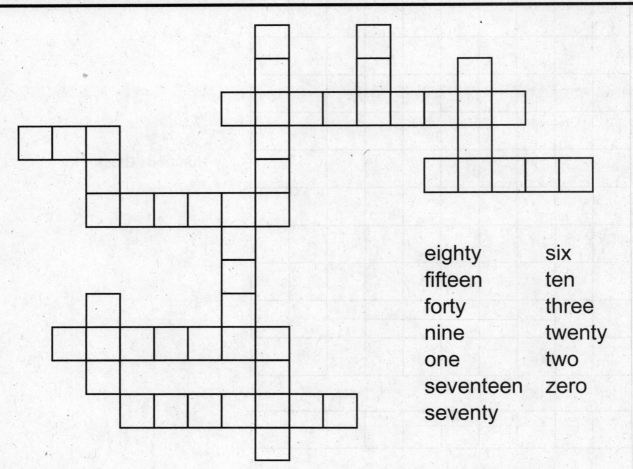

eighty   six
fifteen   ten
forty   three
nine   twenty
one   two
seventeen   zero
seventy

1. Group the words according to the number of their letters.

3 letters	4 letters	5 letters	6 letters
one			
six			
ten			
two			

7 letters	8 letters	9 letters

2. Which word is by itself in a group? Where does it fit?

3. Solve the puzzle. HINT: Cross out the words as you use them.

Number Word Search

Find:

~~one~~	ten	eleven	two	twenty
twelve	three	thirty	four	forty
fifty	zero	seventeen	eight	

w	t	i	t	w	e	n	t	y
n	w	t	e	o	e	r	t	s
f	o	u	r	v	n	y	w	p
s	e	v	e	n	t	e	e	n
z	t	l	e	r	r	i	l	f
e	e	f	i	f	t	y	v	o
r	n	h	g	n	g	a	e	r
o	t	t	h	r	e	e	n	t
d	s	u	t	m	m	e	r	y

Use the leftover letters to finish the message.

The four seasons are fall, ___ ___ ___ ___ ___ ___ ,

___ ___ ___ ___ ___ ___ ___ ___ ___ ___ ___ ___ ___ ___ ___ ___ ___ .

This puzzle was made using the Internet tool at http://www.superkids.com/aweb/tools/words/search

Number Words Crossword Puzzle

Across

2. Four less than ten
4. Rhymes with fine
7. Ten + Seven
8. Fifty + Thirty
10. Twenty + Twenty
11. Nothing

Down

1. Eleven − Ten
2. Two more than sixty-eight
3. Twenty − Five
5. Two tens
6. Seven + Three
9. Seven − Four

No unauthorized copying   **Games, Activities, and Puzzles**

Recognizing Number Words

☐ Circle the number words.

☐ Cross out the words that only sound like number words.

1. Eight children ate pie.

2. Ravi ate eight cookies.

3. She won two games.

4. He only won one game.

5. Four friends played soccer for fun.

6. She had to fix six bikes.

No unauthorized copying Games, Activities, and Puzzles

Spelling Number Words

Circle the spelling of the number words.

HINT: Look at the words you circled.

1	one	won	wun
2	to	too	two
4	for	four	fore
6	six	sicks	siks
8	ate	eight	ait

No unauthorized copying **Games, Activities, and Puzzles**

Always, Sometimes or Never True (Numbers)

A A 4-digit number is greater than a 3-digit number.	B The product of two multiples of 5 is odd.	C If you multiply a 2-digit number by a 1-digit number, the answer will be a 2-digit number.
D If you multiply a number by zero, the answer will be zero.	E When you subtract a 1-digit number from a multiple of 100 you will have to regroup.	F The product of two even numbers is even.
G When you divide, the remainder is less than the number you divide by.	H The product of two numbers is greater than the sum.	I If you have two fractions, the one with the smaller denominator is the larger fraction.
J Multiples of 8 end in even numbers.	K Tenths are larger than hundredths.	L 10 thousands is the same as 10 thousandths.
M Multiples of 5 are divisible by 2.	N The product of 0 and a number is 0.	O A number that ends in an even number is divisible by 2.

Choose a statement from the chart above and say whether it is **always** true, **sometimes** true, or **never** true. Give reasons for your answer.

1. What statement did you choose? Statement Letter _____

    This statement is…

    Always True   **Sometimes True**   **Never True**

    Explain: _____

    _____

    _____

2. Choose a statement that is sometimes true, and reword it so that it is always true.

    What statement did you choose? Statement Letter _____

    Your reworded statement: _____

    _____

3. Repeat the exercise with another statement.

Define a Number

Each statement describes at least one whole number between 1 and 100.

A The number is even.	B The number is odd.	C You can count to the number by 4s.
D You can count to the number by 3s.	E You can count to the number by 25s.	F You can count to the number by 100s.
G If you multiplied the number by 5, the product would be larger than 100.	H The number has 3 digits.	I The ones digit is one less than the tens digit. The ones digit is 5.
J The number has 3 or more digits.	K The sum of its digits is greater than 9.	L The number has 2 digits and the ones digit is greater than the tens digit.
M The number is less than 40.	N If you rolled two dice and added the numbers together, you could get the number.	O The number is less than 25.
P The ones digit of this number is divisible by 3.	Q You can get this number by multiplying another number by itself (**EXAMPLE:** 9 = 3 × 3).	R The ones digit of this number is more than the tens digit.

1. Name a number that statement **D** applies to: _____

2. Name a number that statement **C** and **O** apply to: _____

3. Name three numbers that statements **N** and **A** apply to: _____, _____, _____

4. a) Name a number that statements **B**, **D**, **G** and **O** apply to: _____

   b) Name a number that statements **D**, **L** and **O** apply to: _____

5. a) Which statements apply to both the number 22 and the number 30? _____

   b) Which statements apply to both the number 12 and the number 32? _____

6. Can you find four numbers that statement **Q** applies to? _____, _____, _____, _____

Games, Activities, and Puzzles

Money Matching Memory Game

$0.75	75¢	$7.50
750¢	20¢	$0.20
200¢	$2	$1
1¢	100¢	$0.01
$2.02	$2.20	22¢
202¢	220¢	$0.22

Games, Activities, and Puzzles

PA3-1: Counting

Tom finds the **difference** between 9 and 6 by counting on his fingers. He says "6" with his fist closed, then counts to 9, raising one finger at a time.

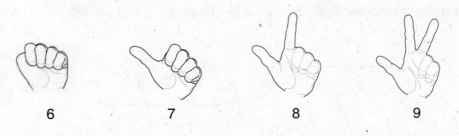

6   7   8   9

When he says "9," he has raised 3 fingers. So the difference or "gap" between 9 and 6 is 3.

----

1. Count the gap between the numbers. Write your answer in the circle. (If you know your subtraction facts, you may find the answer without counting.)

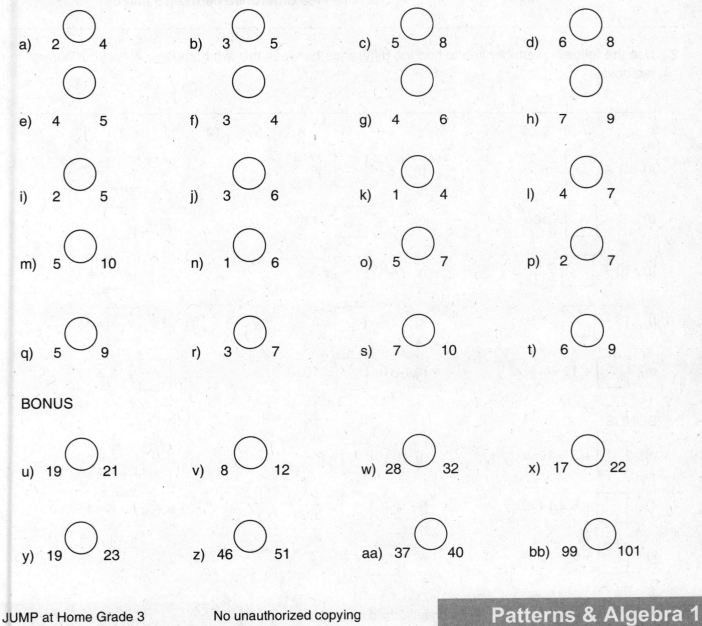

a) 2 ◯ 4   b) 3 ◯ 5   c) 5 ◯ 8   d) 6 ◯ 8

e) 4 ◯ 5   f) 3 ◯ 4   g) 4 ◯ 6   h) 7 ◯ 9

i) 2 ◯ 5   j) 3 ◯ 6   k) 1 ◯ 4   l) 4 ◯ 7

m) 5 ◯ 10   n) 1 ◯ 6   o) 5 ◯ 7   p) 2 ◯ 7

q) 5 ◯ 9   r) 3 ◯ 7   s) 7 ◯ 10   t) 6 ◯ 9

BONUS

u) 19 ◯ 21   v) 8 ◯ 12   w) 28 ◯ 32   x) 17 ◯ 22

y) 19 ◯ 23   z) 46 ◯ 51   aa) 37 ◯ 40   bb) 99 ◯ 101

Patterns & Algebra 1

PA3-1: Counting *(continued)*

What number added to 6 gives 9? $6 + \boxed{?} = 9$

Anne finds the answer using a **number line**. She puts her finger on 6 and counts the number of spaces between 6 and 9.

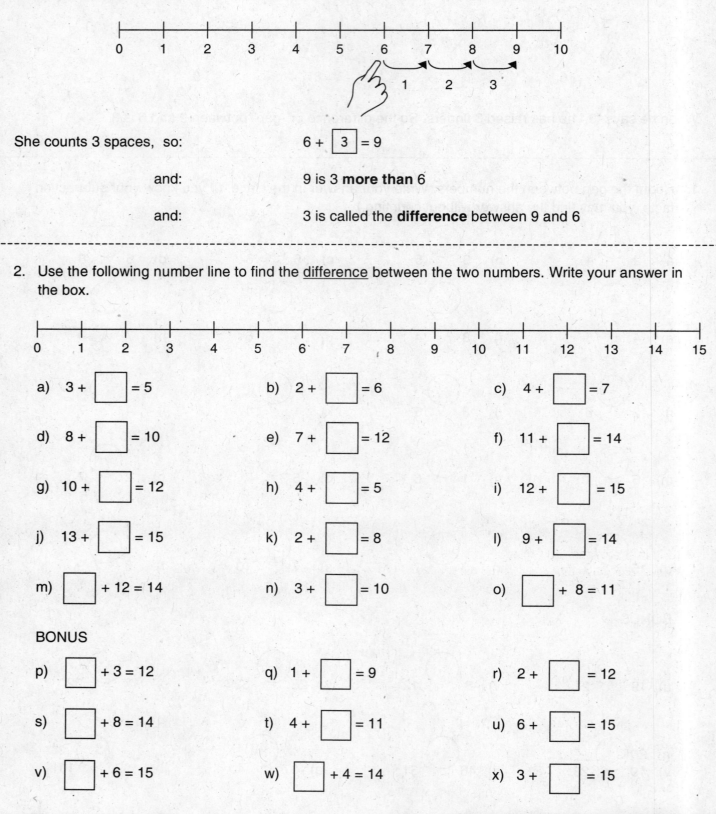

She counts 3 spaces, so: $6 + \boxed{3} = 9$

and: 9 is 3 **more than** 6

and: 3 is called the **difference** between 9 and 6

----

2. Use the following number line to find the <u>difference</u> between the two numbers. Write your answer in the box.

a) $3 + \boxed{} = 5$

b) $2 + \boxed{} = 6$

c) $4 + \boxed{} = 7$

d) $8 + \boxed{} = 10$

e) $7 + \boxed{} = 12$

f) $11 + \boxed{} = 14$

g) $10 + \boxed{} = 12$

h) $4 + \boxed{} = 5$

i) $12 + \boxed{} = 15$

j) $13 + \boxed{} = 15$

k) $2 + \boxed{} = 8$

l) $9 + \boxed{} = 14$

m) $\boxed{} + 12 = 14$

n) $3 + \boxed{} = 10$

o) $\boxed{} + 8 = 11$

BONUS

p) $\boxed{} + 3 = 12$

q) $1 + \boxed{} = 9$

r) $2 + \boxed{} = 12$

s) $\boxed{} + 8 = 14$

t) $4 + \boxed{} = 11$

u) $6 + \boxed{} = 15$

v) $\boxed{} + 6 = 15$

w) $\boxed{} + 4 = 14$

x) $3 + \boxed{} = 15$

PA3-1: Counting *(continued)*

3. Use the following number line to find the <u>difference</u> between the two numbers. Write your answer in the circle.

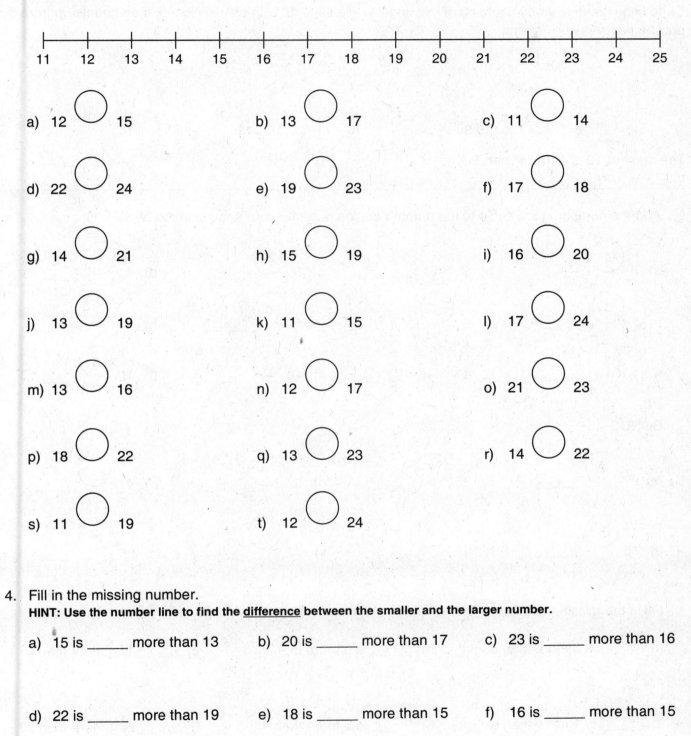

a) 12 ◯ 15

b) 13 ◯ 17

c) 11 ◯ 14

d) 22 ◯ 24

e) 19 ◯ 23

f) 17 ◯ 18

g) 14 ◯ 21

h) 15 ◯ 19

i) 16 ◯ 20

j) 13 ◯ 19

k) 11 ◯ 15

l) 17 ◯ 24

m) 13 ◯ 16

n) 12 ◯ 17

o) 21 ◯ 23

p) 18 ◯ 22

q) 13 ◯ 23

r) 14 ◯ 22

s) 11 ◯ 19

t) 12 ◯ 24

4. Fill in the missing number.
   HINT: Use the number line to find the <u>difference</u> between the smaller and the larger number.

   a) 15 is _____ more than 13

   b) 20 is _____ more than 17

   c) 23 is _____ more than 16

   d) 22 is _____ more than 19

   e) 18 is _____ more than 15

   f) 16 is _____ more than 15

   g) 20 is _____ more than 19

   h) 17 is _____ more than 13

   i) 23 is _____ more than 18

Patterns & Algebra 1

PA3-2: Preparation for Increasing Sequences

What number is 4 **more than** 8? (Or: What is 8 + 4?)

Carlo finds the answer by counting on his fingers. He says "8" with his fist closed, then counts up from 8 until he has raised 4 fingers.

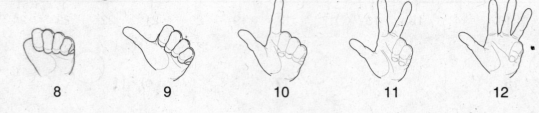

| 8 | 9 | 10 | 11 | 12 |

The number 12 is 4 **more than** 8.

----

1. Add the number in the circle to the number beside it. Write your answer in the blank.

a) 3 ④ __7__

b) 9 ② ____

c) 6 ③ ____

d) 4 ④ ____

e) 7 ⑤ ____

f) 6 ④ ____

g) 2 ⑧ ____

h) 9 ⑥ ____

i) 10 ⑧ ____

j) 17 ⑨ ____

k) 14 ⑦ ____

l) 12 ⑤ ____

BONUS

m) 27 ② ____

n) 35 ⑤ ____

o) 52 ③ ____

p) 47 ④ ____

q) 36 ⑥ ____

r) 82 ⑤ ____

s) 97 ④ ____

t) 95 ⑧ ____

2. Fill in the missing numbers.

a) _____ is 3 more than 6

b) _____ is 2 more than 7

c) _____ is 4 more than 6

d) _____ is 1 more than 8

e) _____ is 5 more than 4

f) _____ is 4 more than 13

g) _____ is 6 more than 9

h) _____ is 7 more than 7

i) _____ is 5 more than 17

No unauthorized copying

Patterns & Algebra 1

PA3-3: Increasing Sequences

Tara wants to continue the number pattern.

$$6, 8, 10, 12, \underline{?}$$

She finds the **difference** between the first two numbers by counting on her fingers.
She says "6" with her fist closed and counts until she reaches 8.

6   7   8

She has raised 2 fingers so the difference between 6 and 8 is 2.

$$\overset{\textstyle\bigcirc\!\!\!\!\!\!{\scriptstyle 2}}{6}, 8, 10, 12, \underline{?}$$

She checks that the difference between the other numbers is 2.

$$6, 8, 10, 12, \underline{?}$$
(2) (2) (2)

To continue the pattern, Tara adds 2 to the last number in the sequence.
She says "12" with her fist closed and counts up until she has raised 2 fingers.

12   13   14

(2) (2) (2) (2)
$$6, 8, 10, 12, \underline{14}$$

----

1. Extend the following patterns.
   NOTE: It is important to start by finding the gap between the numbers.

   a)   1 , 3 , 5 , ___ , ___ , ___

   b)   0 , 2 , 4 , ___ , ___ , ___

   c)   2 , 5 , 8 , ___ , ___ , ___

   d)   0 , 3 , 6 , ___ , ___ , ___

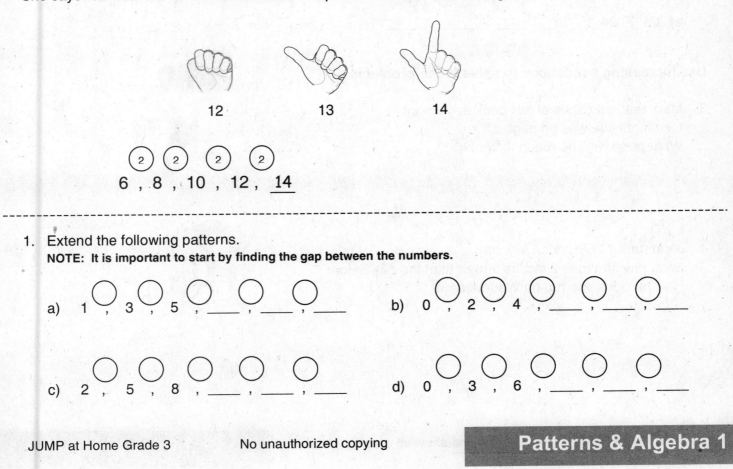

e) 0 , 5 , 10 , ___ , ___ , ___

f) 5 , 7 , 9 , ___ , ___ , ___

g) 3 , 7 , 11 , ___ , ___ , ___

h) 2 , 6 , 10 , ___ , ___ , ___

i) 4 , 8 , 12 , ___ , ___ , ___

j) 10 , 15 , 20 , ___ , ___ , ___

k) 1 , 4 , 7 , ___ , ___ , ___

l) 5 , 9 , 13 , ___ , ___ , ___

m) 11 , 13 , 15 , ___ , ___ , ___ , ___ , ___ , ___

BONUS

2. Extend the following patterns.

a) 1 , 6 , 11 , ___ , ___ , ___

b) 5 , 12 , 19 , ___ , ___ , ___

c) 21 , 24 , 27 , ___ , ___ , ___

d) 86 , 88 , 90 , ___ , ___ , ___

Use increasing sequences to solve these problems.

3. Mary reads 3 pages of her book each night.
Last night she was on page 34.
What page will she reach tonight?

4. Jane runs 10 blocks on Monday.
Each day she runs 2 blocks farther than the day before.
How far does she run on Wednesday?

PA3-4: Counting Backwards

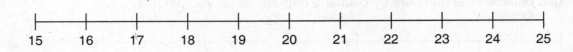

What number must you **subtract** from 22 to get 18?
Dana finds the answer by counting backwards on her fingers. She uses the number line to help.

Dana has raised 4 fingers. So 4 subtracted from 22 gives 18.

------

1. What number must you <u>subtract</u> from the bigger number to get the smaller number?

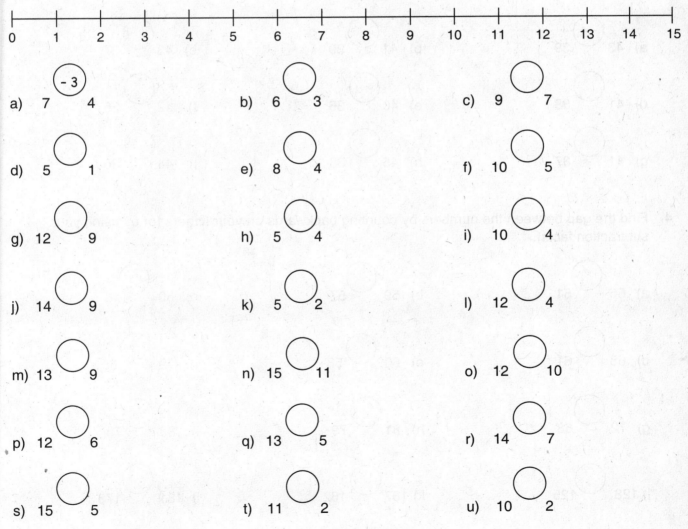

a) 7 ⟨− 3⟩ 4   b) 6 ◯ 3   c) 9 ◯ 7

d) 5 ◯ 1   e) 8 ◯ 4   f) 10 ◯ 5

g) 12 ◯ 9   h) 5 ◯ 4   i) 10 ◯ 4

j) 14 ◯ 9   k) 5 ◯ 2   l) 12 ◯ 4

m) 13 ◯ 9   n) 15 ◯ 11   o) 12 ◯ 10

p) 12 ◯ 6   q) 13 ◯ 5   r) 14 ◯ 7

s) 15 ◯ 5   t) 11 ◯ 2   u) 10 ◯ 2

2. Find the gap between the numbers by counting backwards on your fingers.

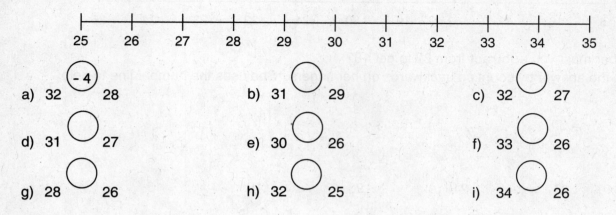

a) 32 −4 28   b) 31 ◯ 29   c) 32 ◯ 27

d) 31 ◯ 27   e) 30 ◯ 26   f) 33 ◯ 26

g) 28 ◯ 26   h) 32 ◯ 25   i) 34 ◯ 26

3. Find the gap between the numbers by counting backwards on your fingers.

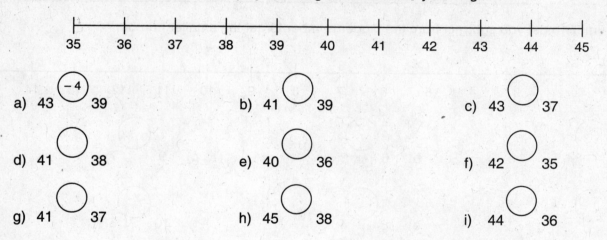

a) 43 −4 39   b) 41 ◯ 39   c) 43 ◯ 37

d) 41 ◯ 38   e) 40 ◯ 36   f) 42 ◯ 35

g) 41 ◯ 37   h) 45 ◯ 38   i) 44 ◯ 36

4. Find the gap between the numbers by counting backwards on your fingers (or by using your subtraction facts).

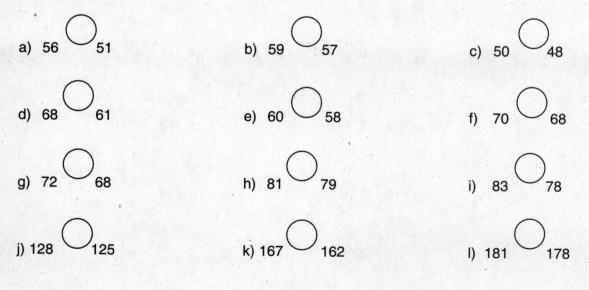

a) 56 ◯ 51   b) 59 ◯ 57   c) 50 ◯ 48

d) 68 ◯ 61   e) 60 ◯ 58   f) 70 ◯ 68

g) 72 ◯ 68   h) 81 ◯ 79   i) 83 ◯ 78

j) 128 ◯ 125   k) 167 ◯ 162   l) 181 ◯ 178

PA3-4: Counting Backwards *(continued)*

What number **subtracted** from 8 gives 5? $8 - \boxed{?} = 5$

Rita puts her finger on 8 on a **number line**.

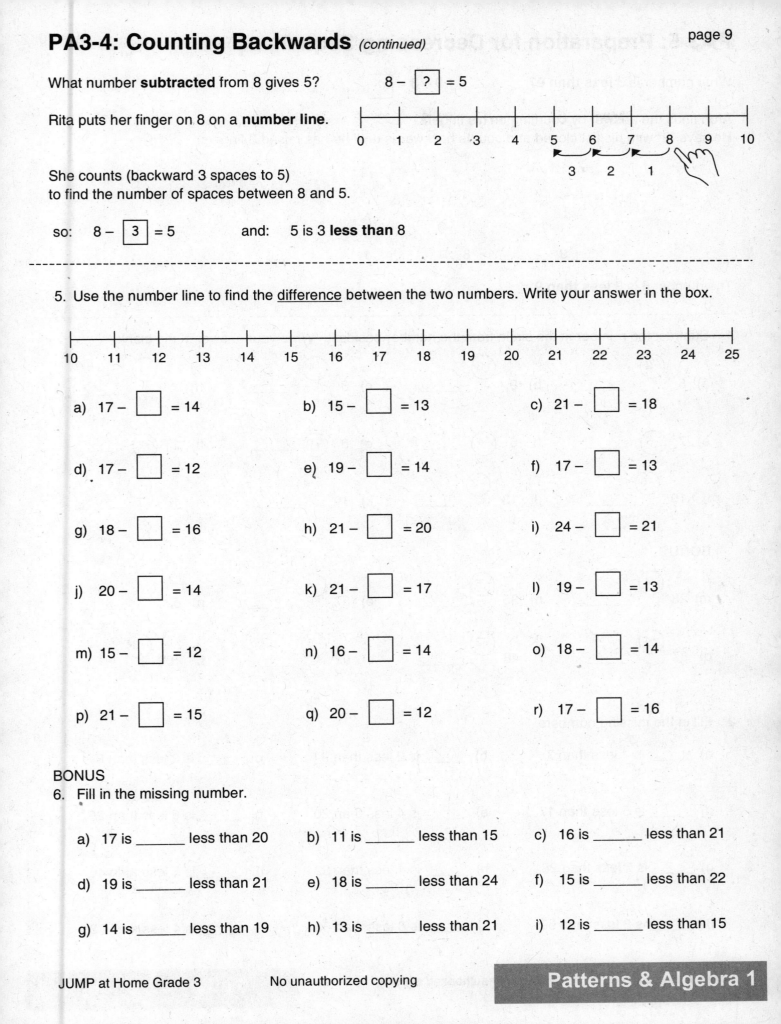

She counts (backward 3 spaces to 5)
to find the number of spaces between 8 and 5.

so: $8 - \boxed{3} = 5$ and: 5 is 3 **less than** 8

----

5. Use the number line to find the <u>difference</u> between the two numbers. Write your answer in the box.

a) $17 - \boxed{} = 14$ b) $15 - \boxed{} = 13$ c) $21 - \boxed{} = 18$

d) $17 - \boxed{} = 12$ e) $19 - \boxed{} = 14$ f) $17 - \boxed{} = 13$

g) $18 - \boxed{} = 16$ h) $21 - \boxed{} = 20$ i) $24 - \boxed{} = 21$

j) $20 - \boxed{} = 14$ k) $21 - \boxed{} = 17$ l) $19 - \boxed{} = 13$

m) $15 - \boxed{} = 12$ n) $16 - \boxed{} = 14$ o) $18 - \boxed{} = 14$

p) $21 - \boxed{} = 15$ q) $20 - \boxed{} = 12$ r) $17 - \boxed{} = 16$

BONUS
6. Fill in the missing number.

a) 17 is _____ less than 20   b) 11 is _____ less than 15   c) 16 is _____ less than 21

d) 19 is _____ less than 21   e) 18 is _____ less than 24   f) 15 is _____ less than 22

g) 14 is _____ less than 19   h) 13 is _____ less than 21   i) 12 is _____ less than 15

PA3-5: Preparation for Decreasing Sequences

What number is 3 **less than** 9? $9 - 3 = \boxed{?}$

Aron finds the answer by counting on his fingers.
He says "9" with his fist closed and counts backwards until he has raised 3 fingers.

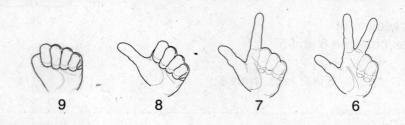

  9   8   7   6

The number 6 is 3 **less than** 9.

----

1. Subtract the number in the circle from the number beside it. Write your answer in the blank.

    a) 5 (−2) _____   b) 9 (−3) _____   c) 8 (−4) _____   d) 7 (−1) _____

    e) 7 (−5) _____   f) 6 (−4) _____   g) 3 (−1) _____   h) 11 (−2) _____

    i) 10 (−6) _____   j) 13 (−2) _____   k) 19 (−4) _____   l) 18 (−3) _____

    BONUS

    m) 28 (−4) _____   n) 35 (−6) _____   o) 57 (−8) _____   p) 62 (−4) _____

    q) 87 (−4) _____   r) 48 (−2) _____   s) 92 (−5) _____   t) 100 (−3) _____

2. Fill in the missing numbers.

    a) _____ is 4 less than 7   b) _____ is 2 less than 9   c) _____ is 3 less than 8

    d) _____ is 5 less than 17   e) _____ is 4 less than 20   f) _____ is 6 less than 25

    g) _____ is 7 less than 28   h) _____ is 4 less than 32   i) _____ is 5 less than 40

    j) _____ is 8 less than 59   k) _____ is 6 less than 63   l) _____ is 4 less than 78

Patterns & Algebra 1

PA3-6: Decreasing Sequences

1. Extend the **decreasing** patterns.
   NOTE: It is important to start by finding the gap between the numbers.

Example:

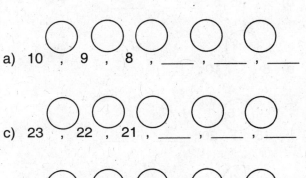

11 , 9 , 7 , ___ , ___ , ___

Step 1: 11 , 9 , 7 , ___ , ___ , ___

Step 2: 11 , 9 , 7 , 5 , 3 , 1

a) 10 , 9 , 8 , ___ , ___ , ___

b) 14 , 12 , 10 , ___ , ___ , ___

c) 23 , 22 , 21 , ___ , ___ , ___

d) 24 , 21 , 18 , ___ , ___ , ___

e) 90 , 80 , 70 , ___ , ___ , ___

f) 45 , 40 , 35 , ___ , ___ , ___

g) 15 , 13 , 11 , ___ , ___ , ___

h) 33 , 30 , 27 , ___ , ___ , ___

i) 23 , 21 , 19 , ___ , ___ , ___

j) 28 , 25 , 22 , ___ , ___ , ___

BONUS

k) 95 , 90 , 85 , ___ , ___ , ___

l) 110 , 100 , 90 , ___ , ___ , ___

m) 44 , 40 , 36 , ___ , ___ , ___ , ___ , ___ , ___

PA3-7: Increasing and Decreasing Sequences

1. Extend the patterns, using the gap provided.

   Example 1:

   (+1)

   6 , 7 , _8_ , _9_

   Example 2:

   (−2)

   8 , 6 , _4_ , _2_

   a) (+5) 5 , 10 , ___ , ___

   b) (+3) 2 , 5 , ___ , ___

   c) (+3) 3 , 6 , ___ , ___

   d) (+2) 8 , 10 , ___ , ___

   e) (+2) 14 , 16 , ___ , ___

   f) (+5) 15 , 20 , ___ , ___

   g) (−1) 13 , 12 , ___ , ___

   h) (−2) 18 , 16 , ___ , ___

   i) (−5) 25 , 20 , ___ , ___

   j) (−2) 9 , 7 , ___ , ___

   k) (−3) 22 , 19 , ___ , ___

   l) (−4) 17 , 13 , ___ , ___

   m) (−5) 29 , 24 , ___ , ___

   n) (+5) 32 , 37 , ___ , ___

   o) (+3) 21 , 24 , ___ , ___

   p) (−2) 102 , 100 , ___ , ___

BONUS
2. Rachel has a box of 24 tangerines. She eats 3 each day for 5 days.
   How many are left?

3. Extend the patterns by first finding the gap.
   HINT: You should first check that the gap is the same between each pair of numbers!

Example:

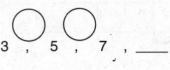

3 , 5 , 7 , ____

Step 1:

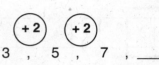

+2   +2

3 , 5 , 7 , ____

Step 2:

+2   +2

3 , 5 , 7 , __9__

a) 5 , 8 , 11 , ____   b) 2 , 4 , 6 , ____

c) 6 , 10 , 14 , ____   d) 1 , 3 , 5 , ____

e) 21 , 24 , 27 , ____   f) 12 , 17 , 22 , ____

g) 25 , 23 , 21 , ____   h) 29 , 24 , 19 , ____

i) 12 , 9 , 6 , ____ , ____   j) 30 , 25 , 20 , ____ , ____

BONUS

k) 45 , 48 , 51 , ____   l) 105 , 95 , 85 , ____ , ____

m) 32 , 34 , 36 , ____ , ____ , ____ , ____ , ____ , ____ , ____

PA3-8: Extending Repeating Patterns

1. The box shows the core of the pattern Karen made with red (R) and yellow (Y) blocks.
   Continue her pattern.

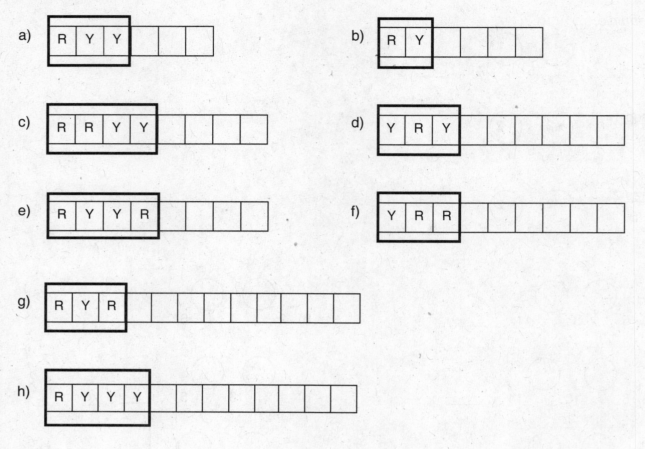

a) | R | Y | Y |

b) | R | Y |

c) | R | R | Y | Y |

d) | Y | R | Y |

e) | R | Y | Y | R |

f) | Y | R | R |

g) | R | Y | R |

h) | R | Y | Y | Y |

2. The core of Rachel's pattern is in the rectangle.
   Stan tried to continue the pattern.
   Did he continue the pattern correctly?
   HINT: Shade the reds if it helps.

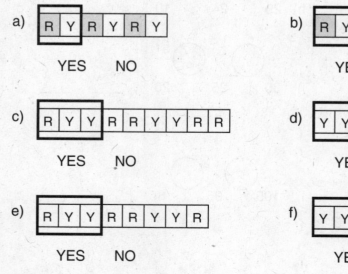

a) | R | Y | R | Y | R | Y |

   YES   NO

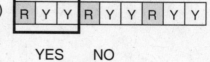

b) | R | Y | Y | R | Y | Y | R | Y | Y |

   YES   NO

c) | R | Y | Y | R | R | Y | Y | R | R |

   YES   NO

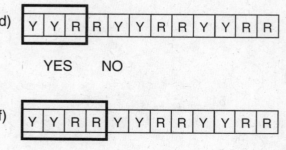

d) | Y | Y | R | R | Y | Y | R | R | Y | Y | R | R |

   YES   NO

e) | R | Y | Y | R | R | Y | Y | R |

   YES   NO

f) | Y | Y | R | R | Y | Y | R | R | Y | Y | R | R |

   YES   NO

PA3-9: Finding Cores in Patterns

1. Are the blocks in the rectangle the <u>core</u> of the pattern?

a) R Y R Y R Y

   YES   NO

b) R Y Y R Y Y R Y Y

   YES   NO

c) R Y Y R R Y Y R

   YES   NO

d) Y Y R R Y Y R R Y Y R R

   YES   NO

e) Y R Y R R Y R Y R R

   YES   NO

f) R Y R Y Y R Y R Y Y

   YES   NO

2. Put a rectangle around the blocks that make up the core of the pattern.

a) Y R R Y R R Y R R

b) R R R Y R R R Y

c) Y Y R R Y Y R R Y Y R R

d) Y R R Y Y R R Y

e) R Y R Y Y Y R Y R Y Y Y

f) R Y R Y R Y R Y R

g) Y R Y Y R Y R Y Y R Y R

h) R Y Y Y R R Y Y Y R

3. Continue the pattern below to show 20 blocks altogether.

1	2	3	4	5	6	7	8	9	10	11	12	13	14	15	16	17	18	19	20
R	Y	R	Y	R	Y	R	Y	R	Y										

a) What colour are the following blocks?

   i) block 12   ii) block 14   iii) block 15   iv) block 18

b) What colour are the blocks of the even numbers (2, 4, 6, 8, ...)? _____

c) If you continued the pattern, what colour would the following blocks be?

   i) block 22   ii) block 27   iii) block 35   iv) block 44

     Patterns & Algebra 1

PA3-10: Making Patterns with Squares

1. Add a square to the figure (along the edge shown by the arrow).

Example 1: 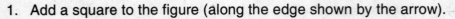   *Example 2:*

a)   b)   c)   d)

e)   f)   g)   h)

2. Shade the square that was added to Figure 1 to make Figure 2.

a)   Figure 1   Figure 2

b)   Figure 1   Figure 2

c)   Figure 1   Figure 2

d)   Figure 1   Figure 2

e)   Figure 1   Figure 2

f)   Figure 1   Figure 2

g)   Figure 1   Figure 2

h)   Figure 1   Figure 2

i)   Figure 1   Figure 2

3. Shade the <u>two</u> squares that were added to Figure 1 to make Figure 2.

a)   Figure 1   Figure 2

b)   Figure 1   Figure 2

c)   Figure 1   Figure 2

d)   Figure 1   Figure 2

e)   Figure 1   Figure 2

f)   Figure 1   Figure 2

Patterns & Algebra 1

4. Shade any squares that were added to make the <u>next</u> figure in the pattern.

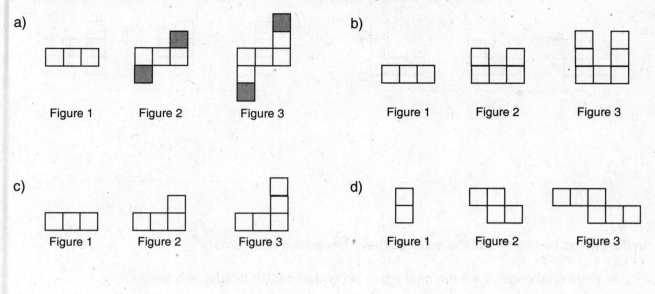

a)
Figure 1   Figure 2   Figure 3

b)
Figure 1   Figure 2   Figure 3

c)
Figure 1   Figure 2   Figure 3

d)
Figure 1   Figure 2   Figure 3

5. Shade any squares that were added to make the next figure.
    Then draw Figure 4 in the box provided.

a)
Figure 1   Figure 2   Figure 3

Figure 4

b)
Figure 1   Figure 2   Figure 3

Figure 4

c)
Figure 1   Figure 2   Figure 3

Figure 4

d)
Figure 1   Figure 2   Figure 3

Figure 4

PA3-11: Making Patterns with Squares (Advanced)

1. Draw the next figure (or build it using blocks).

a)

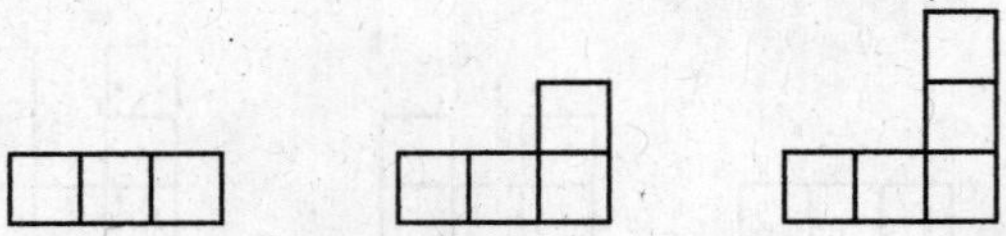

b)

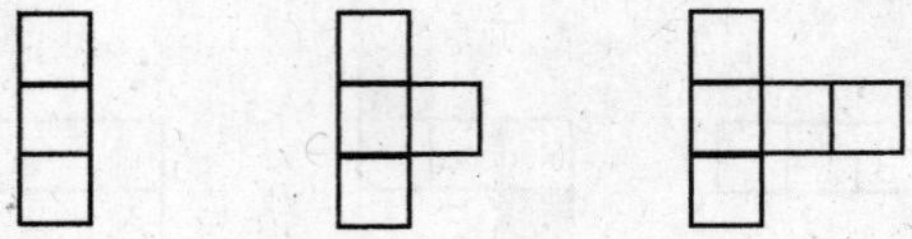

BONUS

2. In the figures below, shade the squares that were added each time.

   For an extra challenge, draw the next figure on grid paper (or build it with blocks).

a)

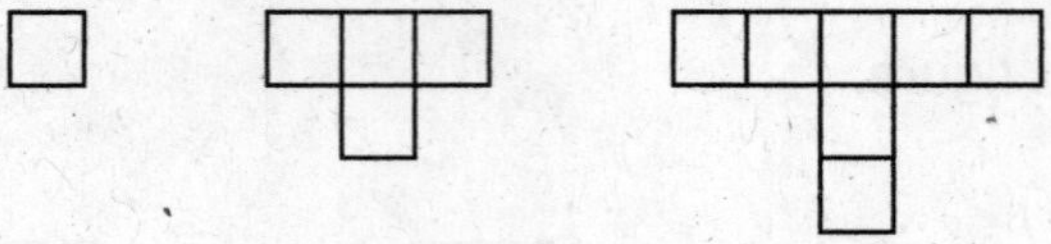

b)

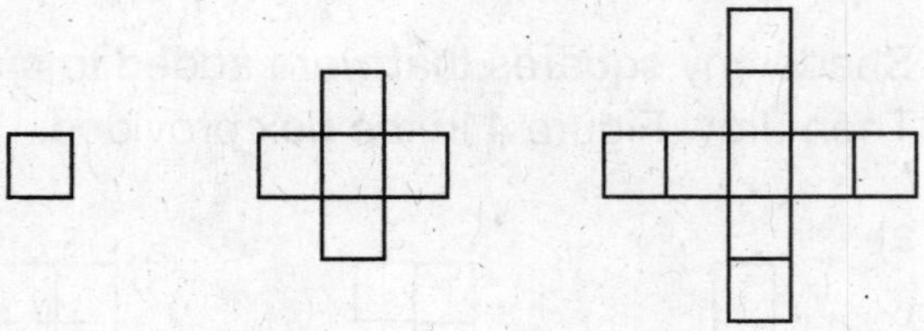

c)

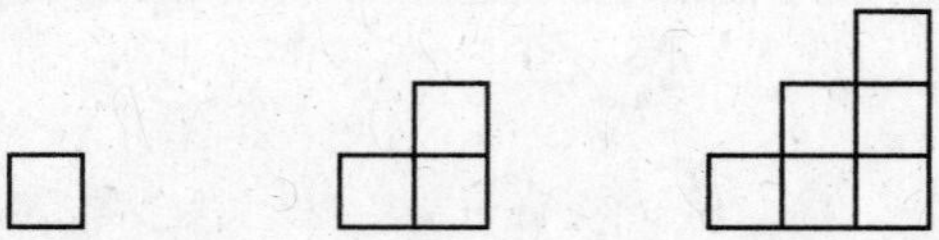

d)

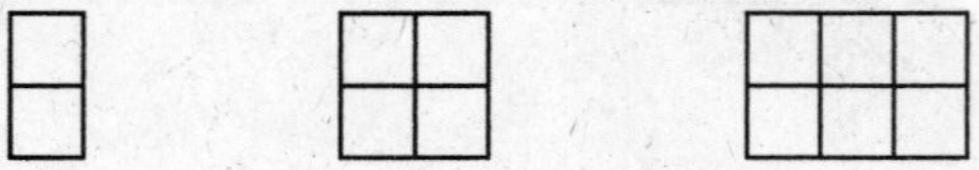

e)

f)

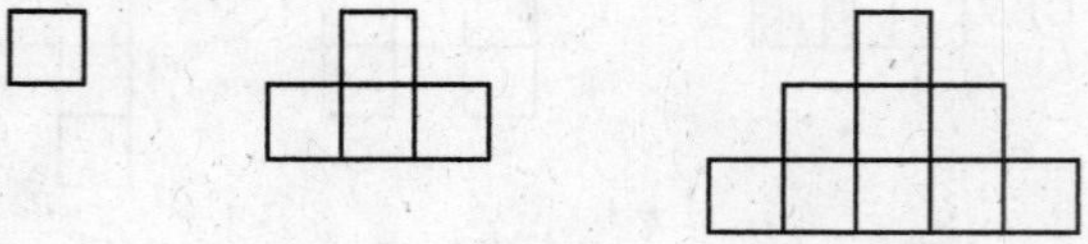

g)

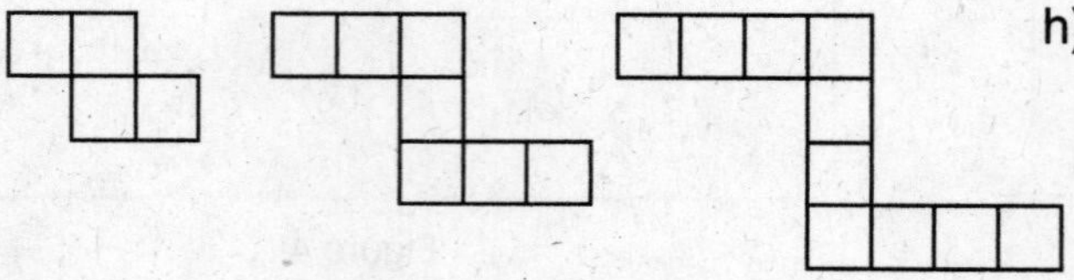

h)

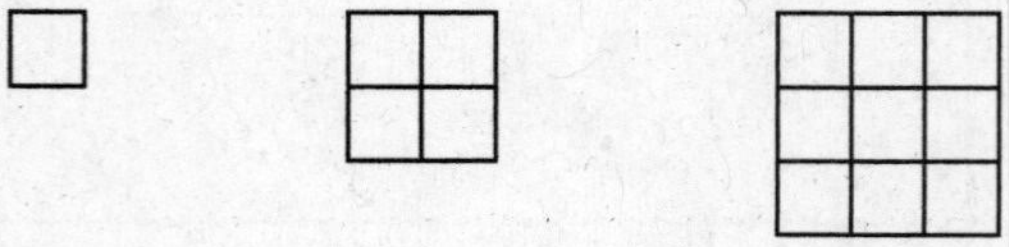

Patterns & Algebra 1

PA3-12: Extending a Pattern Using a Rule

1. Continue the following sequences by <u>adding</u> the number given.

   a) (add 3)   30, 33, _____ , _____ , _____   b) (add 5)   60, 65, _____ , _____ , _____

   c) (add 2)   26, 28, _____ , _____ , _____   d) (add 10) 20, 30, _____ , _____ , _____

   e) (add 3)   12, 15, _____ , _____ , _____   f) (add 5)   46, 51, _____ , _____ , _____

   g) (add 5) 105, 110, _____ , _____ , _____   h) (add 5)   4, 9, _____ , _____ , _____

2. Continue the following sequences by <u>subtracting</u> the number given.

   a) (subtract 2)   12, 10, _____ , _____ , _____   b) (subtract 3)   18, 15, _____ , _____ , _____

   c) (subtract 5)   55, 50, _____ , _____ , _____   d) (subtract 3)   63, 60, _____ , _____ , _____

   e) (subtract 2)   88, 86, _____ , _____ , _____   f) (subtract 5)   79, 74, _____ , _____ , _____

   g) (subtract 3)   30, 27, _____ , _____ , _____   h) (subtract 5) 200, 195, _____ , _____ , _____

BONUS
3. Which of the following sequences were made by adding 3? Circle them.
   HINT: Check all the numbers in each sequence.

   a) 3, 7, 9, 11   b) 3, 6, 9, 11   c) 3, 6, 9, 12

   d) 19, 22, 25, 28   e) 15, 18, 21, 24   f) 18, 21, 24, 29

4.   **2, 6, 10, 14 ...**

   Ann says the above pattern was made by adding 4 each time. Is she right? Explain how you know.

   _____

   _____

PA3-12: Extending a Pattern Using a Rule (continued)

5. Continue the following sequences by <u>adding</u> the number given.

    a) (add 4)   30, 34, _____, _____, _____

    b) (add 9)   11, 20, _____, _____, . _____

    c) (add 6)   10, 16, _____, _____, _____

    d) (add 7)   70, 77, _____, _____, _____

    e) (add 11)   10, 21, _____, _____, _____

    f) (add 4)   56, 60, _____, _____, _____

    g) (add 8)   73, 81, _____, _____, _____

    h) (add 10)   71, 81, _____, _____, _____

6. Continue the following sequences by <u>subtracting</u> the number given.

    a) (subtract 4)   45, 41, _____, _____, _____

    b) (subtract 7)   48, 41, _____, _____, _____

    c) (subtract 3)   92, 89, _____, _____, _____

    d) (subtract 8)   142, 134, _____, _____, _____

    e) (subtract 5)   230, 225, _____, _____

    f) (subtract 5)   565, 560, _____, _____

    g) (subtract 6)   366, 360, _____, _____

    h) (subtract 10)   423, 413, _____, _____

BONUS
7. Create a pattern of your own. Write your pattern in the blanks. Then give the rule you used.

    _____ , _____ , _____ , _____ , _____   My rule: _____

8.   **67, 59, 51, 43, 35 ...**

    Tariq says this sequence was made by subtracting 9 each time. Sharon says it was made by subtracting 8. Who is right?

    _____

    _____

PA3-13: Identifying Pattern Rules

1. The following sequences were made by <u>adding</u> a number repeatedly. In each case, say what number was added.

   a) ☐ 2, 4, 6, 8   add _____   b)   3, 6, 9, 12   add _____

   c) ☐ 15, 18, 21, 24   add _____   d)   42, 44, 46, 48   add _____

   e) ☐ 41, 46, 51, 56   add _____   f)   19, 23, 27, 31   add _____

   g) ☐ 243, 245, 247, 249 add _____   h)   21, 27, 33, 39   add _____

2. The following sequences were made by <u>subtracting</u> a number repeatedly. In each case, say what number was subtracted.

   a) 16, 14, 12, 10   subtract _____   b)   30, 25, 20, 15   subtract _____

   c) 100, 99, 98, 97   subtract _____   d)   42, 39, 36, 33   subtract _____

   e) 17, 14, 11, 8   subtract _____   f)   99, 97, 95, 93   subtract _____

   g) 190, 180, 170, 160   subtract _____   h)   100, 95, 90, 85   subtract _____

3. State the rule for the following patterns.

   a) 117, 110, 103, 96, 89   subtract _____   b) 1, 9, 17, 25, 33, 41   add _____

   c) 101, 105, 109, 113   _____   d) 99, 88, 77, 66   _____

BONUS

4. Continue the pattern by filling in the blanks. Then write a rule for the pattern.

   13, 18, 23, _____, _____, _____   The rule is: _____

5.   **5, 8, 11, 14, 17 ...**

   Keith says the pattern rule is: "Start at 5 and subtract 3 each time."

   Jane says the rule is: "Add 4 each time."

   Molly says the rule is: "Start at 5 and add 3 each time."

   a) Whose rule is correct?

   b) What mistakes did the others make? Explain.

PA3-14: Introduction to T-tables

Abdul makes a **growing** pattern with squares. He records the number of squares in each figure in a T-table. He also records the number of squares he adds each time he makes a new figure.

Figure 1

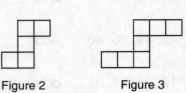

Figure 2   Figure 3

Figure	Number of Squares
1	3
2	5
3	7

② ← Number of squares added each time

②

The number of squares in the figures are 3, 5, 7, …
Abdul writes a rule for this number pattern.

RULE: Start at 3 and add 2 each time.

---

1. Abdul makes another <u>growing</u> pattern with squares. How many squares does he add to make each new figure? Write your answer in the circles provided. Then write a rule for the pattern.

a)

Figure	Number of Squares
1	4
2	7
3	10

Rule:

b)

Figure	Number of Squares
1	2
2	5
3	8

Rule:

c)

Figure	Number of Squares
1	4
2	6
3	8

Rule:

d)

Figure	Number of Squares
1	1
2	5
3	9

Rule:

e)

Figure	Number of Squares
1	5
2	7
3	9

Rule:

f)

Figure	Number of Squares
1	6
2	12
3	18

Rule:

PA3-14: Introduction to T-tables (continued)

g)

Figure	Number of Squares
1	2
2	8
3	14

Rule:

h)

Figure	Number of Squares
1	3
2	6
3	9

Rule:

i)

Figure	Number of Squares
1	5
2	12
3	19

Rule:

BONUS

2. Extend the number pattern. How many squares would be used in Figure 6?

a)

Figure	Number of Squares
1	2
2	5
3	8
4	
5	
6	

b)

Figure	Number of Squares
1	6
2	9
3	12

c)

Figure	Number of Squares
1	1
2	6
3	11

d)

Figure	Number of Squares
1	4
2	9
3	14

e)

Figure	Number of Squares
1	10
2	13
3	16

f)

Figure	Number of Squares
1	12
2	16
3	20

3. Make a T-table and record the number of squares or circles in each figure. Write a rule for the pattern.

a)

b)

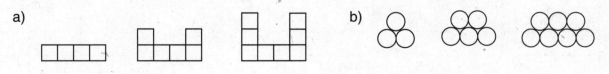

No unauthorized copying

Patterns & Algebra 1

PA3-14: Introduction to T-tables *(continued)*

4. Amy makes a growing pattern with squares. After making Figure 3, she only has 14 squares left. Does she have enough squares to complete Figure 4?

a)

Figure	Number of Squares
1	4
2	7
3	10

YES   NO

b)

Figure	Number of Squares
1	6
2	9
3	12

YES   NO

c)

Figure	Number of Squares
1	1
2	6
3	11

YES   NO

5. Extend the pattern to find out how many eggs 5 birds would lay.

a)

Bald Eagle	Number of Eggs
1	2
2	4
3	
4	
5	

b)

Sand-piper	Number of Eggs
1	4
2	8

c)

Snow Goose	Number of Eggs
1	3
2	6

d)

Marsh Hawk	Number of Eggs
1	5
2	10

6. How many young would 5 animals have?

a)

Polar Bear	Number of Cubs
1	2
2	4

b)

Swift Fox	Number of Pups
1	4
2	8

c)

Bearded Seal	Number of Pups
1	5
2	10

d)

Coyote	Number of Cubs
1	6
2	12

7. How much money would Alice earn for 4 hours of work?

a)

Hours Worked	Dollars Earned in an Hour
1	$7

b)

Hours Worked	Dollars Earned in an Hour
1	$8

c)

Hours Worked	Dollars Earned in an Hour
1	$6

1. How many squares or triangles would be used for Figure 6? Explain how you know.

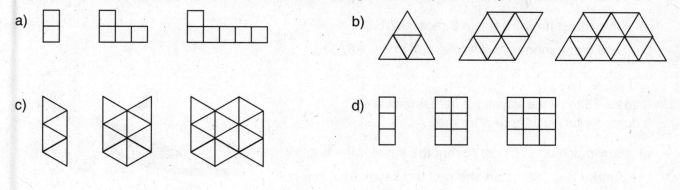

a)

b)

c)

d)

2. Priya makes a sequence of Ls with nickels.

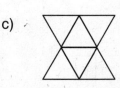

Figure 1   Figure 2   Figure 3

   a) How many nickels will be in Figure 5?

   b) What is the value of the coins in Figure 5?

3. Indra makes broaches with triangles. She has 16 triangles.

   Does she have enough triangles to make 5 broaches if there are:

   a)

   4 triangles in
   each broach?

   b)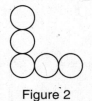

   3 triangles in
   each broach?

   c)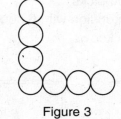

   6 triangles in
   each broach?

   d) Explain how you know the answer for part a).

BONUS
4. The even numbers (greater than 0) are the numbers you say when counting by 2s:

   2, 4, 6, 8, 10, 12, 14 ...

   Predict whether the number of squares in Figure 10 in Question 1 d) above will be even or not.

PA3-16: Problems and Puzzles

> **Answer the following questions in your notebook.**

1. Bill saves $6 each month.

   a) How much he will save in 3 months?

   b) How many months will it take him to save $30?

2. It costs $5 to rent a kayak for the first hour.
   It costs $4 for each hour after that.

   a) How much does it cost to rent the kayak for 4 hours?

   b) Sandra has $26. Can she rent the kayak for 6 hours?

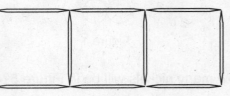

3. Karla has 20 toothpicks.
   Can she make a design with 6 squares?
   Explain how you know.

   Step 1   Step 2   Step 3

4. How many squares and circles would be in Design E?

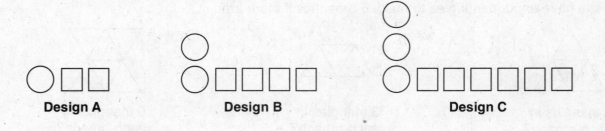

   Design A   Design B   Design C

5. Each pattern was made by adding a number repeatedly.
   Find the mistake and correct it.

   a)   5, 8, 9, 11, 13

   b)   7, 10, 13, 15, 19

6. Find an increasing pattern and a repeating pattern in your classroom.

Patterns & Algebra 1

NS3-1: Place Value – Ones, Tens, and Hundreds

1. Write the place value of the underlined digit.

REMEMBER:

375

| hundreds | tens | ones |

a) 1<u>7</u> — ones

b) 9<u>8</u>

c) <u>2</u>4

d) 6<u>3</u>

e) <u>3</u>81

f) 97<u>2</u>

g) 4<u>5</u>7

h) 7<u>9</u>

i) <u>2</u>61

j) <u>8</u>

2. Give the place value of the number 5 in each of the numbers below.
   HINT: Underline the 5 in each question first.

a) 50

b) 15

c) 251

d) 586

e) 375

f) 584

3. You can also write numbers using a place value chart.

Example:
In a place value chart, 431 is:

hundreds	tens	ones
4	3	1

Write the following numbers into the place value chart.

		hundreds	tens	ones
a)	65	0	6	5
b)	283			
c)	17			
d)	942			
e)	408			

		hundreds	tens	ones
f)	130			
g)	753			
h)	4			
i)	201			
j)	989			

JUMP at Home Grade 3 — No unauthorized copying — **Number Sense 1**

NS3-2: Place Value

The number 475 is a **3-digit number**.

- ♣ The **digit** 4 stands for 400 – the **value** of the digit 4 is 400.
- ♣ The **digit** 7 stands for 70 – the **value** of the digit 7 is 70.
- ♣ The **digit** 5 stands for 5 – the **value** of the digit 5 is 5.

---

1. Write the **value** of each digit.

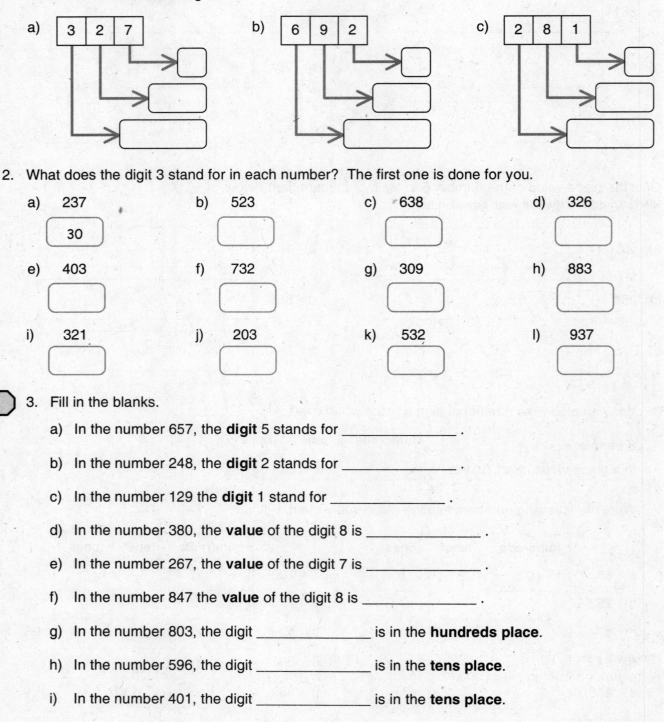

a) | 3 | 2 | 7 |

b) | 6 | 9 | 2 |

c) | 2 | 8 | 1 |

2. What does the digit 3 stand for in each number? The first one is done for you.

a) 237

30

b) 523

c) 638

d) 326

e) 403

f) 732

g) 309

h) 883

i) 321

j) 203

k) 532

l) 937

3. Fill in the blanks.

a) In the number 657, the **digit** 5 stands for _____ .

b) In the number 248, the **digit** 2 stands for _____ .

c) In the number 129 the **digit** 1 stand for _____ .

d) In the number 380, the **value** of the digit 8 is _____ .

e) In the number 267, the **value** of the digit 7 is _____ .

f) In the number 847 the **value** of the digit 8 is _____ .

g) In the number 803, the digit _____ is in the **hundreds place**.

h) In the number 596, the digit _____ is in the **tens place**.

i) In the number 401, the digit _____ is in the **tens place**.

NS3-3: Representation with Base Ten Materials

1. What number is shown in the picture?

   Write your answer in **expanded form** (as shown in the example).

> **Base ten blocks** are used to represent ones, tens, and hundreds:
>
>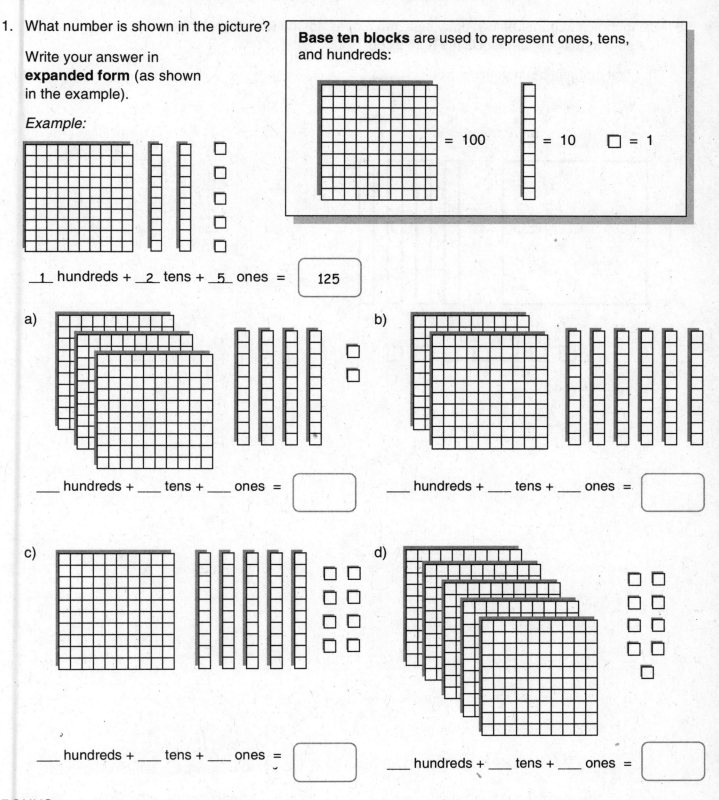
>
> = 100   = 10   ☐ = 1

Example:

__1__ hundreds + __2__ tens + __5__ ones = [125]

a)

___ hundreds + ___ tens + ___ ones = [   ]

b)

___ hundreds + ___ tens + ___ ones = [   ]

c)

___ hundreds + ___ tens + ___ ones = [   ]

d)

___ hundreds + ___ tens + ___ ones = [   ]

BONUS

2. Make your own model of a number using base ten blocks.
   Write your number in expanded form in the space below.

_____

3. Using the chart paper below, draw base ten models for the following numbers.
   (Be sure to make your models the right size!)

   The first one has been done for you.

a) 147

b) 63

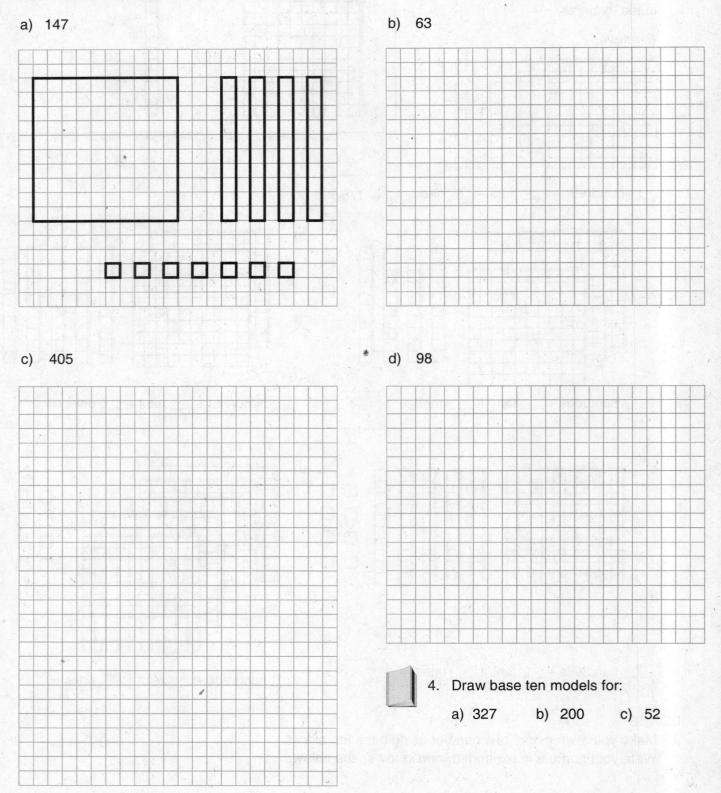

c) 405

d) 98

4. Draw base ten models for:

   a) 327   b) 200   c) 52

1. Expand the following numbers in numerals and words.

   a) 427 = __4__ hundreds + __2__ tens + __7__ ones

   b) 893 = ____ hundreds + ____ tens + ____ ones

   c) 56 = ____ hundreds + ____ tens + ____ ones

   d) 2 = ____ hundreds + ____ tens + ____ ones

   e) 671 = _____

   f) 304 = _____

2. Expand the numbers using numerals. The first one is done for you.

   a) 953 = __900 + 50 + 3__

   b) 139 = _____

   c) 27 = _____

   d) 604 = _____

   e) 470 = _____

   f) 201 = _____

   g) 32 = _____

   h) 493 = _____

3. Write the number for each sum.

   a) 200 + 50 + 3 = _____

   b) 400 + 60 + 8 = _____

   c) 20 + 7 = _____

   d) 900 + 90 + 9 = _____

   e) 600 + 7 = _____

   f) 500 + 60 = _____

   g) 300 + 20 + 7 = _____

   h) 800 + 2 = _____

   i) 900 + 40 = _____

4. Find the missing numbers.

   a) 800 + _____ + 7 = 827

   b) 400 + _____ + 5 = 475

   c) 900 + _____ + 2 = 982

   d) 500 + 20 + _____ = 526

   e) 200 + _____ = 202

   f) 300 + _____ = 320

   g) _____ + 30 = 730

   h) 600 + _____ = 680

   i) 900 + _____ + _____ = 926

   j) 100 + _____ + _____ = 173

5. Write each number in **expanded form**. Then draw a base ten model.

Example: 634 = | 600 + 30 + 4 |

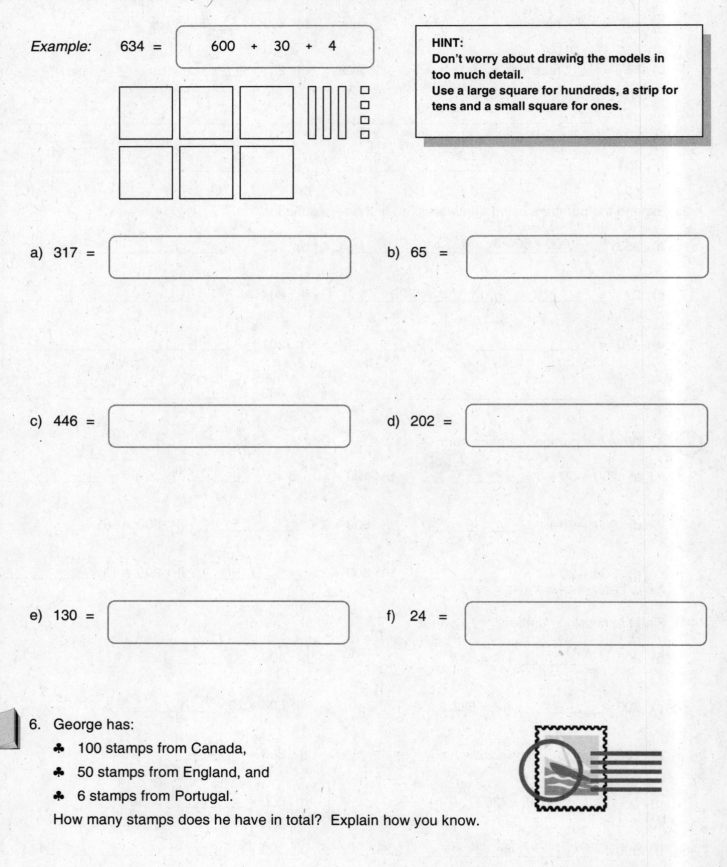

HINT:
Don't worry about drawing the models in too much detail.
Use a large square for hundreds, a strip for tens and a small square for ones.

a) 317 =

b) 65 =

c) 446 =

d) 202 =

e) 130 =

f) 24 =

6. George has:
    ♣ 100 stamps from Canada,
    ♣ 50 stamps from England, and
    ♣ 6 stamps from Portugal.
    How many stamps does he have in total? Explain how you know.

Patrick makes a **model** of the number 27 using base ten blocks.
He writes the number in **expanded form**, using **words and numerals**, and using **numerals alone**.

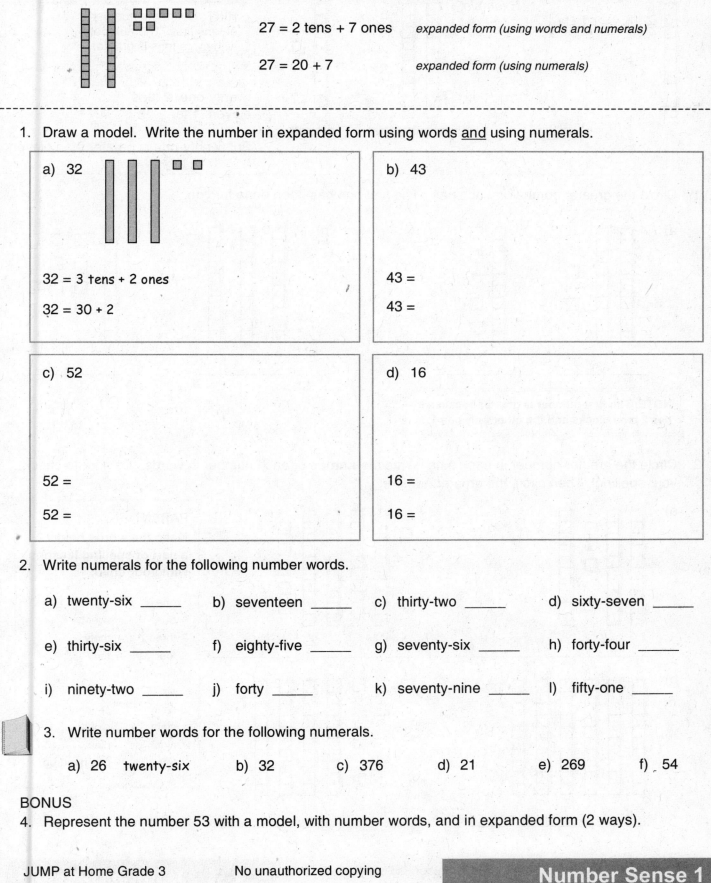

27 = 2 tens + 7 ones   *expanded form (using words and numerals)*

27 = 20 + 7   *expanded form (using numerals)*

----

1. Draw a model. Write the number in expanded form using words <u>and</u> using numerals.

a) 32

32 = 3 tens + 2 ones

32 = 30 + 2

b) 43

43 =

43 =

c) 52

52 =

52 =

d) 16

16 =

16 =

2. Write numerals for the following number words.

a) twenty-six ـــــ   b) seventeen ـــــ   c) thirty-two ـــــ   d) sixty-seven ـــــ

e) thirty-six ـــــ   f) eighty-five ـــــ   g) seventy-six ـــــ   h) forty-four ـــــ

i) ninety-two ـــــ   j) forty ـــــ   k) seventy-nine ـــــ   l) fifty-one ـــــ

3. Write number words for the following numerals.

a) 26   twenty-six   b) 32   c) 376   d) 21   e) 269   f) 54

BONUS
4. Represent the number 53 with a model, with number words, and in expanded form (2 ways).

NS3-6: Comparing Numbers

Compare the base ten models to determine which amount is greater.

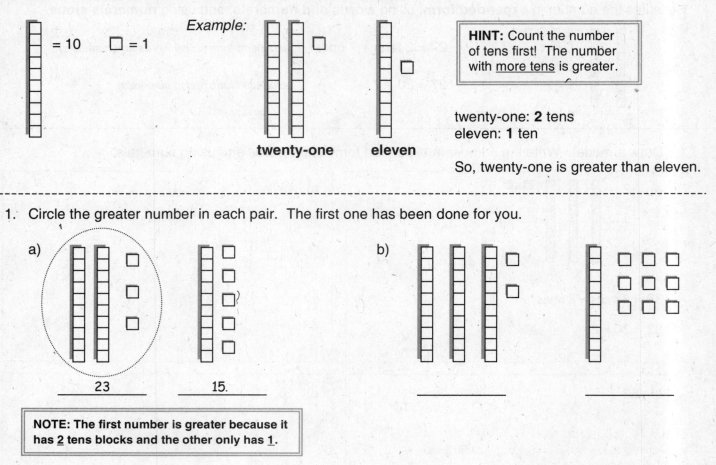

Example:

twenty-one   **eleven**

HINT: Count the number of tens first! The number with <u>more tens</u> is greater.

twenty-one: **2** tens
eleven: **1** ten

So, twenty-one is greater than eleven.

---

1. Circle the greater number in each pair. The first one has been done for you.

   a)

   _____23_____   _____15._____

   NOTE: The first number is greater because it has <u>2</u> tens blocks and the other only has <u>1</u>.

   b)

   _____   _____

2. Circle the greater number in each pair. Write the **names** of each number in words. Be sure to check your spelling! Then circle the greater number.

   a)

   _____   _____

   b)

   _____   _____

   PARENT:
   Make the words below a part of spelling lessons with your child:

one	
two	twenty
three	thirty
four	forty
five	fifty
six	sixty
seven	seventy
eight	eighty
nine	ninety
ten	one hundred

3. Write a number for each model in the box. Write the words for each number on the line below. Then, circle the greater number in each pair.

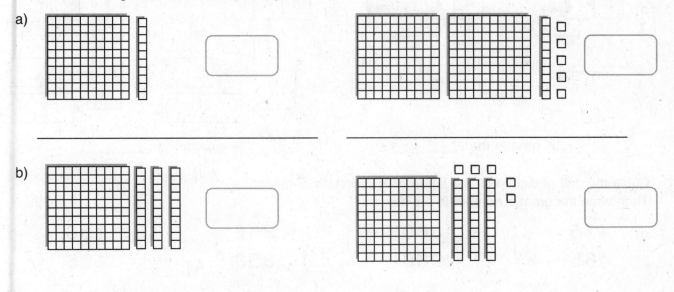

a)

b)

4. Explain how you knew which number in Question 3 a) was greater.

_____

_____

5. Write words for each number. Then circle the greater number in each pair.

HINT: If there is the same number of hundreds, count the number of tens.

a)

b)

6. Circle the greater number in each pair.

a) 34   forty-two   b) eighty-two   91   c) fifty-six   63

d) three hundred six   217   e) one hundred thirty-two   140

1. Write the **value** of each digit. Then complete the sentence.

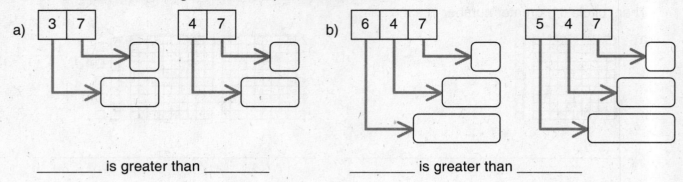

a)
| 3 | 7 |

| 4 | 7 |

b)
| 6 | 4 | 7 |

| 5 | 4 | 7 |

_____ is greater than _____   _____ is greater than _____

2. Circle the pair of digits that are different in each pair of numbers.
   Then write the greater number in the box.

a) 4⁷5   b) 360   c) 852   d) 136
    4⁶5   260   858   126

   [475]   [   ]   [   ]   [   ]

3. Read the numbers from left to right.
   Circle the first pair of digits you find that are different. Then write the greater number in the box.

a) 5⁸3   b) 629   c) 576   d) 432
    5⁹7   654   603   431

   [597]   [   ]   [   ]   [   ]

e) 384   f) 906   g) 875   h) 238
    597   904   869   221

   [   ]   [   ]   [   ]   [   ]

4. Circle the greater number.

   a) 111 or 311   b) 625 or 525   c) 321 or 721

   d) 843 or 867   e) 480 or 412   f) 219 or 220

   g) 125 or 122   h) 854 or 859   i) 336 or 330

5. a) Sindi earns $18 an hour. Bianca earns $13 an hour. Who earns more?

   _____

   b) Anthony's grandfather is 83. Nita's grandfather is 81. Whose grandfather is older?

   _____

1. Write "10 more" or "10 less" in the blanks.

   a) 80 is _____ than 70   b) 20 is _____ than 30

   c) 50 is _____ than 60   d) 90 is _____ than 80

2. Write "100 more" or "100 less" in the blanks.

   a) 500 is _____ than 400   b) 300 is _____ than 400

   c) 700 is _____ than 600   d) 800 is _____ than 900

3. Write the value of the digits. Then say how much more or less the first number is than the second.

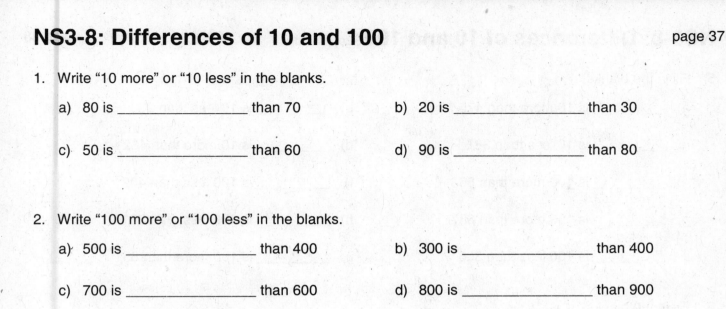

   647 is _____ than 657   482 is _____ than 382

4. Circle the pair of digits that are different. Then fill in the blanks.

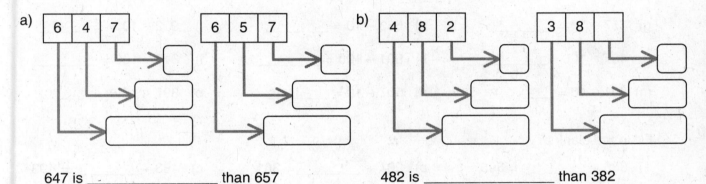

   a) 265
       275

   265 is _____10 less_____
   than 275

   b) 392
       492

   392 is _____
   than 492

   c) 687
       677

   687 is _____
   than 677

   d) 362
       262

   362 is _____
   than 262

   e) 405
       415

   405 is _____
   than 415

   f) 587
       687

   587 is _____
   than 687

5. Fill in the blanks.

a) _____ is 10 more than 475

b) _____ is 10 less than 263

c) _____ is 10 less than 387

d) _____ is 10 more than 482

e) _____ is 100 more than 563

f) _____ is 100 less than 402

g) _____ is 100 more than 687

h) _____ is 100 less than 291

i) _____ is 100 less than 305

j) _____ is 100 more than 851

6. Fill in the blanks.

a) 375 + 10 = _____

b) 252 + 10 = _____

c) 972 + 10 = _____

d) 127 + 100 = _____

e) 863 + 100 = _____

f) 821 + 100 = _____

g) 357 − 10 = _____

h) 683 − 10 = _____

i) 932 − 10 = _____

j) 487 − 100 = _____

k) 901 − 100 = _____

l) 316 − 100 = _____

m) 301 − 10 = _____

n) 507 − 10 = _____

o) 397 − 10 = _____

7. Fill in the blanks.

a) 385 + _____ = 395

b) 201 + _____ = 301

c) 483 + _____ = 493

d) 617 + _____ = 717

e) 286 − _____ = 276

f) 837 − _____ = 737

BONUS

8. Continue the number patterns.

a) 508, 518, 528, _____, _____

b) 572, 672, 772, _____, _____

c) 482, 492, _____, 512, _____

d) 363, _____, _____, 393, 403

9. Circle the pair of digits that are different. Then fill in the blanks.

a) 2④1
   2③1

b) 485
   585

c) 682
   692

__231__ is __10__

_____ is _____

_____ is _____

less than __241__

greater than _____

less than _____

NS3-9: Comparing Numbers (Advanced)

1. Circle the greater number in each pair.

   a) 35   or   thirty-two   b) eighty-eight   or   91   c) seventy-six   or   71

   d) 99   or   ninety   e) 42   or   fifty-five   f) eleven   or   21

   g) one hundred six   or   107   h) 375   or   three hundred eighty-five

2. List the two-digit numbers you can make using one or both digits.

   a) 4 and 5   b) 6 and 1   c) 3 and 9   d) 6 and 7

3. Create the largest possible **two-digit** number using both the digits given.

   a) 3, 2 [ ]   b) 8, 9 [ ]   c) 4, 1 [ ]   d) 7, 4 [ ]

4. Use all the digits given to create the greatest three-digit number and the least three-digit number.

   a)

Digits	Greatest Number	Least Number
5 7 2		

   b)

Digits	Greatest Number	Least Number
3 6 2		

5. Arrange the numbers in order, starting with the **least** number.

   a) 75, 62, 87

   _____ , _____ , _____

   b) 251, 385, 256

   _____ , _____ , _____

   c) 395, 385, 327, 357

   _____ , _____ , _____ , _____

   d) 432, 484, 402, 434

   _____ , _____ , _____ , _____

6. Arrange the lengths of these ocean animals from shortest to longest.

   13 m   4 m   14 m   30 m

   Giant Squid   Tiger Shark   Whale Shark   Giant Blue Whale

7. List all the **three-digit** numbers you can make using the digits 5, 3 and 2.
   (Use each digit only once in a number.)
   What is the largest number you can make?
   Explain how you know.

1. a) Underline the ones digits of the numbers you say when counting by 2s.

1	2	3	4	5	6	7	8	9	10
11	12	13	14	15	16	17	18	19	20
21	22	23	24	25	26	27	28	29	30
31	32	33	34	35	36	37	38	39	40

The **even** numbers are the numbers you say when counting by 2s (i.e. 2, 4, 6, 8, …).

b) What pattern do you see in the ones digits of the even numbers?

_____

c) Using the pattern, continue the following sequences.

   i) 46, 48, 50, _____, _____, _____   ii) 76, 78, 80, _____, _____, _____

   iii) 52, 54, 56, _____, _____, _____   iv) 80, 82, 84, _____, _____, _____

2. a) Underline the ones digits of the numbers you don't say when counting by 2s.

1	2	3	4	5	6	7	8	9	10
11	12	13	14	15	16	17	18	19	20
21	22	23	24	25	26	27	28	29	30
31	32	33	34	35	36	37	38	39	40

The **odd** numbers are the numbers you don't say when counting by 2s (i.e. 1, 3, 5, 7, …).

b) What pattern do you see in the ones digits of the odd numbers?

_____

c) Using the pattern, continue the following sequences.

   i) 47, 49, 51, _____, _____, _____   ii) 67, 69, 71, _____, _____, _____

   iii) 53, 55, 57, _____, _____, _____   iv) 81, 83, 85, _____, _____, _____

NS3-11: Counting by 5s and 25s

1. Start at 23. Mark the numbers you say when counting on by 5s. Underline the ones digit.

What pattern do you see in the underlined ones digits?

_____

2. Here are some number sequences formed by counting by 5s. Underline the ones digit in each number, then write the pattern.

   a) 1<u>2</u>, 1<u>7</u>, 2<u>2</u>, 2<u>7</u>, 3<u>2</u>, 3<u>7</u>   Pattern in the ones digits: _2_ , ___ , ___ , ___ , ___ , ___

   b) 7<u>1</u>, 76, 81, 86, 91, 96   Pattern in the ones digits: _1_ , ___ , ___ , ___ , ___ , ___

   c) 8<u>4</u>, 89, 94, 99, 104, 109   Pattern in the ones digits: _4_ , ___ , ___ , ___ , ___ , ___

3. Complete the number sequence below by counting on by 5s.

   a) 29, 34, _____, _____, _____   b) 79, 84, _____, _____, _____

   c) 43, 48, _____, _____, _____   d) 56, 61, _____, _____, _____

   e) 31, 36, _____, _____, _____   f) 82, 87, _____, _____, _____

   g) 107, 112, _____, _____, _____   h) 213, 218, _____, _____, _____

4. Explain what all the patterns above have in common.

5. Start at 25. Circle the numbers you say when counting by 25s.

Write the pattern in the <u>ones</u> digits of the numbers you circled:

   _5_ , _0_ , _____ , _____ , _____ , _____

6. Complete the number sequence below by skip counting by 25s.

   a) 75, 100, _____, _____, _____   b) 375, 400, _____, _____, _____

   c) 125, 150, _____, _____, _____   d) 600, 625, _____, _____, _____

   e) 200, 225, _____, _____, _____   f) 850, 875, _____, _____, _____

No unauthorized copying   **Number Sense 1**

1. Count by 5s.

    _____5_____, _____, _____, _____, _____, _____, _____, _____, _____

    _____, _____, _____, _____, _____, _____, _____, _____, _____

2. Count on by 5s.

    a) 65, _____, _____, _____

    b) 105, _____, _____, _____

    c) 245, _____, _____, _____

    d) 315, _____, _____, _____

    e) 560, _____, _____, _____

    f) 785, _____, _____, _____

3. The numbers below are the numbers you say counting by 3s.
    Use the pattern in the first two rows to fill in the missing numbers.

    ___3___, ___6___, ___9___, ___12___, ___15___, ___18___, ___21___, ___24___, ___27___, ___30___,

    ___33___, ___36___, ___39___, ___42___, ___45___, _____, ___51___, _____, _____, ___60___,

    _____, ___66___, _____, _____, _____, _____, _____, _____, _____,

    _____, _____, _____

4. Hien counted by 2s, 3s or 5s.
    Fill in the missing numbers and say what he counted by.

    a)

    20   □   30   35

    He counted by _____.

    b)

    4   □   8

    He counted by _____.

    c)

    9   □

    He counted by _____.

    d)

    22   □   □   28

    He counted by _____.

    e)

    40   □   □   55

    He counted by _____.

    f)

    33   □   □   42

    He counted by _____.

5. Explain how you found your answer to Question 4 e).

NS3-13: Counting Backward by 2s and 5s

1. Circle the numbers that you would say when counting backward by 2s starting at 52.

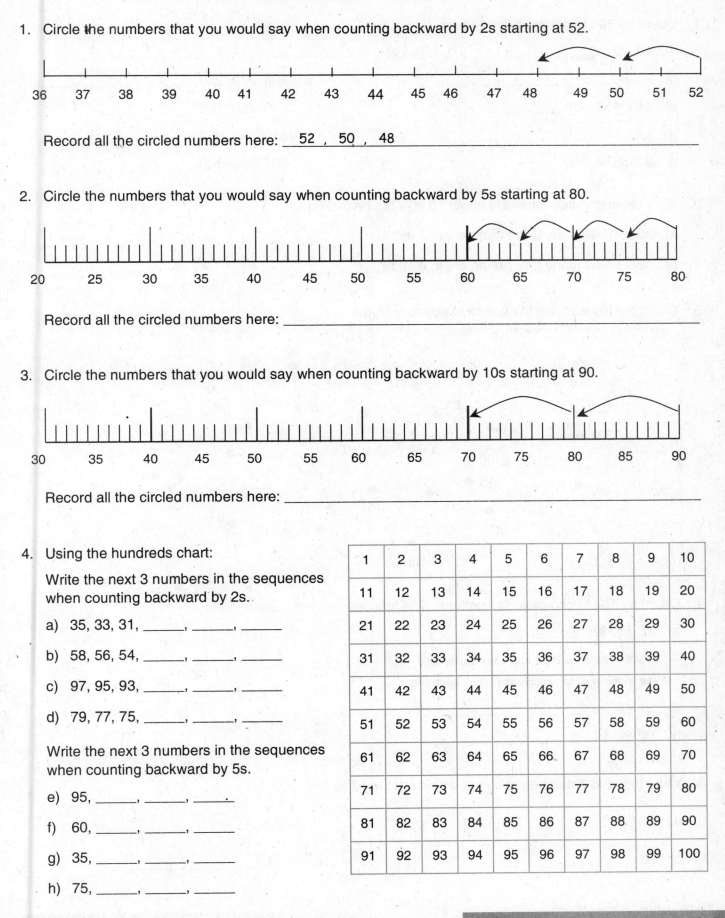

Record all the circled numbers here: __52 , 50 , 48_____

2. Circle the numbers that you would say when counting backward by 5s starting at 80.

Record all the circled numbers here: _____

3. Circle the numbers that you would say when counting backward by 10s starting at 90.

Record all the circled numbers here: _____

4. Using the hundreds chart:

Write the next 3 numbers in the sequences when counting backward by 2s.

a) 35, 33, 31, _____, _____, _____

b) 58, 56, 54, _____, _____, _____

c) 97, 95, 93, _____, _____, _____

d) 79, 77, 75, _____, _____, _____

Write the next 3 numbers in the sequences when counting backward by 5s.

e) 95, _____, _____, _____

f) 60, _____, _____, _____

g) 35, _____, _____, _____

h) 75, _____, _____, _____

1	2	3	4	5	6	7	8	9	10
11	12	13	14	15	16	17	18	19	20
21	22	23	24	25	26	27	28	29	30
31	32	33	34	35	36	37	38	39	40
41	42	43	44	45	46	47	48	49	50
51	52	53	54	55	56	57	58	59	60
61	62	63	64	65	66	67	68	69	70
71	72	73	74	75	76	77	78	79	80
81	82	83	84	85	86	87	88	89	90
91	92	93	94	95	96	97	98	99	100

Number Sense 1

NS3-14: Counting by 10s

1. Count by 10s to continue the pattern.

   a) 10, 20, 30, _____, _____, _____

   b) 40, 50, 60, _____, _____, _____

   c) 70, 80, 90, _____, _____, _____

   d) 200, 210, 220, _____, _____, _____

   e) 440, 450, 460, _____, _____, _____

   f) 240, 250, 260, _____, _____, _____

   g) 170, 180, 190, _____, _____, _____

   h) 330, 340, 350, _____, _____, _____

   i) 360, 370, 380, _____, _____, _____

   j) 680, 690, 700, _____, _____, _____

2. Kara estimates that there are about 10 jelly beans in a jar.

   a) About how many jelly beans are in 2 jars? _____

   b) About how many jelly beans are in 4 jars? _____

3. Count by 10s and join the points to create a shape.

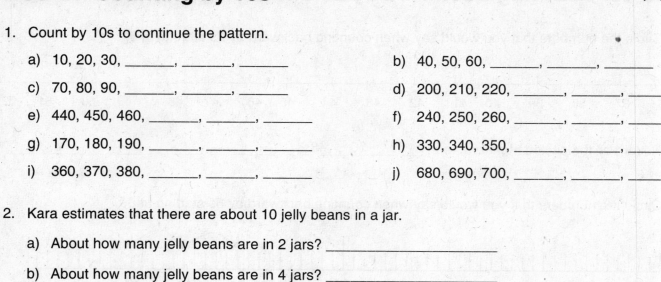

4. Count by 10s to complete the pattern. The first one has been done for you.

   a) 47, 57, 67, __77__, __87__, __97__

   **NOTE: The ones digit stays the same, and
   the number of tens increases by 1 each time.**

   b) 48, 58, 68, _____, _____, _____

   c) 25, 35, 45, _____, _____, _____

   e) 57, 67, 77, _____, _____, _____

   d) 36, 46, 56, _____, _____, _____

   f) 72, 82, 92, _____, _____, _____

   g) 161, 171, 181, _____, _____, _____

5. Write the next 3 numbers when counting backward by 10s.

   a) 80, _____, _____, _____

   b) 70, _____, _____, _____

   c) 50, _____, _____, _____

   d) 100, _____, _____, _____

NS3-15: Counting by 2s, 3s, 4s, 5s and 10s

1. Continue the pattern counting by 4s.

    <u> 4 </u> , <u> 8 </u> , <u> 12 </u> , <u> 16 </u> , <u> 20 </u> ,

    <u> 24 </u> , <u> 28 </u> , <u> 32 </u> , <u> 36 </u> , <u> 40 </u> ,

    <u>   </u> , <u>   </u> , <u> 52 </u> , <u>   </u> , <u>   </u> ,

    <u>   </u> , <u>   </u> , <u>   </u> , <u>   </u> , <u>   </u> ,

2. Karla counted by 2s, 3s, 4s, 5s, or 10s.
   Fill in the missing numbers.

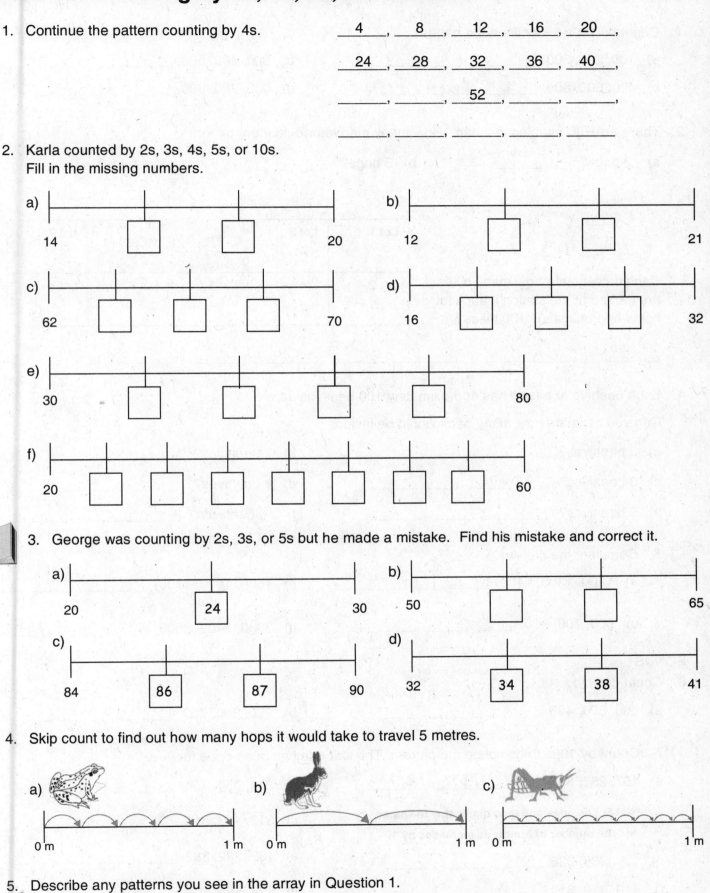

3. George was counting by 2s, 3s, or 5s but he made a mistake. Find his mistake and correct it.

4. Skip count to find out how many hops it would take to travel 5 metres.

    a)
    0 m   1 m
    b)
    0 m   1 m
    c)
    0 m   1 m

5. Describe any patterns you see in the array in Question 1.

1. Count by 100s to continue the pattern.

   a) 100, 200, 300, _____, _____, _____   b) 300, 400, 500, _____, _____, _____

   c) 400, 500, 600, _____, _____, _____   d) 600, 700, 800, _____, _____, _____

2. There are 200 marbles in a bag. How many marbles would there be in:

   a) 2 bags? _____   b) 3 bags? _____   c) 4 bags? _____

3.

   Can you estimate how many bikes
   are parked at the station if each lot
   holds approximately 100 bikes?

Lot 1	Lot 3	TRAIN STATION		Lot 7
Lot 2	Lot 4	Lot 5	Lot 6	Lot 8

   _____

4. Each beehive at a farm has approximately 100 bees inside.

   Can you estimate how many bees would be inside:

   a) 2 beehives? _____   b) 7 beehives? _____

   c) 3 beehives? _____   d) 8 beehives? _____

   e) 9 beehives? _____   f) 10 beehives? _____

5. Complete the pattern.

   a) 1200, 1300, 1400, 1_____, 1_____   b) 1500, 1600, 1700, _____, _____

   c) 600, 700, 800, _____, _____   d) 3300, 3400, 3500, _____, _____

BONUS

6. Count down by 100s.

   a) 600, 500, 400, _____, _____, _____   b) 900, 800, 700, _____, _____, _____

7. Count by 100s to complete the pattern. The first one has been done for you.

   a) 157, 257, 357, __457__, __557__, __657__   b) 254, 354, 454, _____, _____, _____

   NOTE: The ones and tens digits stay the same,
   and the number of hundreds increases by 1.

   c) 313, 413, 513, _____, _____, _____

   d) 136, 236, 336, _____, _____, _____   e) 182, 282, 382, _____, _____, _____

   f) 419, 519, 619, _____, _____, _____   g) 438, 538, 638, _____, _____, _____

Selma has 2 tens blocks and 12 ones blocks. She regroups 10 ones blocks as 1 tens block.

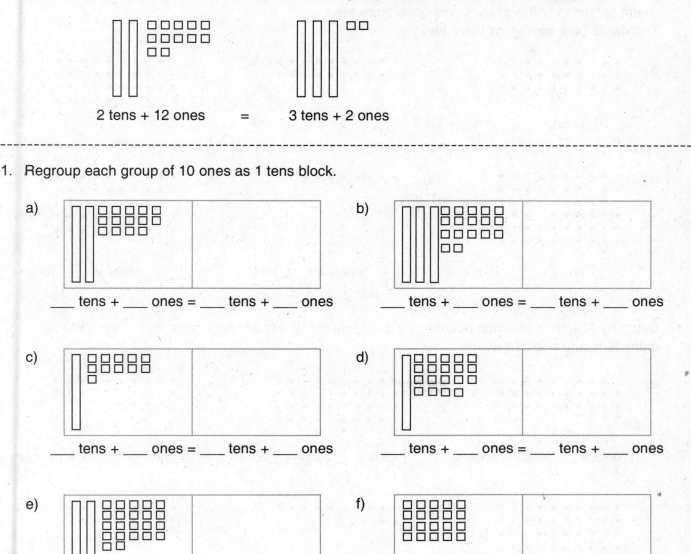

2 tens + 12 ones   =   3 tens + 2 ones

----

1. Regroup each group of 10 ones as 1 tens block.

a) ___ tens + ___ ones = ___ tens + ___ ones

b) ___ tens + ___ ones = ___ tens + ___ ones

c) ___ tens + ___ ones = ___ tens + ___ ones

d) ___ tens + ___ ones = ___ tens + ___ ones

e) ___ tens + ___ ones = ___ tens + ___ ones

f) ___ tens + ___ ones = ___ tens + ___ ones

2. Complete the charts by regrouping 10 ones as 1 ten. The first one has been done for you.

a)

tens	ones
4	13
4 + 1 = 5	3

b)

tens	ones
6	14

c)

tens	ones
8	15

d)

tens	ones
2	19

e)

tens	ones
6	17

f)

tens	ones
1	18

NS3-17: Regrouping (continued)

3. There are 10 dots in each row.
   Count by 10s to find out how many ones there are.
   Then write how many tens there are.

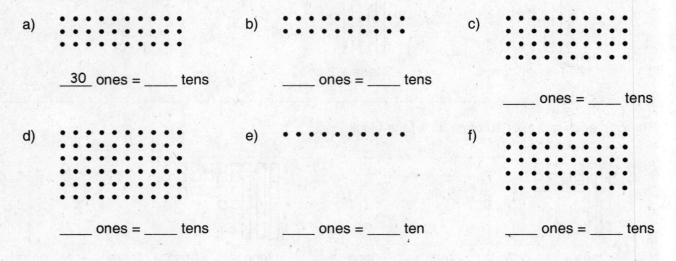

a) __30__ ones = ____ tens

b) ____ ones = ____ tens

c) ____ ones = ____ tens

d) ____ ones = ____ tens

e) ____ ones = ____ ten

f) ____ ones = ____ tens

4. Count by 10s, then continue counting by 1s to find out how many dots there are. Then write how many tens and ones there are.

a) ____ ones = ___ tens + ___ ones

b) ____ ones = ___ tens + ___ ones

c) ____ ones = ___ tens + ___ ones

d) ____ ones = ___ tens + ___ one

e) ____ ones = ___ ten + ___ ones

f) ____ ones = ___ ten + ___ ones

5. Regroup the ones as tens. The first one has been done for you.

a) 68 ones = __6__ tens + __8__ ones

b) 42 ones = _____ tens + _____ ones

c) 93 ones = _____ tens + _____ ones

d) 35 ones = _____ tens + _____ ones

e) 17 ones = _____ ten + _____ ones

f) 84 ones = _____ tens + _____ ones

g) 8 ones = _____ tens + _____ ones

h) 30 ones = _____ tens + _____ ones

Paul has 3 hundreds blocks, 12 tens blocks, and 3 ones blocks.
He regroups 10 tens blocks as 1 hundreds block.

3 hundreds + 12 tens + 3 ones   4 hundreds + 2 tens + 3 ones

----

1. Regroup 10 tens as 1 hundred, or 10 ones as 1 ten.

   a) 4 hundreds + 15 tens + 6 ones = _____ hundreds + _____ tens + _____ ones

   b) 3 hundreds + 14 tens + 2 ones = _____ hundreds + _____ tens + _____ ones

   c) 6 hundreds + 19 tens + 3 ones = _____ hundreds + _____ tens + _____ ones

   d) 6 hundreds + 3 tens + 15 ones = _____ hundreds + _____ tens + _____ ones

   e) 9 hundreds + 8 tens + 16 ones = _____

   _____

2. Regroup as many pennies for dimes as you can.
   REMEMBER: 10 pennies = 1 dime; 20 pennies = 2 dimes; 30 pennies = 3 dimes, etc.)

   a)

dimes	pennies
3	27
3 + 2	7
5	7

   b)

dimes	pennies
5	23

   c)

dimes	pennies
4	37

   d)

dimes	pennies
2	32

   Regroup 20 pennies as 2 dimes.

3. Write the money amounts using the fewest possible number of coins. The first one is done for you.

   a)

	dollars	dimes	pennies
	4	34	27
Step 1	4	34 + 2 = 36	7
Step 2	4 + 3 = 7	6	7

   b)

dollars	dimes	pennies
2	37	21

   c)

dollars	dimes	pennies
3	56	28

   d)

dollars	dimes	pennies
1	31	68

NS3-19: Adding 2-Digit Numbers

1. Find the <u>sum</u> of the numbers below by drawing a picture and by adding the digits.
   Don't worry about drawing the model in too much detail.

a) **24 + 32**

with base ten materials		with numerals	
tens	ones	tens	ones
24	▫▫▫▫	2	4
32	▫▫	3	2
sum	▫▫▫▫▫ ▫	5	6

b) **13 + 22**

with base ten materials		with numerals	
tens	ones	tens	ones
13			
22			
sum			

c) **23 + 33**

with base ten materials		with numerals	
tens	ones	tens	ones
23			
33			
sum			

d) **21 + 22**

with base ten materials		with numerals	
tens	ones	tens	ones
21			
22			
sum			

2. Add the numbers by adding the digits.

a) $\begin{array}{r} 2\ 1 \\ +\ 2\ 3 \\ \hline \end{array}$ b) $\begin{array}{r} 1\ 3 \\ +\ 2\ 2 \\ \hline \end{array}$ c) $\begin{array}{r} 4\ 1 \\ +\ 2\ 2 \\ \hline \end{array}$ d) $\begin{array}{r} 1\ 2 \\ +\ 4\ 5 \\ \hline \end{array}$ e) $\begin{array}{r} 5\ 2 \\ +\ 3\ 2 \\ \hline \end{array}$

f) $\begin{array}{r} 2\ 4 \\ +\ 3\ 1 \\ \hline \end{array}$ g) $\begin{array}{r} 1\ 2 \\ +\ 1\ 5 \\ \hline \end{array}$ h) $\begin{array}{r} 2\ 1 \\ +\ 3\ 1 \\ \hline \end{array}$ i) $\begin{array}{r} 4\ 2 \\ +\ 1\ 3 \\ \hline \end{array}$ j) $\begin{array}{r} 3\ 1 \\ +\ 2\ 2 \\ \hline \end{array}$

NS3-20: Adding with Regrouping (or Carrying)

1. Add the numbers below by drawing a picture and by adding the digits.
   Use base ten materials to show how to combine the numbers and how to regroup.

a) **25 + 17**

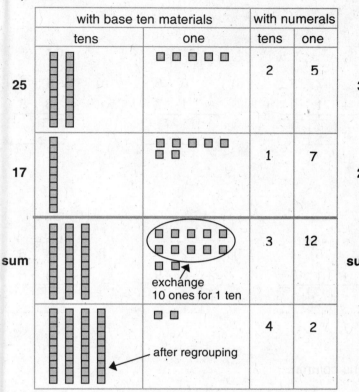

with base ten materials		with numerals	
tens	one	tens	one
25		2	5
17		1	7
sum		3	12
		4	2

exchange 10 ones for 1 ten

after regrouping

b) **33 + 29**

with base ten materials		with numerals	
tens	one	tens	one
33			
29			
sum			

c) **14 + 58**

with base ten materials		with numerals	
tens	one	tens	one
14			
58			
sum			

d) **19 + 5**

with base ten materials		with numerals	
tens	one	tens	one
19			
5			
sum			

2. Add the numbers by regrouping.

   Step 1:   Regroup 10 ones as 1 ten.

tens go here

a)
```
   1
   1 5
 + 1 8
 ─────
   3
```
ones go here

b)
```
 
   6 4
 + 1 6
 ─────
 ▓ □
```

c)
```
 
   7 5
 + 1 9
 ─────
 ▓ □
```

d)
```
 
   6 6
 + 1 7
 ─────
 ▓ □
```

e)
```
 
   1 5
 + 3 8
 ─────
 ▓ □
```

f)
```
   1
   1 3
 + 1 9
 ─────
 ▓ □
```

g)
```
 
   2 4
 + 3 8
 ─────
 ▓ □
```

h)
```
 
   5 4
 + 1 8
 ─────
 ▓ □
```

i)
```
 
   2 7
 + 6 9
 ─────
 ▓ □
```

j)
```
 
   4 6
 + 4 8
 ─────
 ▓ □
```

   Step 2:   Add the numbers in the tens column.

k)
```
   1
   1 2
 + 1 8
 ─────
   3 0
```

l)
```
   1
   1 3
 + 1 7
 ─────
   □ 0
```

m)
```
   1
   1 5
 + 2 8
 ─────
   □ 3
```

n)
```
   1
   2 6
 + 2 6
 ─────
   □ 2
```

o)
```
   1
   3 8
 + 2 7
 ─────
   □ 5
```

3. Add the numbers by regrouping (or carrying).

a)
```
   1
   2 5
 + 1 7
 ─────
   4 2
```

b)
```
   2 6
 + 1 6
 ─────
```

c)
```
   3 8
 + 1 4
 ─────
```

d)
```
   2 8
 + 2 3
 ─────
```

e)
```
   4 6
 + 2 5
 ─────
```

f)
```
   4 9
 + 1 4
 ─────
```

g)
```
   3 9
 + 4 6
 ─────
```

h)
```
   2 8
 + 1 7
 ─────
```

i)
```
   1 6
 + 2 8
 ─────
```

j)
```
   4 8
 + 2 8
 ─────
```

1. Rewrite each money amount in dimes and pennies.

   a) 51¢ = __5__ dimes + __1__ penny   b) 23¢ = _____ dimes + _____pennies

   c) 67¢ = _____ dimes + _____pennies   d) 92¢ = _____ dimes + _____ pennies

   e) 84¢ = _____ dimes + _____pennies   f) 70¢ = _____ dimes + _____pennies

   g) 2¢ = _____ dimes + _____pennies   h) 5¢ = _____ dimes + _____pennies

2. Show how to regroup ten pennies as 1 dime.

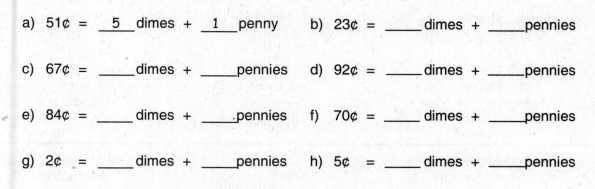

a)

dimes	pennies
2	12
3	2

After regrouping

b)

dimes	pennies
5	13

c)

dimes	pennies
7	17

d)

dimes	pennies
4	18

3. Find the total number of dimes and pennies. Then regroup.

a)

dimes	pennies
3	5
2	6
5	11
6	1

Total after regrouping {

b)

dimes	pennies
2	6
3	6

c)

dimes	pennies
5	2
2	9

d)

dimes	pennies
3	3
4	9

4. Add by regrouping 10 pennies as 1 dime.

a) 3 7 ¢
  + 2 5 ¢
  _____ ¢

b) 2 3 ¢
  + 4 9 ¢
  _____ ¢

c) 2 6 ¢
  + 3 7 ¢
  _____ ¢

d) 4 7 ¢
  + 6 7 ¢
  _____ ¢

e) 2 8 ¢
  + 4 8 ¢
  _____ ¢

5. Add by lining the dimes and pennies up in the grid.

   a) 15¢ + 17¢   b) 23¢ + 27¢   c) 48¢ + 59¢   d) 26¢ + 34¢   e) 27¢ + 85¢

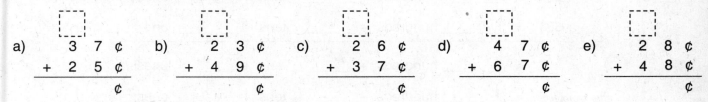

	1	5	¢
+	1	7	¢

NS3-22: Adding 3-Digit Numbers

Marzuk adds 142 + 275 using base ten materials.

142 = 1 hundred + 4 tens + 2 ones

+ 275 = 2 hundreds + 7 tens + 5 ones

= 3 hundreds + 11 tens + 7 ones

Then, to get the final answer, Marzuk regroups 10 tens as 1 hundred.

= 4 hundreds + 1 ten + 7 ones

----

1. Add the numbers using base ten materials or a picture (and record your work below).

a)   **242** = ___2___ hundreds + ___4___ tens + ___2___ ones

    + 384 = ___3___ hundreds + ___8___ tens + ___4___ ones

    = ___5___ hundreds + ___12___ tens + ___6___ ones

    after regrouping = ___6___ hundreds + ___2___ tens + ___6___ ones

b)   **394** = _____ hundreds + _____ tens + _____ ones

    + 531 = _____ hundreds + _____ tens + _____ one

    = _____ hundreds + _____ tens + _____ ones

    after regrouping = _____ hundreds + _____ tens + _____ ones

c)   **156** = _____ hundred + _____ tens + _____ ones

    + 483 = _____ hundreds + _____ tens + _____ ones

    = _____ hundreds + _____ tens + _____ ones

    after regrouping = _____ hundreds + _____ tens + _____ ones

2. Add. You will need to regroup the tens. The first one is started for you.

a)
```
   [1]
   4 2 5
 + 3 8 1
 ───────
     0 6
```
b)
```
   [ ]
   7 3 2
 + 1 9 1
 ───────
```
c)
```
   [ ]
   4 6 2
 + 2 5 1
 ───────
```
d)
```
   3 7 4
 + 3 6 5
 ───────
```
e)
```
   3 9 1
 + 1 2 7
 ───────
```

3. Add. You will need to regroup the ones as tens.

a)
```
   [ ]
   4 5 6
 +   2 9
 ───────
```
b)
```
   [ ]
   1 7 5
 + 4 1 8
 ───────
```
c)
```
   [ ]
   6 4 4
 +   5 7
 ───────
```
d)
```
   2 3 8
 + 3 4 5
 ───────
```
e)
```
   7 2 7
 + 5 3 8
 ───────
```

4. Add, regrouping where necessary.

a)
```
   4 2 1
 + 2 9 3
 ───────
```
b)
```
   2 6 3
 + 3 7 2
 ───────
```
c)
```
   2 4 3
 + 5 1 6
 ───────
```
d)
```
   4 2 8
 + 3 6 7
 ───────
```
e)
```
   6 2 7
 + 2 3 1
 ───────
```
f)
```
   7 3 5
 + 1 8 7
 ───────
```

5. Add by lining the numbers up correctly in the grid. The first one has been started for you.

a) 28 + 26   b) 272 + 213   c) 643 + 718   d) 937 + 25

	2	8													
+	2	6													

e) 126 + 48   f) 380 + 428   g) 925 + 77   h) 765 + 5

BONUS

6. How do you think you might add the following numbers? Write what you think the answer might be.

a)
```
   2 3 5 1
 + 5 1 3 4
 ─────────
```
b)
```
   3 5 8 1
 + 4 3 1 7
 ─────────
```
c)
```
   3 8 9 5
 + 2 0 1 3
 ─────────
```
d)
```
   4 5 1 2 3
 + 5 4 1 7 5
 ───────────
```

NS3-23: Subtracting 2- and 3-Digit Numbers

Nevina subtracts 37 – 24 using base ten materials. She makes a model of 37. Then she takes away
2 tens and 4 ones (because 24 = 2 tens + 4 ones).

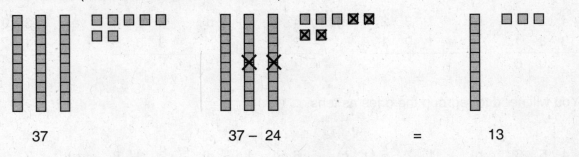

| 37 | | 37 – 24 | = | 13 |

----

1. Perform the subtractions by crossing out tens blocks and ones blocks. Draw your final answer in the
   right-hand box. The first one has been done for you.

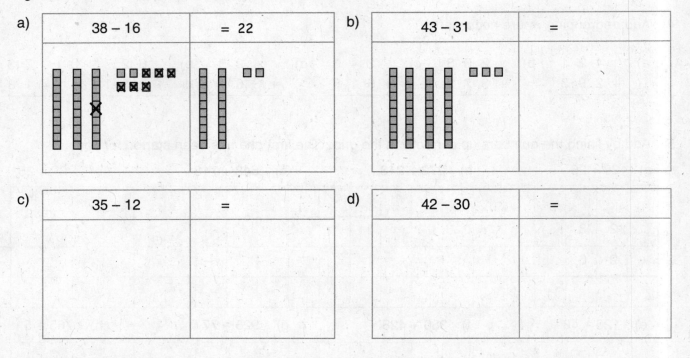

a)

| 38 – 16 | = 22 |

b)

| 43 – 31 | = |

c)

| 35 – 12 | = |

d)

| 42 – 30 | = |

2. Write the number of tens and ones in each number. Then subtract the number.

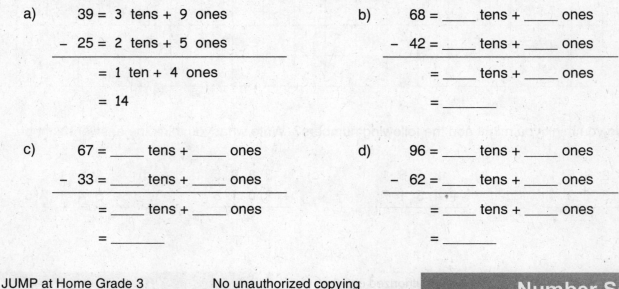

a)
$$39 = 3 \text{ tens} + 9 \text{ ones}$$
$$- 25 = 2 \text{ tens} + 5 \text{ ones}$$
$$= 1 \text{ ten} + 4 \text{ ones}$$
$$= 14$$

b)
$$68 = \underline{\quad} \text{ tens} + \underline{\quad} \text{ ones}$$
$$- 42 = \underline{\quad} \text{ tens} + \underline{\quad} \text{ ones}$$
$$= \underline{\quad} \text{ tens} + \underline{\quad} \text{ ones}$$
$$= \underline{\quad}$$

c)
$$67 = \underline{\quad} \text{ tens} + \underline{\quad} \text{ ones}$$
$$- 33 = \underline{\quad} \text{ tens} + \underline{\quad} \text{ ones}$$
$$= \underline{\quad} \text{ tens} + \underline{\quad} \text{ ones}$$
$$= \underline{\quad}$$

d)
$$96 = \underline{\quad} \text{ tens} + \underline{\quad} \text{ ones}$$
$$- 62 = \underline{\quad} \text{ tens} + \underline{\quad} \text{ ones}$$
$$= \underline{\quad} \text{ tens} + \underline{\quad} \text{ ones}$$
$$= \underline{\quad}$$

3. Subtract by writing the number of tens and ones in each number.

    a)
    $$
    \begin{array}{rcl}
    46 &=& 40 + 6 \\
    -\ 32 &=& 30 + 2 \\
    \hline
    &=& 10 + 4 \\
    &=& 14
    \end{array}
    $$

    b)
    $$
    \begin{array}{rcl}
    95 &=& \\
    -\ 62 &=& \\
    \hline
    &=& \\
    &=&
    \end{array}
    $$

    c)
    $$
    \begin{array}{rcl}
    37 &=& \\
    -\ 11 &=& \\
    \hline
    &=& \\
    &=&
    \end{array}
    $$

    d)
    $$
    \begin{array}{rcl}
    63 &=& \\
    -\ 20 &=&
    \end{array}
    $$

    e)
    $$
    \begin{array}{rcl}
    29 &=& \\
    -\ 4 &=&
    \end{array}
    $$

    f)
    $$
    \begin{array}{rcl}
    58 &=& \\
    -\ 41 &=&
    \end{array}
    $$

4. Subtract the numbers by subtracting the digits.

    a)
    $$
    \begin{array}{r}
    2\ 8 \\
    -\ 1\ 2 \\
    \hline
    \end{array}
    $$
    b)
    $$
    \begin{array}{r}
    4\ 8 \\
    -\ 2\ 7 \\
    \hline
    \end{array}
    $$
    c)
    $$
    \begin{array}{r}
    6\ 9 \\
    -\ 5\ 3 \\
    \hline
    \end{array}
    $$
    d)
    $$
    \begin{array}{r}
    4\ 9 \\
    -\ 4\ 5 \\
    \hline
    \end{array}
    $$
    e)
    $$
    \begin{array}{r}
    8\ 7 \\
    -\ 5\ 3 \\
    \hline
    \end{array}
    $$
    f)
    $$
    \begin{array}{r}
    6\ 2 \\
    -\ 3\ 0 \\
    \hline
    \end{array}
    $$

    g)
    $$
    \begin{array}{r}
    5\ 6 \\
    -\ 2\ 1 \\
    \hline
    \end{array}
    $$
    h)
    $$
    \begin{array}{r}
    3\ 9 \\
    -\ 1\ 5 \\
    \hline
    \end{array}
    $$
    i)
    $$
    \begin{array}{r}
    7\ 2 \\
    -\ 6\ 0 \\
    \hline
    \end{array}
    $$
    j)
    $$
    \begin{array}{r}
    6\ 2 \\
    -\ 4\ 1 \\
    \hline
    \end{array}
    $$
    k)
    $$
    \begin{array}{r}
    9\ 6 \\
    -\ 4\ 3 \\
    \hline
    \end{array}
    $$
    l)
    $$
    \begin{array}{r}
    8\ 7 \\
    -\ 3\ 4 \\
    \hline
    \end{array}
    $$

5. a) Draw a picture of 325 using hundreds blocks, tens blocks and ones blocks.
        Show how you would subtract 325 – 112 by crossing out parts of your picture.

    b) Now subtract the numbers by lining up the digits and subtracting. Do you get the same answer?

BONUS
6. Subtract.

    a)
    $$
    \begin{array}{r}
    7\ 2\ 9 \\
    -\ 3\ 1\ 6 \\
    \hline
    \end{array}
    $$
    b)
    $$
    \begin{array}{r}
    8\ 9\ 5 \\
    -\ 2\ 5\ 4 \\
    \hline
    \end{array}
    $$
    c)
    $$
    \begin{array}{r}
    5\ 2\ 4 \\
    -\ 4\ 0\ 1 \\
    \hline
    \end{array}
    $$
    d)
    $$
    \begin{array}{r}
    3\ 9\ 8 \\
    -\ 1\ 6\ 3 \\
    \hline
    \end{array}
    $$
    e)
    $$
    \begin{array}{r}
    5\ 9\ 2 \\
    -\ 1\ 7\ 0 \\
    \hline
    \end{array}
    $$

NS3-24: Subtracting by Regrouping

Rina subtracts 34 – 19 using base ten materials.

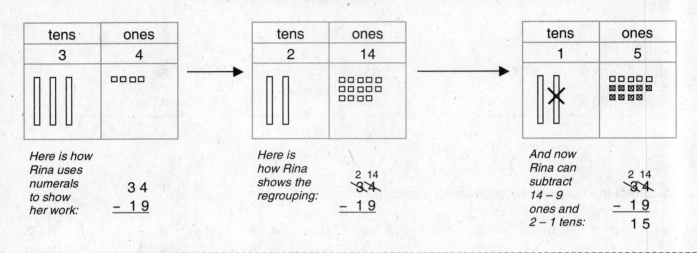

Step 1:
Rina represents 34 using base ten materials:

Step 2:
9 (the ones digit of 19) is greater than 4 (the ones digit of 34), so Rina regroups 1 ten as 10 ones:

Step 3:
Rina subtracts 19 (she takes away 1 tens block and 9 ones):

tens	ones
3	4

Here is how Rina uses numerals to show her work:

$$\begin{array}{r} 3\,4 \\ -\ 1\,9 \end{array}$$

tens	ones
2	14

Here is how Rina shows the regrouping:

tens	ones
1	5

And now Rina can subtract 14 – 9 ones and 2 – 1 tens:

---

1. In these questions, Rina doesn't have enough ones to subtract. Help her by regrouping 1 tens block as 10 ones. Show how she would rewrite her subtraction statement.

a) **33 – 18**

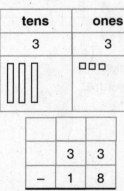

b) **54 – 28**

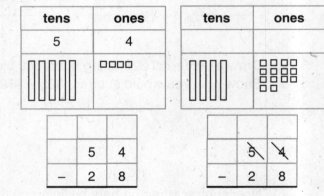

c) **32 – 17**

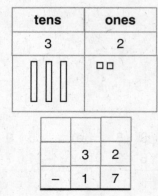

d) **23 – 19**

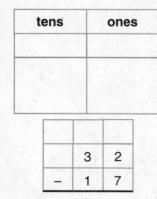

2. Subtract by regrouping.

a)

	2	11
	~~3~~	~~1~~
−	1	9
	1	2

b)

	4	4
−	2	8

c)

	5	3
−	3	6

d)

	6	2
−	1	5

e)

	8	5
−		8

3. For the questions where you need to regroup, write "Help!" in the space provided. If you don't need to regroup, write "OK."

a)   2 3   _Help!_
    − 1 7   3 is less than 7

b)   3 5   _OK_
    − 1 3   _____

c)   8 5   _____
    − 2 9

d)   2 2   _____
    − 1 7

e)   8 5   _____
    − 1 7

f)   2 2   _____
    − 1 9

g)   8 1   _____
    − 6 7

h)   8 8   _____
    − 3 4

i)   2 7   _____
    − 1 6

j)   3 4   _____
    − 1 5

k)   8 5   _____
    − 6 7

l)   7 5   _____
    − 3 9

m)   2 1   _____
    − 1 7

n)   3 2   _____
    − 1 8

o)   2 1   _____
    −   8

p)   6 7   _____
    − 2 9

q)   4 7   _____
    − 2 3

r)   5 7   _____
    − 3 2

4. Go back and finish the subtraction questions above.

To subtract 325 – 172, Samir regroups 1 hundreds block as 10 tens blocks.

hundreds	tens	ones
3	2	5

hundreds	tens	ones
2	12	5

hundreds	tens	ones
1	5	3

```
    3 2 5
  - 1 7 2
```

```
    2 12
    3̸ 2̸ 5
  - 1 7 2
```

```
    2 12
    3̸ 2̸ 5
  - 1 7 2
  ─────────
    1 5 3
```

---

1. Subtract by regrouping the **hundreds**. The first one has been started for you.

a)
```
  3  12
  4̸  2̸  7
- 2  9  2
```

b)
```
  5  3  8
- 2  9  5
```

c)
```
  3  1  7
- 1  8  6
```

d)
```
  9  4  2
- 5  7  0
```

2. Subtract by regrouping the **tens**. The first one has been started for you.

a)
```
     2 13
  8  3̸  3̸
- 3  1  9
```

b)
```
  5  8  3
- 2  7  7
```

c)
```
  9  6  3
- 4  1  7
```

d)
```
  4  5  0
- 1  3  6
```

3. For the questions below, you will have to regroup **twice**.

Example:

Step 1:
```
    2 11
    5 3̸ 1̸
  - 2 7 9
```

Step 2:
```
    2 11
    5 3̸ 1̸
  - 2 7 9
  ─────────
        2
```

Step 3:
```
       12
    4 2̸ 11
    5̸ 3̸ 1̸
  - 2 7 9
  ─────────
        2
```

Step 4:
```
       12
    4 2̸ 11
    5̸ 3̸ 1̸
  - 2 7 9
  ─────────
      5 2
```

Step 5:
```
       12
    4 2̸ 11
    5̸ 3̸ 1̸
  - 2 7 9
  ─────────
    2 5 2
```

a)
```
  5  3  2
- 2  9  8
```

b)
```
  3  1  2
- 1  8  6
```

c)
```
  8  2  3
- 2  7  9
```

d)
```
  1  0  0
-    5  7
```

NS3-26: Mental Math

1. Show all the ways you can decompose the number.

   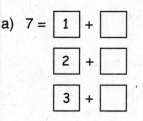

   a) 7 = [1] + [ ]

   [2] + [ ]

   [3] + [ ]

   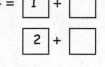

   b) 4 = [1] + [ ]

   [2] + [ ]

   c) 6 = [ ] + [ ]

   [ ] + [ ]

   [ ] + [ ]

2. Show all the ways you can decompose 10.

   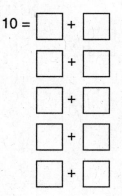

   10 = [ ] + [ ]

   [ ] + [ ]

   [ ] + [ ]

   [ ] + [ ]

   [ ] + [ ]

3. Circle the pair that adds to 10.

   a) (2)   7   (8)

   b) 3   7   4

   c) 5   3   5

   d) 6   4   5

   e) 1   8   9

4. Find the pair that adds to 10. Rewrite the addition statement.

   a) 4 + 5 + 6 = 10 + [5]

   b) 7 + 3 + 4 = 10 + [ ]

   c) 8 + 3 + 2 = 10 + [ ]

   d) 6 + 9 + 4 = 10 + [ ]

   e) 9 + 1 + 7 = 10 + [ ]

   f) 5 + 8 + 2 = 10 + [ ]

5. Use the pattern in a), b), and c) below to add.

   a) 10 + 5 = __15__

   b) 10 + 7 = __17__

   c) 40 + 8 = __48__

   d) 50 + 9 = _____

   e) 60 + 1 = _____

   f) 20 + 3 = _____

   g) 40 + 4 = _____

   h) 30 + 6 = _____

   i) 90 + 8 = _____

   j) 90 + 7 = _____

   k) 120 + 5 = _____

   l) 160 + 4 = _____

Number Sense 1

6. Fill in the boxes.

a) $8 + 6 = 8 + \boxed{2} + \boxed{4}$

        these make 10   left over

b) $9 + 5 = 9 + \boxed{} + \boxed{}$

        these make 10   left over

c) $6 + 5 = 6 + \boxed{} + \boxed{}$

d) $5 + 7 = 5 + \boxed{} + \boxed{}$

e) $9 + 4 = 9 + \boxed{} + \boxed{}$

f) $8 + 8 = 8 + \boxed{} + \boxed{}$

g) $7 + 6 = 7 + \boxed{} + \boxed{}$

h) $9 + 6 = 9 + \boxed{} + \boxed{}$

7. Add by following the steps.

a) $7 + 5 = \boxed{7} + \boxed{3} + \boxed{2} = 10 + 2 = 12$

      these make 10   left over

b) $26 + 5 = 26 + \boxed{} + \boxed{} =$ _____

      these make 30   left over

c) $78 + 6 = 78 + \boxed{} + \boxed{} =$ _____

      these make 80   left over

d) $45 + 8 = 45 + \boxed{} + \boxed{} =$ _____

      these make 50   left over

8. Find the answers mentally.

a) Roger has saved $38.
His parents gave him $7.
How much money does Roger have?

_____

b) Damon has 26 stickers.
Chloe has 7 stickers.
How many do they have altogether?

_____

9. Explain how you would add $37 + 5$ mentally.

NS3-27: Parts and Totals

1. Shade boxes to show the number of marbles. Then find:

- the total number of marbles
- the difference between the number of green and blue marbles

a) 5 green marbles
3 blue marbles

difference: _____2 marbles_____

green

blue

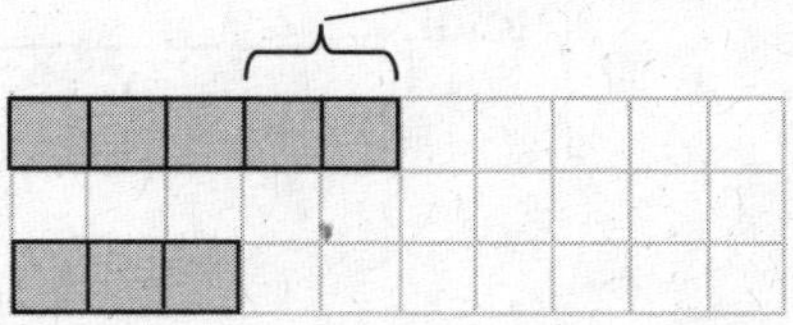

total: _____8 marbles_____

b) 4 green marbles
6 blue marbles

difference: _____

green

blue

total: _____

c) 8 green marbles
4 blue marbles

difference: _____

green

blue

total: _____

BONUS

d) 5 green marbles
2 more green marbles than blue marbles

difference: _____

green

blue

total: _____

e) 3 green marbles
_____ blue marbles

difference: _____

green

blue

total: _____4 marbles_____

NS3-27: Parts and Totals (continued)

2. Follow the steps in Question 1.
   Put the colour of marble that you have more of on top.

   a) 4 green marbles
      5 blue marbles

      difference: _____

      _____blue_____

      _____green_____

      total: _____

   b) 3 green marbles
      7 blue marbles

      difference: _____

      _____

      _____

      total: _____

   c) 9 green marbles
      5 blue marbles

      difference: _____

      _____

      _____

      total: _____

   d) ___ blue marbles
      2 green marbles

      difference: _____

      _____

      _____

      total: _____6 marbles_____

   e) 3 green marbles
      4 more blue marbles than green

      difference: _____

      _____

      _____

      total: _____

3. Draw a picture (as in Question 1) and make a chart for each question.

   a) 3 green marbles
      2 more blue marbles than
      green marbles

   b) 11 marbles in total
      6 green marbles

   c) 12 marbles in total
      7 blue marbles

NS3-28: Parts and Totals (Advanced)

1. Write the missing numbers.

Green Marbles	Blue Marbles	Total Number of Marbles	How many more marbles of one colour than the other?
3	5	8	2 more blue marbles than green
4		6	
	2	3	
3			1 more blue marble than green
	2		1 more green marble than blue
	4		1 more blue marble than green

2. The fact family for the addition statement **2 + 4 = 6** is: **4 + 2 = 6**; **6 − 4 = 2** and **6 − 2 = 4**.

   Write the fact family of equations for the following statements:

   a)   3 + 4 = 7 _____

   b)   5 + 4 = 9 _____

3. Fill in the chart.

	Green Marbles	Blue Marbles	Total Number of Marbles	Fact Family	How many more marbles of one colour than the other?
a)	7	2	9	9 − 2 = 7 7 + 2 = 9 9 − 7 = 2 2 + 7 = 9	5 more green than purple
b)	6		10		
c)	2	9			
d)		5			4 more green than purple

Number Sense 1

4. Use the correct symbol (+ or −).

a) Number of green marbles ⬜ Number of blue marbles = Total number of marbles

b) Number of green marbles ⬜ Number of blue marbles = How many more green marbles than blue marbles?

c) Number of green apples ⬜ Number of red apples = Total number of apples

d) Number of green grapes ⬜ Number of purple grapes = How many more green grapes than purple grapes?

e) Number of yellow beans ⬜ Number of green beans = How many more yellow beans?

f) Number of red marbles ⬜ Number of blue marbles = How many more red marbles?

5. Draw a picture on grid paper (as in Question 1 in "Parts and Totals") for each question.

a) Kate has 3 green fish and 4 yellow fish.
How many fish does she have?

b) Ed has 5 green marbles. He has 3 more green marbles than blue marbles.
How many marbles does he have?

c) Serge has 5 pets. 3 are cats. The rest are dogs.
How many dogs does he have?

d) Leesa walked 4 km. Mark walked 3 km.
How much farther did Leesa walk?

1. Ken has $7 and Reg has $15.
   How much money do they have altogether?

2. Anne is 12 years old. Her sister is 23.
   How much older is her sister?

3. A school library has 520 books.
   150 were borrowed.
   How many books are left?

4. 52 children went on a school trip.
   27 of the children were girls.
   How many were boys?

5. Leslie paid 75¢ for a pen that cost 49¢.
   How much change did he get back?

6. Shelly has 57¢. Gerome has 42¢.
   How much more money does Shelly have?

7. Alice's mother is 47. Her aunt is 33.
   How much older is Alice's mother than
   Alice's aunt?

8. Sam sold 27 raffle tickets in two days.
   On Thursday, he sold 13 tickets.
   How many tickets did he sell on
   Wednesday?

9. Midori had 35 pencil crayons.
   She lost 4.
   How many does she have left?

10. Imogen read 2 books by Roald Dahl.
    The BFG is 208 pages long.
    Charlie and the Chocolate Factory
    is 155 pages long.
    How many pages did she read altogether?

11. A single woolly mammoth skull weighs
    110 kg. How much would
    2 skulls weigh?

12. Calvin explored 2 caves in the Rocky
    Mountains from end to end. Wapiabi
    Cave is 540 metres long and Serendipity
    Cave is 470 metres long. How far did
    Calvin travel in the caves altogether?

Answer the following questions in your notebook.

1. Tanya has 12 pencil crayons. Some are at school and 8 are at home.

   a) How many pencil crayons are at school?

   b) How did you solve the problem? (Did you use a calculation?
   Make a model? Draw a picture?)

---

2. Here are the heights of some of Canada's tallest towers.

   a) Write the heights in order from least to greatest.

   b) How much higher than the Calgary Tower is the
   Scotia Plaza?

   c) How much higher than the shortest tower is the
   tallest tower?

Heights of Buildings	
First Canadian Place, Toronto	298 m
Scotia Plaza, Toronto	275 m
Calgary Tower, Calgary	191 m

---

3. Place the numbers 1, 2, 3, and 4 in the top four
   boxes to make the greatest possible sum and
   the greatest possible difference.

4. Find the error in Bob's sum.

$$\begin{array}{r} 2 \\ 4\,7 \\ +\,2\,5 \\ \hline 8\,1 \end{array}$$

---

5. A baby whale drinks about 100 litres of milk
   each day.

   a) How many litres of milk will a baby whale
   drink in 7 days?

   b) What method of computation did you use
   to solve the problem?

6. a) Write the number that is 10 greater
   than 200.

   b) Write the number that is 10 less
   than 200.

---

7. Pens cost 53¢.
   Erasers cost 44¢.
   Eric has 98¢.

   Does he have enough money
   to buy a pen and an eraser?

   Explain how you know.

8. Sam wants to add the numbers below.
   He starts by adding the ones digits.

$$\begin{array}{r} 1 \\ 2\,5 \\ +\,3\,7 \\ \hline 2 \end{array}$$

   *Explain why Sam wrote
   the number 1 here.*

NS3-31: Arrays

In the **array** below, there are 3 **rows** of dots. There are 5 dots **in each row**.

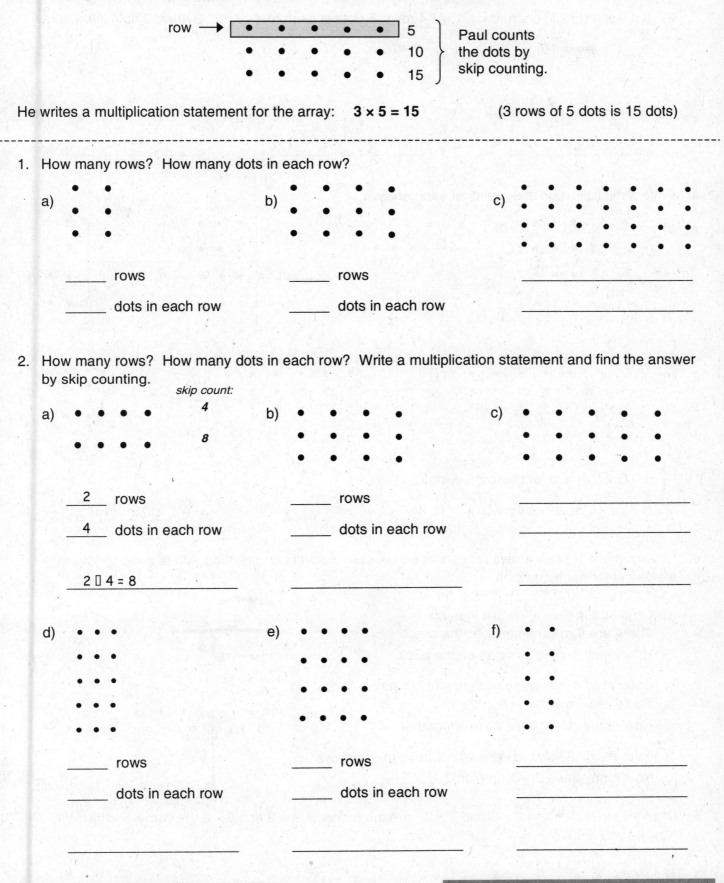

row → • • • • • 5
      • • • • • 10   ⎫ Paul counts
      • • • • • 15   ⎬ the dots by
                        ⎭ skip counting.

He writes a multiplication statement for the array: **3 × 5 = 15**   (3 rows of 5 dots is 15 dots)

----

1. How many rows? How many dots in each row?

a)

_____ rows

_____ dots in each row

b)

_____ rows

_____ dots in each row

c)

_____

_____

2. How many rows? How many dots in each row? Write a multiplication statement and find the answer by skip counting.

a)   skip count: **4**
                    8

___2___ rows

___4___ dots in each row

___2 ⬚ 4 = 8_____

b)

_____ rows

_____ dots in each row

_____

c)

_____

_____

d)

_____ rows

_____ dots in each row

_____

e)

_____ rows

_____ dots in each row

_____

f)

_____

_____

3. Draw an array and write a multiplication sentence for each question.

    a) 3 rows; 4 dots in each row   b) 4 rows; 5 dots in each row   c) 2 rows; 3 dots in each row

    _____   _____   _____

4. Write a multiplication statement for each array.

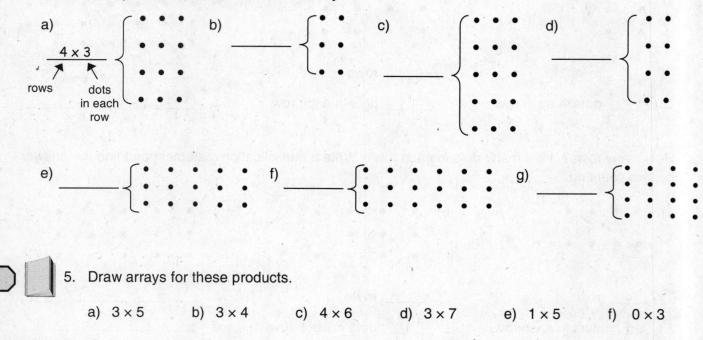

    a)
         4 × 3
       ↑   ↑
     rows   dots
            in each
             row

    b) _____

    c) _____

    d) _____

    e) _____

    f) _____

    g) _____

5. Draw arrays for these products.

    a) 3 × 5   b) 3 × 4   c) 4 × 6   d) 3 × 7   e) 1 × 5   f) 0 × 3

6. Use counters or draw arrays (of dots or squares) to model each question. Write a multiplication statement for each question.

    a) On a bus, 4 people can sit in a row.
        There are 5 rows of seats on the bus.
        How many people can ride on the bus?

    b) Peter puts 6 stamps in each row of his stamp book.
        There are 3 rows of stamps.
        How many stamps are there altogether?

    c) John plants 5 rows of trees with 3 trees in each row.
        How many trees did John plant?

7. Draw an array showing 2 × 3 and 3 × 2. Are the products 2 × 3 and 3 × 2 the same or different?
    How do you know?

NS3-32: Adding Sequences of Numbers

1. Add the following numbers. (Keep a record of your sums in the boxes.)

Example $2 + 3 + 6 =$ ___   add 2 + 3 (= 5) $\boxed{5}$ $2 + 3 + 6 =$ ___   add 5 + 6 (= 11) $\boxed{5}$ $2 + 3 + 6 = 11$

a) $3 + 4 + 1 =$ ___

b) $2 + 4 + 3 =$ ___

c) $1 + 3 + 2 =$ ___

d) $2 + 3 + 4 =$ ___

e) $3 + 2 + 3 =$ ___

f) $2 + 1 + 5 =$ ___

g) $3 + 2 + 1 + 4 =$ ___

h) $2 + 2 + 2 + 2 =$ ___

i) $5 + 5 + 5 + 5 =$ ___

2. Write an addition statement for each picture.
   Then add the numbers to find out how many apples there are altogether.

   a) 3 boxes; 2 apples in each box

   b) 4 boxes; 3 apples in each box

   c) 2 boxes; 4 apples in each box

   d) 4 boxes; 5 apples in each box

3. Draw a picture for each amount and write an addition statement for your picture.

   a) 4 boxes
      2 apples in each box

   b) 3 boxes
      5 pencils in each box

   c) 3 fish bowls
      4 fish in each bowl

   d) 3 boats
      3 kids in each boat

4. Write an addition statement for each amount.

   a) 4 boxes
      3 dimes in each box

   b) 4 wagons
      2 kids in each wagon

   c) 5 baskets
      6 oranges in each basket

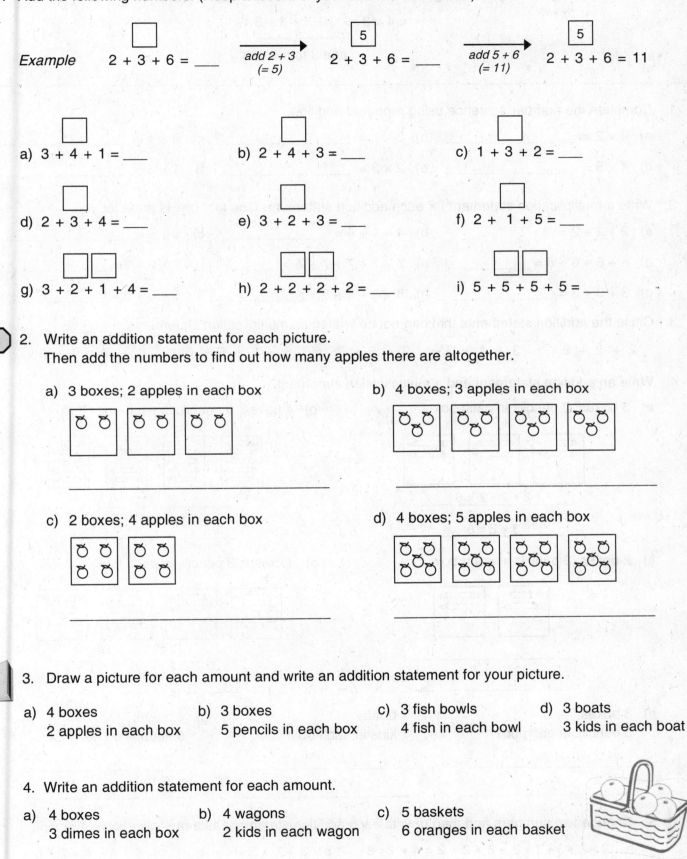

     No unauthorized copying   **Number Sense 1**

NS3-33: Multiplication and Repeated Addition

Multiplication is a short way of writing the addition of the same number many times.

$$4 \times 3 = \underbrace{3 + 3 + 3 + 3}$$

add 3 four times

---

1. Complete the number sentence using repeated addition.

    a) $4 \times 2 =$ _____

    b) $3 \times 2 =$ _____

    c) $3 \times 4 =$ _____

    d) $4 \times 5 =$ _____

    e) $2 \times 3 =$ _____

    f) $1 \times 5 =$ _____

2. Write a multiplication statement for each addition statement. The first one is done for you.

    a) $2 + 2 + 2 = 3 \times 2$

    b) $4 + 4 + 4 =$ _____

    c) $5 + 5 =$ _____

    d) $6 + 6 + 6 + 6 =$ _____

    e) $7 + 7 + 7 + 7 + 7 =$ _____

    f) $9 + 9 + 9 =$ _____

    g) $3 + 3 + 3 =$ _____

    h) $8 + 8 + 8 + 8 =$ _____

    i) $5 + 5 + 5 =$ _____

3. Circle the addition statements that can not be written as multiplication statements.

    $2 + 2 + 2$ $3 + 4 + 3$ $2 + 5 + 7$ $6 + 6 + 6 + 6$ $8 + 8 + 9 + 8$

4. Write an addition statement and a multiplication statement.

    a) 3 boxes; 2 pencils in each box

    b) 4 boxes; 5 pencils in each box

    $\underline{\quad 2 + 2 + 2 = 6 \quad}$

    $\underline{\quad 3 \times 2 = 6 \quad}$

    c) 2 boxes; 2 pencils in each box

    d) 4 boxes; 3 pencils in each box

    e) 3 boxes
        5 pencils in each box

    f) 2 boats
        7 kids in each boat

    g) 4 pages
        5 stamps on each page

5. Change two numbers and then rewrite each addition statement as a multiplication statement.

    a) $2 + 2 + 3 + 1 = \mathbf{2 + 2 + 2 + 2 = 4 \times 2 = 8}$

    b) $3 + 2 + 3 + 4 + 3$

    c) $4 + 4 + 4 + 2 + 6$

NS3-34: Multiplying by Skip Counting

When you multiply a pair of numbers, the result is called the **product** of the numbers.

Lee finds the product of 3 and 4 by skip counting on a number line. He counts off three 4s:

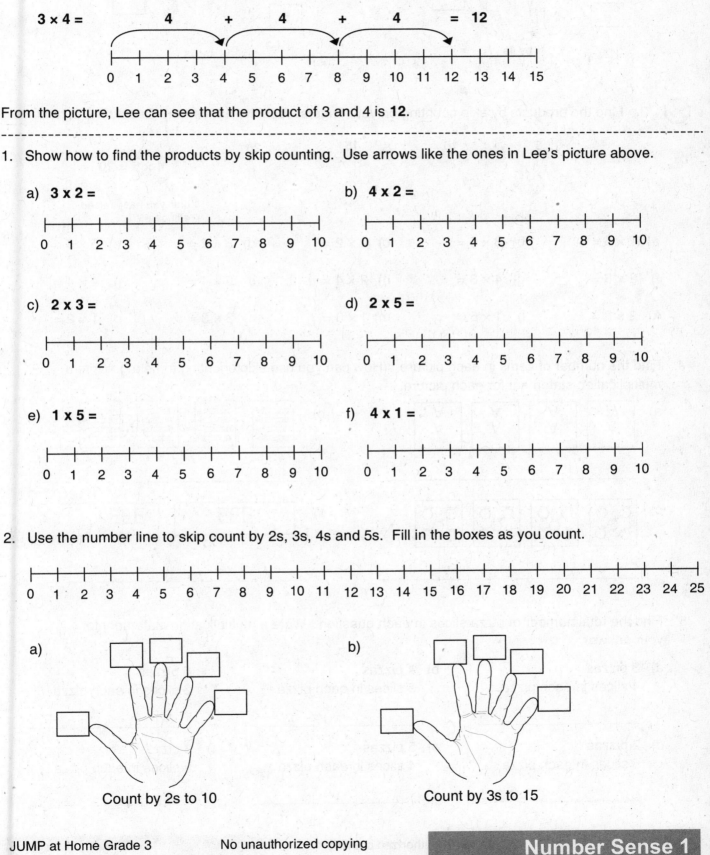

$3 \times 4 =$ **4**   +   **4**   +   **4**   = **12**

From the picture, Lee can see that the product of 3 and 4 is **12**.

- -

1. Show how to find the products by skip counting. Use arrows like the ones in Lee's picture above.

a) **3 x 2 =**

b) **4 x 2 =**

c) **2 x 3 =**

d) **2 x 5 =**

e) **1 x 5 =**

f) **4 x 1 =**

2. Use the number line to skip count by 2s, 3s, 4s and 5s. Fill in the boxes as you count.

a)

Count by 2s to 10

b)

Count by 3s to 15

No unauthorized copying

Number Sense 1

c) 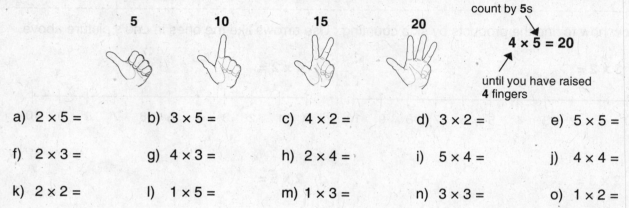   d)

Count by **4s**

Count by **5s**

3. Find the products by skip counting on your fingers. Use the hands from Question 2 to help.

count by 5s

5   10   15   20

$4 \times 5 = 20$

until you have raised **4 fingers**

a) $2 \times 5 =$ b) $3 \times 5 =$ c) $4 \times 2 =$ d) $3 \times 2 =$ e) $5 \times 5 =$

f) $2 \times 3 =$ g) $4 \times 3 =$ h) $2 \times 4 =$ i) $5 \times 4 =$ j) $4 \times 4 =$

k) $2 \times 2 =$ l) $1 \times 5 =$ m) $1 \times 3 =$ n) $3 \times 3 =$ o) $1 \times 2 =$

4. Find the number of items in each picture. (How can you use skip counting to help?) Write a multiplication statement for each picture.

a) 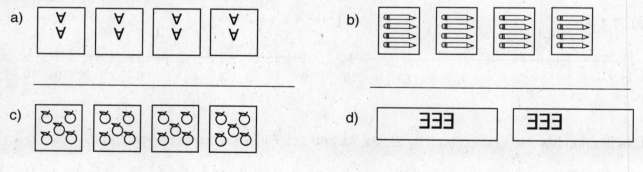   b)

c)   d)

5. Find the total number of pizza slices in each question. Write a multiplication statement for your answer.

a) 3 pizzas
   4 slices in each pizza

b) 4 pizzas
   5 slices in each pizza

c) 5 pizzas
   3 slices in each pizza

d) 2 pizzas
   5 slices in each pizza

e) 5 pizzas
   4 slices in each pizza

f) 3 pizzas
   3 slices in each pizza

NS3-35: Doubles

1. Count by 2s.

   2 , 4 , 6 , _____, _____, _____, _____, _____, _____

2. Double each number mentally by doubling the ones digit and the tens digit separately.

	24	14	12	32	64	22	13
Double	48						

	82	51	34	54	92	74	71
Double							

3. Double the ones and tens separately and add the result: $2 \times 27 = 2 \times 20 + 2 \times 7 = 40 + 14 = 54$.

	16	15	25	37	28	18	48
Double							

	17	45	66	35	46	29	55
Double							

4. Use doubles to find the missing products.

If $2 \times 7 = 14$	$3 \times 7 = 21$	$4 \times 7 = 28$	$2 \times 6 = 12$
Then $4 \times 7 =$	$6 \times 7 =$	$8 \times 7 =$	$4 \times 6 =$

$3 \times 6 = 18$	$4 \times 6 = 24$	$2 \times 8 = 16$	$4 \times 8 = 32$
$6 \times 6 =$	$8 \times 6 =$	$4 \times 8 =$	$8 \times 8 =$

$2 \times 9 = 18$	$3 \times 9 = 27$	$4 \times 9 = 36$	$2 \times 12 = 24$
$4 \times 9 =$	$6 \times 9 =$	$8 \times 9 =$	$4 \times 12 =$

5. Calculate the total cost of 2 items mentally.

   a) 2 oranges for 42¢ each _____

   b) 2 stickers for 37¢ each _____

   c) 2 stamps for 48¢ each _____

   d) 2 goldfish for 35¢ each _____

NS3-36: Topics in Multiplication

1. Use skip counting to find out how many legs the following animals have.

Animals	Number of animals				
	1	**2**	**3**	**4**	**5**
(snail)	0				
(bird)					
(cat)					
(insect)					
(spider)					

2. A hockey line has 5 players.
   Fill in the missing information.

_____ lines	5 + 5 + 5 + 5	4 × 5
3 lines	5 + 5 + 5	
6 lines		
_____ lines		2 × 5

3. Fill in the missing numbers.

   a) 4, 8, _____, 16, 20

   b) 5, _____, 15, _____, 25

   c) _____, 6, _____, 12, 15

   d) _____, _____, _____, 8, 10

4. Philip practises guitar twice a week. How many times will he practise in 4 weeks?

5. Carmen can ride 1 kilometre in 5 minutes. How far can she ride in 20 minutes?

6. Create a multiplication problem using the numbers 4 and 6.

7.
   2 × 4 = 8   2 × 3 = 6   2 × 2 = 4   2 × 1 = 2   2 × 0 = 2

   Draw a similar set of arrays for 3 × 4, 3 × 3, 3 × 2, 3 × 1 and 3 × 0.

No unauthorized copying
Number Sense 1

8. How many times as many circles are in box B as in box A?

   HINT: Put the circles in box B into groups that contain as many circles as box A.

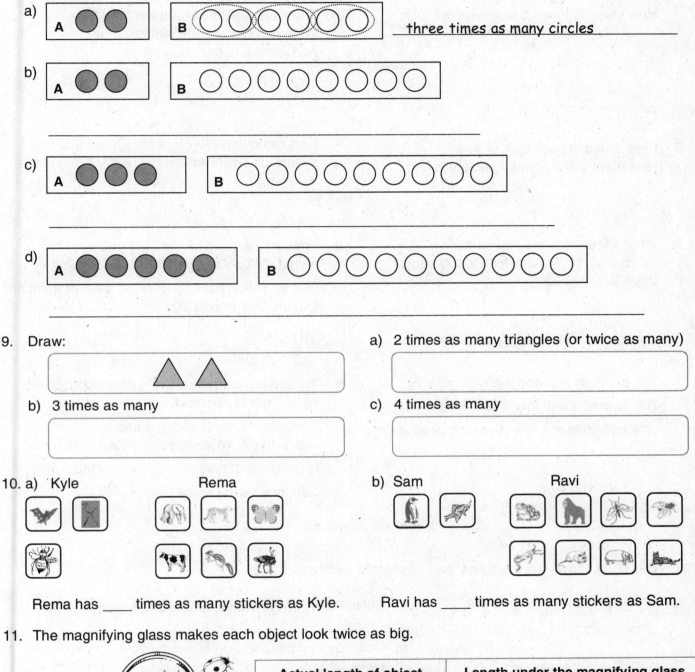

a) A ●●   B ○○○○○○   _three times as many circles_

b) A ●●   B ○○○○○○○○

c) A ●●●   B ○○○○○○○○○

d) A ●●●●●   B ○○○○○○○○○○

9. Draw:
   a) 2 times as many triangles (or twice as many)

   △ △

   b) 3 times as many

   c) 4 times as many

10. a) Kyle   Rema   b) Sam   Ravi

    Rema has ____ times as many stickers as Kyle.   Ravi has ____ times as many stickers as Sam.

11. The magnifying glass makes each object look twice as big.

Actual length of object	Length under the magnifying glass
2 cm	
5 cm	
7 cm	

12. Kyle has 6 books. Ron has three times as many books.
    Explain how you would find out how many books Ron has.

Answer these questions in your notebook.

1. A stool has 3 legs.
   How many legs will 6 stools have?

2. Terry multiplied 5 by a number less than 4.
   The ones digit of her answer was 0.
   What number did she multiply 5 by?
   And what was her answer?

3. Pens come in packages of 4.
   How many pens are in 4 packages?

4. Find two numbers ($\square$ and $\triangle$) so that the
   multiplication statement $\square \times \triangle = \square$ is true.

5. What happens when you multiply a
   number by 1? What does 1×100 equal?
   What is $1 \times 2\,732$?

6. Write all the pairs of numbers you can think
   of that multiply to give 12.

   (For an extra challenge, find all pairs of numbers
   that multiply to give 20.)

7. The **product** of 3 and 2 is 6 ($3 \times 2 = 6$).

   The **sum** of 3 and 2 is 5 ($3 + 2 = 5$).

   Which is greater: the **sum** or the **product**?

8. Try finding the **sum** and the **product** of some
   other pairs of numbers.

   For instance, try 3 and 4, 2 and 5, 5 and 6,
   and 1 and 7. What do you notice?

   Is the product always greater than the sum?

   Can they be the same?

9. This chart shows the multiplication facts for the numbers 1 to 6.

×	1	2	3	4	5	6
1	1	2	3			
2	2	4	6			
3	3	6	9			
4						
5						
6						

a) Fill in the missing numbers in the times table.

b) Describe any patterns you see in the rows of the
   times table.

c) Can you explain the patterns?

NS3-38: Pennies, Nickels and Dimes

1. Write the name and value of each coin.

1¢   Name _____   Value _____

5¢   Name _____   Value _____

10¢   Name _____   Value _____

2. Answer the following questions. **HINT: Look at the pictures.**

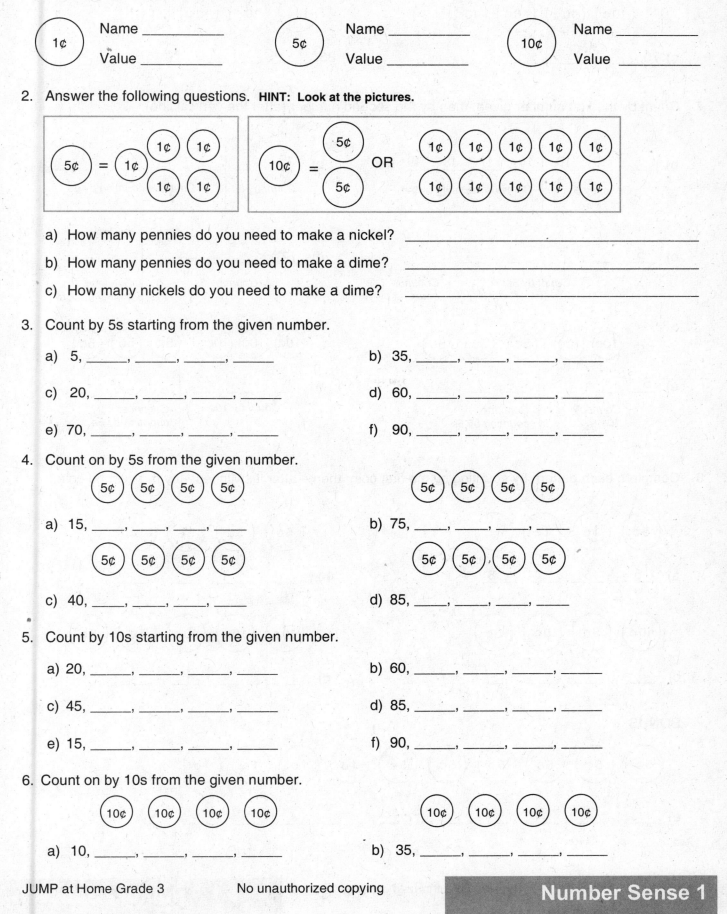

a) How many pennies do you need to make a nickel? _____

b) How many pennies do you need to make a dime? _____

c) How many nickels do you need to make a dime? _____

3. Count by 5s starting from the given number.

a) 5, _____, _____, _____, _____

b) 35, _____, _____, _____, _____

c) 20, _____, _____, _____, _____

d) 60, _____, _____, _____, _____

e) 70, _____, _____, _____, _____

f) 90, _____, _____, _____, _____

4. Count on by 5s from the given number.

a) 15, ____, ____, ____, ____

b) 75, ____, ____, ____, ____

c) 40, ____, ____, ____, ____

d) 85, ____, ____, ____, ____

5. Count by 10s starting from the given number.

a) 20, _____, _____, _____, _____

b) 60, _____, _____, _____, _____

c) 45, _____, _____, _____, _____

d) 85, _____, _____, _____, _____

e) 15, _____, _____, _____, _____

f) 90, _____, _____, _____, _____

6. Count on by 10s from the given number.

a) 10, _____, _____, _____, _____

b) 35, _____, _____, _____, _____

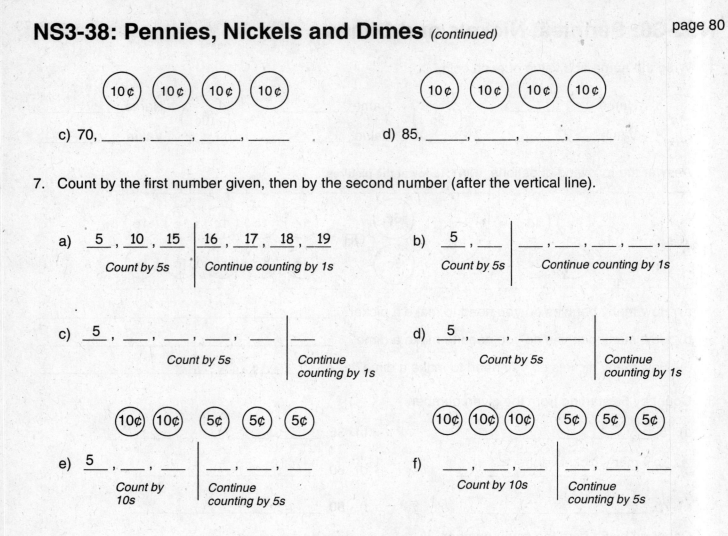

c) 70, _____, _____, _____, _____

d) 85, _____, _____, _____, _____

7. Count by the first number given, then by the second number (after the vertical line).

a) __5__ , __10__ , __15__ | __16__ , __17__ , __18__ , __19__

    Count by 5s | *Continue counting by 1s*

b) __5__ , ___ | ___ , ___ , ___ , ___ , ___

    Count by 5s | *Continue counting by 1s*

c) __5__ , ___ , ___ , ___ , ___ | ___

    Count by 5s | *Continue counting by 1s*

d) __5__ , ___ , ___ , ___ | ___ , ___

    Count by 5s | *Continue counting by 1s*

e) __5__ , ___ , ___ | ___ , ___ , ___

    Count by 10s | *Continue counting by 5s*

f) ___ , ___ , ___ | ___ , ___ , ___

    Count by 10s | *Continue counting by 5s*

8. Complete each pattern by counting by the first coin, then – after it switches – by the second coin.

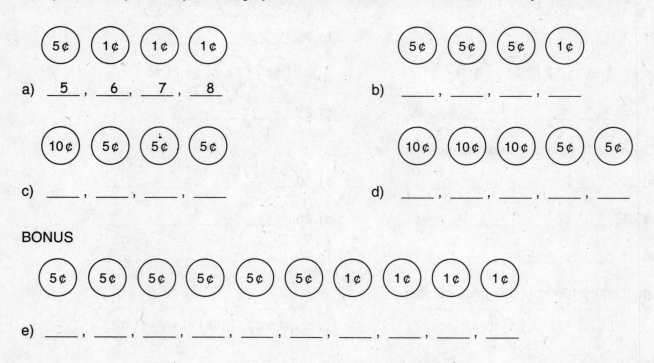

a) __5__ , __6__ , __7__ , __8__

b) ___ , ___ , ___ , ___

c) ___ , ___ , ___ , ___

d) ___ , ___ , ___ , ___ , ___

BONUS

e) ___ , ___ , ___ , ___ , ___ , ___ , ___ , ___ , ___ , ___

NS3-39: Quarters

1. Write the name and the value of the coin.

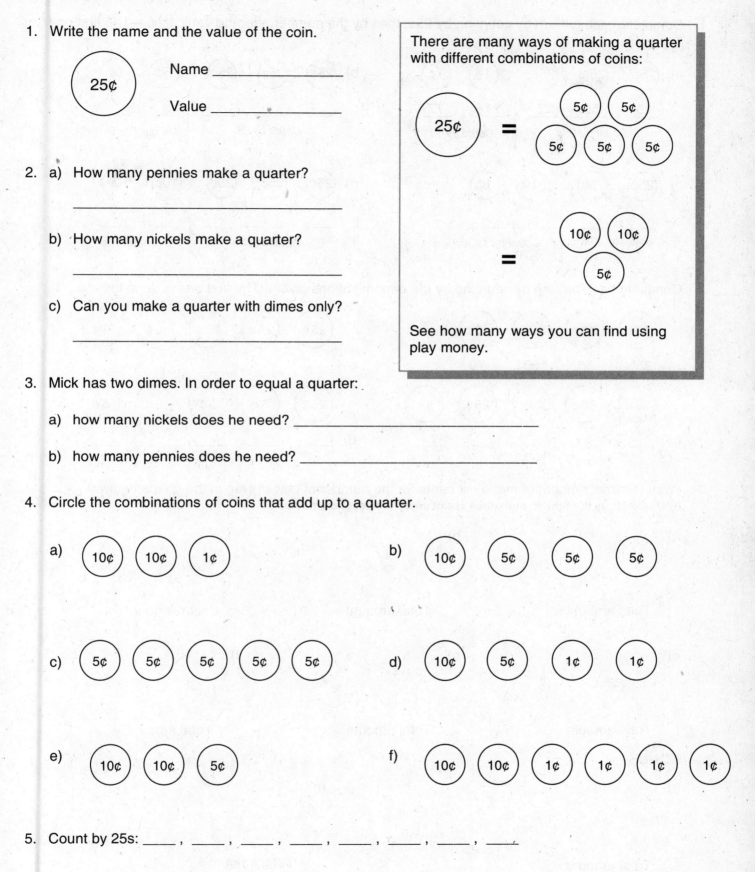

   25¢   Name _____

          Value _____

2. a) How many pennies make a quarter?

   _____

   b) How many nickels make a quarter?

   _____

   c) Can you make a quarter with dimes only?

   _____

There are many ways of making a quarter with different combinations of coins:

25¢ = 5¢ 5¢ 5¢ 5¢ 5¢

= 10¢ 10¢ 5¢

See how many ways you can find using play money.

3. Mick has two dimes. In order to equal a quarter:

   a) how many nickels does he need? _____

   b) how many pennies does he need? _____

4. Circle the combinations of coins that add up to a quarter.

   a) 10¢ 10¢ 1¢   b) 10¢ 5¢ 5¢ 5¢

   c) 5¢ 5¢ 5¢ 5¢ 5¢   d) 10¢ 5¢ 1¢ 1¢

   e) 10¢ 10¢ 5¢   f) 10¢ 10¢ 1¢ 1¢ 1¢ 1¢

5. Count by 25s: _____ , _____ , _____ , _____ , _____ , _____ , _____ , _____

NS3-40: Counting by Two or More Coin Values

1. Complete each pattern by counting by 25s, then by the number after the vertical line. The first one is done for you.

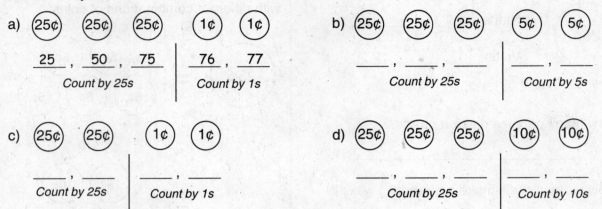

a) 25¢ 25¢ 25¢ | 1¢ 1¢

   25 , 50 , 75 | 76 , 77

   Count by 25s | *Count by 1s*

b) 25¢ 25¢ 25¢ | 5¢ 5¢

   ___ , ___ , ___ | ___ , ___

   Count by 25s | *Count by 5s*

c) 25¢ 25¢ | 1¢ 1¢

   ___ , ___ | ___ , ___

   Count by 25s | *Count by 1s*

d) 25¢ 25¢ 25¢ | 10¢ 10¢

   ___ , ___ , ___ | ___ , ___

   Count by 25s | *Count by 10s*

2. Complete each pattern by counting by the denominations given. The first one is done for you.

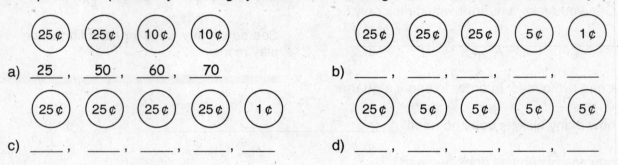

   25¢ 25¢ 10¢ 10¢

a) 25 , 50 , 60 , 70

   25¢ 25¢ 25¢ 5¢ 1¢

b) ___ , ___ , ___ , ___ , ___

   25¢ 25¢ 25¢ 25¢ 1¢

c) ___ , ___ , ___ , ___ , ___

   25¢ 5¢ 5¢ 5¢ 5¢

d) ___ , ___ , ___ , ___ , ___

3. Write the total amount of money in cents for the number of coins given in the charts below.
   HINT: Count by the first amount, then count on by the second amount.

   a)

   b)

   c)

   Total amount =   Total amount =   Total amount =

   d)

   e)

   f)

   Total amount =   Total amount =   Total amount =

   BONUS

   g)   h)

   Total amount =   Total amount =

Number Sense 1

4. Complete each pattern by counting by the numbers given.

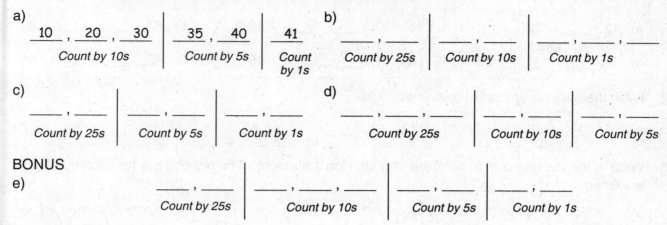

a)

_10_ , _20_ , _30_ | _35_ , _40_ | _41_

Count by 10s   Count by 5s   Count by 1s

b)

___ , ___ | ___ , ___ | ___ , ___ , ___

Count by 25s   Count by 10s   Count by 1s

c)

___ , ___ | ___ , ___ | ___ , ___

Count by 25s   Count by 5s   Count by 1s

d)

___ , ___ , ___ | ___ , ___ , ___ | ___ , ___

Count by 25s   Count by 10s   Count by 5s

BONUS

e)

___ , ___ | ___ , ___ , ___ | ___ , ___ | ___ , ___

Count by 25s   Count by 10s   Count by 5s   Count by 1s

5. Count the given coins and write the total amount.
   HINT: Count the bigger amounts first.

a)  (1¢)(1¢)(5¢)(5¢)(10¢)

Total amount =

b) (10¢)(25¢)(25¢)(1¢)

Total amount =

c) (5¢)(25¢)(10¢)(10¢)

Total amount =

d) (5¢)(10¢)(25¢)(5¢)(1¢)(1¢)

Total amount =

e) 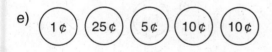 (1¢)(25¢)(5¢)(10¢)(10¢)

Total amount =

f) 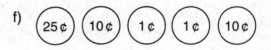 (25¢)(10¢)(1¢)(1¢)(10¢)

Total amount =

g) 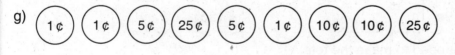 (1¢)(1¢)(5¢)(25¢)(5¢)(1¢)(10¢)(10¢)(25¢)

Total amount =

BONUS

6. Complete each pattern by counting on by each denomination.

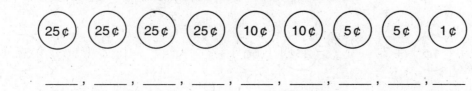 (25¢)(25¢)(25¢)(25¢)(10¢)(10¢)(5¢)(5¢)(1¢)

___ , ___ , ___ , ___ , ___ , ___ , ___ , ___ , ___

PARENT: Allow your child to practise the skill in Question 5 with play money.

NS3-41: Counting by Different Denominations

1. Fill in the missing amounts, counting by 5s.

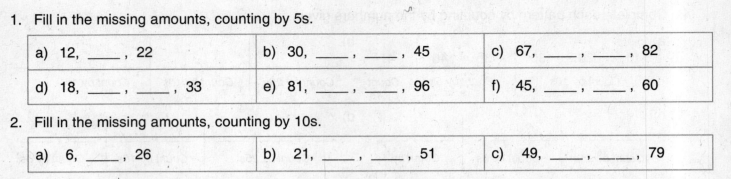

| a) 12, _____, 22 | b) 30, _____, _____, 45 | c) 67, _____, _____, 82 |
| d) 18, _____, _____, 33 | e) 81, _____, _____, 96 | f) 45, _____, _____, 60 |

2. Fill in the missing amounts, counting by 10s.

| a) 6, _____, 26 | b) 21, _____, _____, 51 | c) 49, _____, _____, 79 |

3. Write in the missing coin to complete the addition statement. The possibilities for each question are listed.

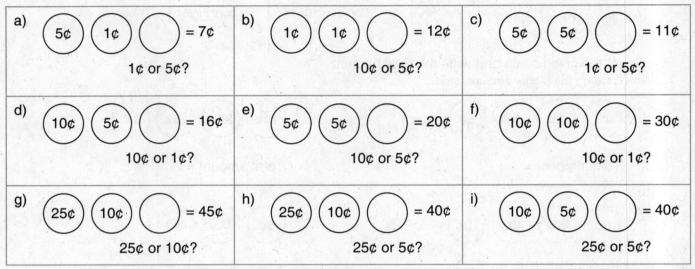

a) 5¢ 1¢ ◯ = 7¢
1¢ or 5¢?

b) 1¢ 1¢ ◯ = 12¢
10¢ or 5¢?

c) 5¢ 5¢ ◯ = 11¢
1¢ or 5¢?

d) 10¢ 5¢ ◯ = 16¢
10¢ or 1¢?

e) 5¢ 5¢ ◯ = 20¢
10¢ or 5¢?

f) 10¢ 10¢ ◯ = 30¢
10¢ or 1¢?

g) 25¢ 10¢ ◯ = 45¢
25¢ or 10¢?

h) 25¢ 10¢ ◯ = 40¢
25¢ or 5¢?

i) 10¢ 5¢ ◯ = 40¢
25¢ or 5¢?

4. Draw the additional **pennies** needed to make the total.

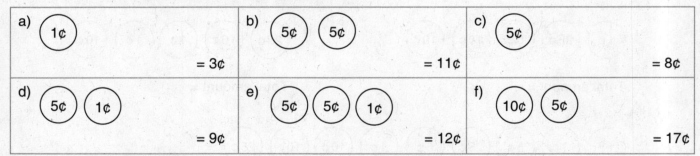

a) 1¢ = 3¢

b) 5¢ 5¢ = 11¢

c) 5¢ = 8¢

d) 5¢ 1¢ = 9¢

e) 5¢ 5¢ 1¢ = 12¢

f) 10¢ 5¢ = 17¢

5. Draw the additional **nickels** needed to make the total.

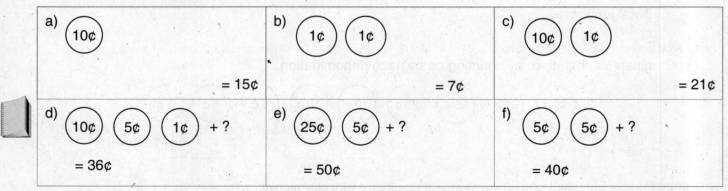

a) 10¢ = 15¢

b) 1¢ 1¢ = 7¢

c) 10¢ 1¢ = 21¢

d) 10¢ 5¢ 1¢ + ? = 36¢

e) 25¢ 5¢ + ? = 50¢

f) 5¢ 5¢ + ? = 40¢

Number Sense 1

6. Draw the additional **dimes** needed to make the total.

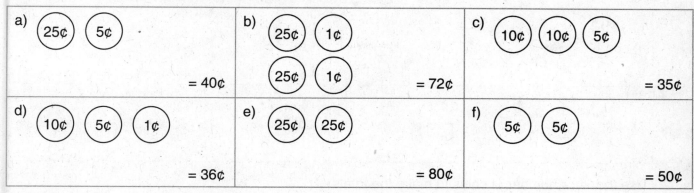

| a) 25¢ 5¢   = 40¢ | b) 25¢ 1¢   25¢ 1¢   = 72¢ | c) 10¢ 10¢ 5¢   = 35¢ |
| d) 10¢ 5¢ 1¢   = 36¢ | e) 25¢ 25¢   = 80¢ | f) 5¢ 5¢   = 50¢ |

7. Draw the additional **coins** needed to make each total.

a) *How many nickels?* 25¢ + = 35¢	b) *How many dimes?* 10¢ + = 50¢
d) *How many dimes?* 25¢ 25¢ + = 70¢	e) *How many nickels?* 25¢ 5¢ + = 35¢
f) *How many nickels?* 10¢ 10¢ + = 35¢	g) *How many quarters?* 25¢ 25¢ + = 75¢

BONUS

8. Draw the additional coins needed to make each total. You can only use **two** coins for each question, either (i) a penny and a nickel, (ii) a penny and a dime, or (iii) a nickel and a dime.

a) 16¢ 10¢	b) 17¢ 10¢ 1¢
c) 30¢ 10¢ 5¢	d) 50¢ 25¢ 10¢
e) 26¢ 10¢ 1¢	f) 61¢ 25¢ 25¢

9. Draw a picture to show the **extra coins** each child will need to pay for the item they want:

    a) Kevin has 25¢. He wants to buy a pen for 35¢.

    b) Sandra has 1 quarter and 2 dimes. She wants to buy a notebook for 70¢.

    c) Laura has 2 quarters, 1 dime and 1 nickel. She wants to buy a snack for 87¢.

10. Can you make 27¢ using only nickels and dimes? Explain why or why not.

NS3-42: Least Number of Coins

1. Use the *least* number of coins to make the totals. Draw in the coins.

a) 6¢	b) 4¢
c) 8¢	d) 9¢

2. Use the *least* number of coins to make the totals.
   HINT: Start by seeing how many dimes you need.

a) 12¢ (10¢)(1¢)(1¢) *correct* ¦ (5¢)(5¢)(1¢)(1¢) *incorrect*	b) 14¢
c) 21¢	d) 23¢

3. Use the *least* number of coins to make the totals.

a) 15¢	b) 20¢

4. Use the *least* number of coins.
   HINT: Start by seeing how many dimes you need (if any), then nickels and then pennies.

a) 16¢	b) 22¢
c) 11¢	d) 8¢
e) 24¢	f) 17¢
g) 14¢	h) 19¢

5. Fill in the amounts: 2 quarters = _____ ¢   3 quarters = _____ ¢   4 quarters = _____ ¢

6. Ron has 85¢ in coins in his pocket. What is the greatest number of coins that could be quarters?

NS3-42: Least Number of Coins *(continued)*

7. For each amount, what is the greatest amount you could pay in quarters?

Amount	Greatest amount you could pay in quarters	Amount	Greatest amount you could pay in quarters
a) 35¢		b) 78¢	
c) 52¢		d) 62¢	
e) 31¢		f) 83¢	
g) 59¢		h) 27¢	

8. For each amount, find the greatest amount you could pay in quarters. Represent the amount remaining using the least number of coins.

Amount	Greatest Amount Paid in Quarters	Amount Remaining	Amount Remaining in Coins
a) 81¢	75¢	81¢ − 75¢ = 6¢	(5¢) (1¢)
c) 57¢			
e) 31¢			
g) 85¢			

9. Use the **least** number of coins to make the totals.

a) 30¢   (10¢)(10¢)(10¢) | (25¢)(5¢)
      incorrect   *correct*

b) 76¢

c) 35¢

d) 50¢

10. Trade coins to make each amount with fewer coins. Draw a picture to show your answer.

a) (10¢)(5¢)(5¢)	b) (25¢)(5¢)(5¢)(5¢)	c) (10¢)(10¢)(5¢)(5¢)
d) (5¢)(5¢)(5¢)(5¢)	e) (5¢)(1¢)(1¢)(1¢)(1¢)(1¢)	f) (10¢)(10¢)(5¢)(5¢)(5¢)

11. How could you trade 3 dimes for fewer coins?

12. Show how you could make 42¢ using the least number of coins. Use play money to help you.

NS3-43: Dimes and Pennies

1. Write the number of dimes and pennies in each collection of coins. Then total each collection.

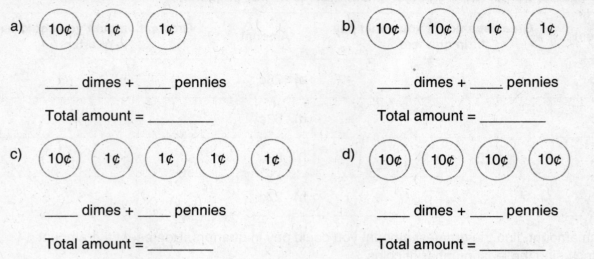

a) 10¢ 1¢ 1¢

_____ dimes + _____ pennies

Total amount = _____

b) 10¢ 10¢ 1¢ 1¢

_____ dimes + _____ pennies

Total amount = _____

c) 10¢ 1¢ 1¢ 1¢ 1¢

_____ dimes + _____ pennies

Total amount = _____

d) 10¢ 10¢ 10¢ 10¢

_____ dimes + _____ pennies

Total amount = _____

2. Give the total amount of money for the number of dimes and pennies in the T-tables below.

a)

dimes	pennies
2	3

= _____ ¢

b)

dimes	pennies
7	0

= _____ ¢

c)

dimes	pennies
4	1

= _____ ¢

d)

dimes	pennies
8	2

= _____ ¢

e)

dimes	pennies
3	9

= _____ ¢

f)

dimes	pennies
1	8

= _____ ¢

3. For each amount, write the number of dimes and pennies needed in each column of the tables.

a)

dimes	pennies

= 25¢

b)

dimes	pennies

= 40¢

c)

dimes	pennies

= 36¢

d)

dimes	pennies

= 2¢

e)

dimes	pennies

= 12¢

f)

dimes	pennies

= 99¢

BONUS

4. Draw the number of dimes and pennies you would need to make each amount.
   Then write the money amount in words.

   a) 30¢   b) 24¢   c) 51¢   d) 45¢   e) 33¢   f) 67¢

NS3-44: Making Change Using Mental Math

1. Calculate the change owing for each purchase.

a) Price of a pen = 48¢
   Amount paid = 50¢

   Change = _____

b) Price of a pencil = 47¢
   Amount paid = 50¢

   Change = _____

c) Price of an eraser = 84¢
   Amount paid = 90¢

   Change = _____

d) Price of a sticker = 52¢
   Amount paid = 60¢

   Change = _____

e) Price of a marker = 74¢
   Amount paid = 80¢

   Change = _____

f) Price of a notebook = 66¢
   Amount paid = 70¢

   Change = _____

2. Find the change owing from a dollar (100¢).

Price	Change	Price	Change	Price	Change
a) 80¢		d) 40¢		h) 50¢	
b) 70¢		e) 60¢		i) 10¢	
c) 20¢		f) 30¢		j) 90¢	

3. Find the change owing for each purchase.

a) Price of a pen = 50¢
   Amount Paid = $1.00

   Change = _____

b) Price of an eraser = 80¢
   Amount paid = $1.00

   Change = _____

c) Price of an apple = 20¢
   Amount paid = $1.00

   Change = _____

d) Price of a banana = 60¢
   Amount paid = $1.00

   Change = _____

e) Price of a patty = 90¢
   Amount paid = $1.00

   Change = _____

f) Price of a pencil = 30¢
   Amount paid = $1.00

   Change = _____

g) Price of a gumball = 10¢
   Amount paid = $1.00

   Change = _____

h) Price of a juice = 40¢
   Amount paid = $1.00

   Change = _____

i) Price of a popsicle = 70¢
   Amount paid = $1.00

   Change = _____

4. Find the smallest number ending in zero (i.e. 10, 20, 30, 40...) that is <u>greater</u> than the number given.

a) 72 | 80 | b) 63 | | c) 49 | | d) 27 | | e) 55 | | f) 6 | |

No unauthorized copying   Number Sense 1

NS3-44: Making Change Using Mental Math (continued)

5. Make change for the amount written below. Follow the steps shown for 17¢.

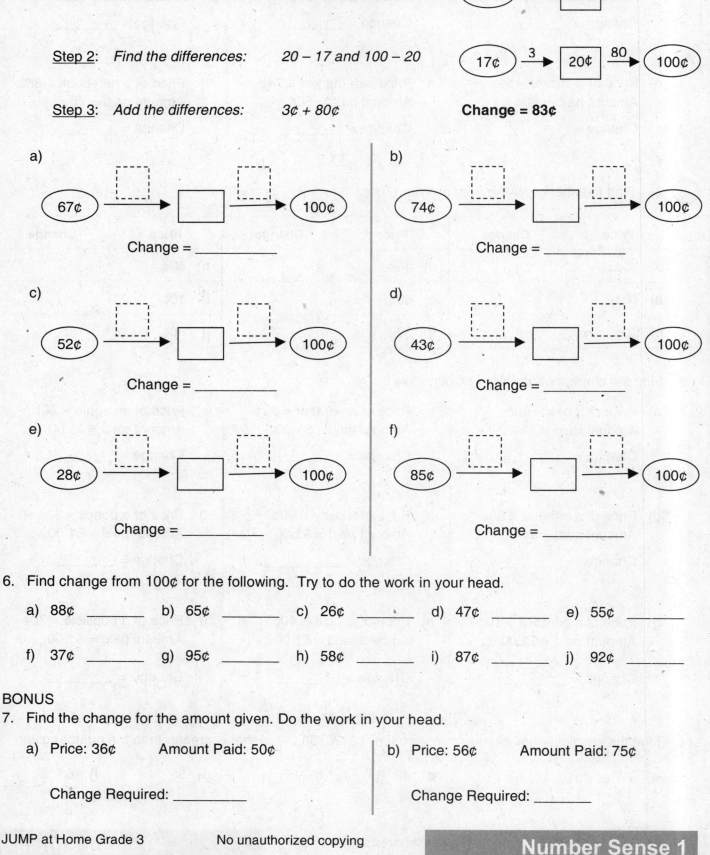

Step 1: *Find the smallest multiple of 10 greater than 17¢.*

Step 2: *Find the differences:* 20 – 17 and 100 – 20

Step 3: *Add the differences:* 3¢ + 80¢   **Change = 83¢**

a)

67¢ → ▢ → 100¢

Change = _____

b)

74¢ → ▢ → 100¢

Change = _____

c)

52¢ → ▢ → 100¢

Change = _____

d)

43¢ → ▢ → 100¢

Change = _____

e)

28¢ → ▢ → 100¢

Change = _____

f)

85¢ → ▢ → 100¢

Change = _____

6. Find change from 100¢ for the following. Try to do the work in your head.

a) 88¢ _____   b) 65¢ _____   c) 26¢ _____   d) 47¢ _____   e) 55¢ _____

f) 37¢ _____   g) 95¢ _____   h) 58¢ _____   i) 87¢ _____   j) 92¢ _____

BONUS

7. Find the change for the amount given. Do the work in your head.

a) Price: 36¢   Amount Paid: 50¢

   Change Required: _____

b) Price: 56¢   Amount Paid: 75¢

   Change Required: _____

1 cm

1. A **centimetre** (cm) is a unit of measurement for **length** (or **height** or **thickness**).

   Your index finger is approximately one centimetre wide.

   Measure the following objects using your index finger (or the finger closest to 1 cm):

   a) My pencil is approximately _____ cm long.   b) My JUMP book is about _____ cm wide.

2. Pick another object in the room to measure with your index finger:

   _____ is approximately _____ cm.

3. **2 cm**   A penny is about 2 cm wide.

   1¢

   How many pennies would you need to line up to make:
   HINT: Skip count by 2s.

   a) 10 cm? _____   b) 20 cm? _____   c) 30 cm? _____

4. Hold up your hand to a ruler.

   How far do you have to spread your fingers to make your hand 10 cm wide?

   10 cm

   Now measure the following objects in your home using your (measured) spread out hand:

   a) My workbook is approx. _____ cm long.

   b) My table is approx. _____ cm wide.

   c) My arm is approx. _____ cm long.

   d) My leg is approx. _____ cm long.

5. Pick another object to measure with your hand:

   The _____ is approximately _____ cm long.

ME3-2: Measuring in Centimetres

Midori counts the number of centimetres between the arrows by counting the number of "hops" it takes to move between them:

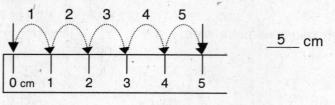

_5_ cm

---

1. Measure the distance between the two arrows by counting the number of centimetres between them.

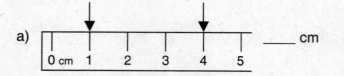

a) _____ cm

b) _____ cm

2. Measure the distance between the arrows.
   Count carefully – the first arrow is not at the beginning of the ruler.

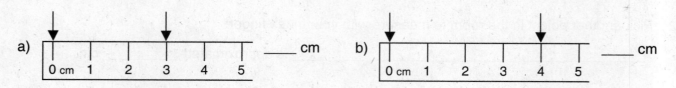

a) _____ cm

b) _____ cm

3. Measure the distance between the arrows.

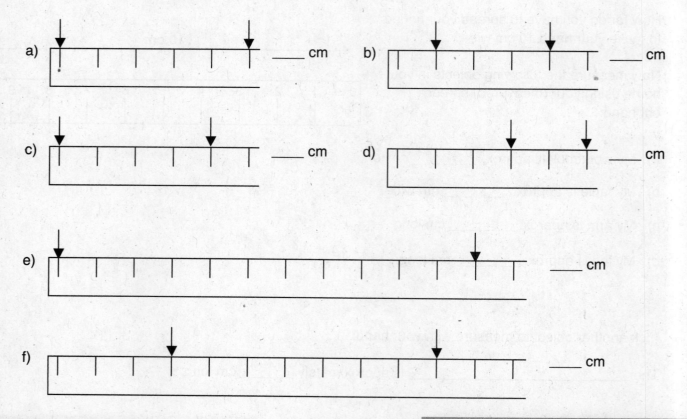

a) _____ cm   b) _____ cm

c) _____ cm   d) _____ cm

e) _____ cm

f) _____ cm

Measurement 1

ME3-3: Rulers

Laura measures the line by lining up her ruler with the endpoint of the line.

She counts the number of centimetre "hops" it takes to reach to the end of the line.

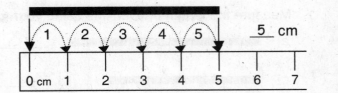

1. Measure the length of each line or object.

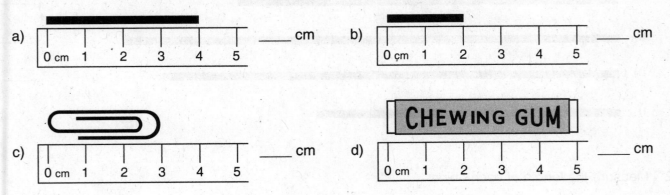

a) _____ cm

b) _____ cm

c) _____ cm

d) _____ cm

2. Measure the length of the lines and objects below.
   BE CAREFUL: The centimetre marks on these rulers are not numbered.

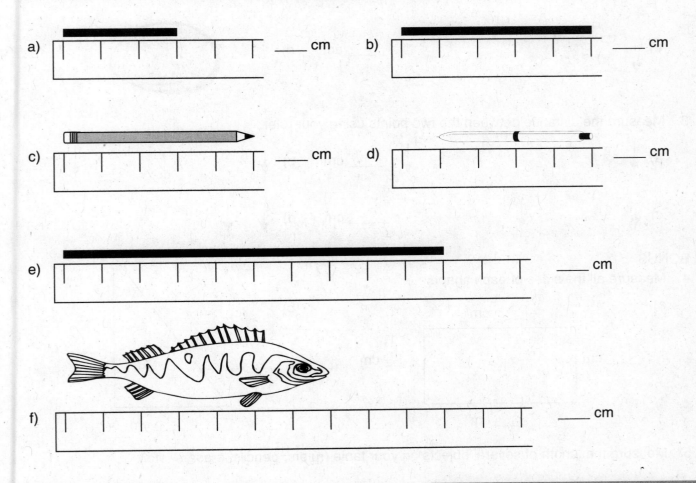

a) _____ cm

b) _____ cm

c) _____ cm

d) _____ cm

e) _____ cm

f) _____ cm

No unauthorized copying   **Measurement 1**

1. Measure the length of each line using your ruler.

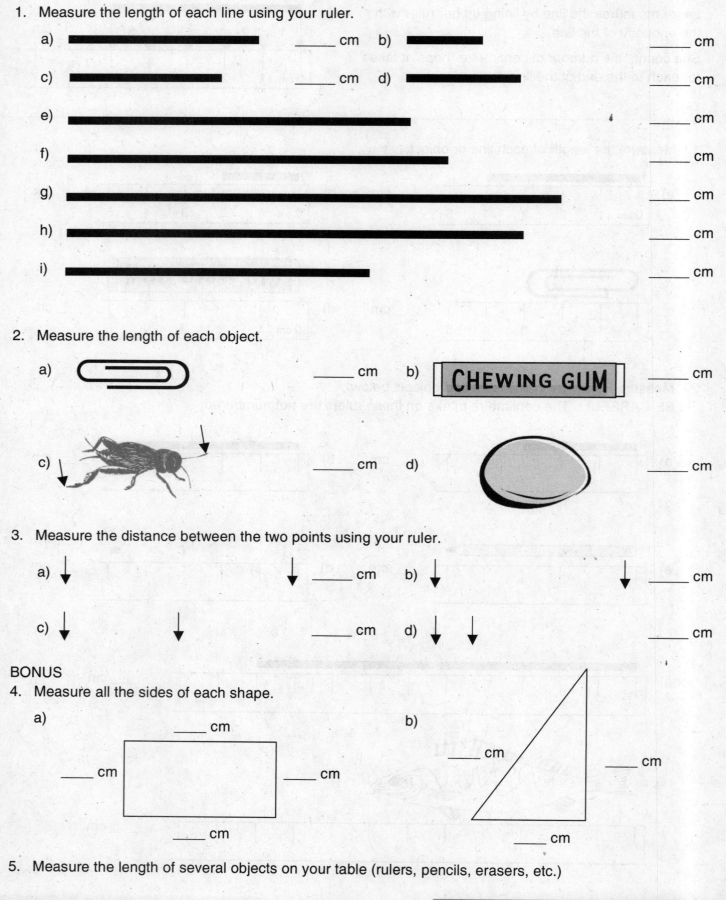

a) _____ cm   b) _____ cm

c) _____ cm   d) _____ cm

e) _____ cm

f) _____ cm

g) _____ cm

h) _____ cm

i) _____ cm

2. Measure the length of each object.

a) _____ cm   b) CHEWING GUM _____ cm

c) _____ cm   d) _____ cm

3. Measure the distance between the two points using your ruler.

a) _____ cm   b) _____ cm

c) _____ cm   d) _____ cm

BONUS
4. Measure all the sides of each shape.

a) _____ cm
_____ cm   _____ cm
_____ cm

b) _____ cm   _____ cm
_____ cm

5. Measure the length of several objects on your table (rulers, pencils, erasers, etc.)

Blake is drawing a line 5 cm long.

He starts by drawing an arrow at the beginning of the ruler and then counting in 5 centimetres:

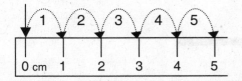

He draws a second arrow on the last centimetre mark that was counted to and then draws a line to connect the two arrows:

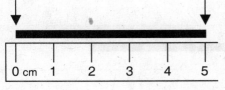

----

1. Draw two arrows on each ruler that are the given distance apart.
    HINT: You may find this easier if you place one of your arrows at the '0' mark.

    a) Two arrows 3 cm apart.

    b) Two arrows 1 cm apart.

    c) Two arrows 4 cm apart.

2. Use a ruler or straight edge to draw a line starting from the '0' mark of the ruler and ending at the given length.

    a) Draw a line 1 cm long.

    b) Draw a line 4 cm long.

    c) Draw a line 5 cm long.

3. Draw a line that is:

    a) 3 cm long

    b) 7 cm long

    c) 10 cm long

4. Draw each object to the exact measurement given:

    a) A caterpillar, 4 cm long.

    b) A leaf, 9 cm long.

    c) A spoon, 9 cm long.

BONUS
5. On grid paper, draw a rectangle with a width of 4 cm and a length of 5 cm.

ME3-6: Estimating in Centimetres

1. Estimate whether each line is <u>less than</u> or <u>more than</u> 10 cm long. Place a checkmark in the appropriate column.

		LESS than 10 cm	MORE than 10 cm
a)			
b)			
c)			
d)			

2. How good were your estimates? Measure the length of each line in Question 1.

a) _____ cm   b) _____ cm   c) _____ cm   d) _____ cm

3. Estimate whether the distance between the points is <u>less</u> than 10 cm or <u>more</u> than 10 cm.

		LESS than 10 cm	MORE than 10 cm
a)	• •		
b)	• •		
c)	• •		
d)	• •		

4. How good were your estimates? Measure the distance between the pairs of dots in Question 3.

a) _____ cm   b) _____ cm   c) _____ cm   d) _____ cm

BONUS

5. Estimate the **length** of the boxes below to the nearest cm. Then check your estimate.

a) [ ]   b) [ ]

Estimate: _____ cm   Actual: _____ cm   Estimate: _____ cm   Actual: _____ cm

A **metre** is a unit of measurement for **length** (or **height** or **thickness**) equal to 100 cm.

A metre stick is 100 cm long: |‖‖‖‖‖‖‖‖‖‖‖‖‖‖‖‖‖‖‖‖‖‖‖‖‖‖‖‖‖‖‖‖‖‖‖‖‖‖‖|

----

1. Ten interlocking centimetre cubes are 10 cm long.

   How many groups of ten cubes would make a metre?

   _____

   You can estimate metres using parts of your body:

   • A giant step is about one metre long.

   • If you stretch your arms out the distance between
     the tips of your fingers is about one metre.
     (This distance is called your *arm span*.)

2. Take a giant step and ask a friend or parent to measure your step with a piece of string.

   Hold the string up to a metre stick. Is your step more or less than a metre long?

   _____

3. Ask a friend to measure your arm span using a piece of string.

   Is your arm span more or less than a metre?

   _____

4. Stand against a wall and ask a parent or friend to measure your height with chalk and a metre stick:

   Your height is _____ cm.   Are you taller than 1 metre? _____

5. Estimate each distance to the nearest metre. Then measure the distance:

   a) The length of the bed in your room: Estimate - _____ m   Actual - _____ m

   b) The length of your table: Estimate - _____ m   Actual - _____ m

   c) The distance from the floor to the door handle: Estimate - _____ m   Actual - _____ m

6. Find (or think of) an object in your home or outside that is approximately 2 metres long.

   _____

Here are some measurements you can use for estimating in metres:

about 2 metres	*about 2 metres*	*about 10 metres*	*about 100 metres*

The height of a (tall) adult	The length of an adult's bicycle	The length of a school bus	The length of a football field

1. Five bikes (end to end) can park along a school wall. About how long is the wall?
    Use the estimates given above.

2. a) How many adults do you think could lie head to foot across your room?

    b) Approximately how wide is your room?

3. a) A typical floor in a building is about 4 m high. About how high is your home?

    b) If a school bus was tipped up on its end, would it be as high as your school?

    c) A car is about 3 metres long. How many cars high is your home?

4. a) About how many school buses can park along your school playground?

    b) How many metres long do you think your school playground is? Explain.

5.   Count by 25s: 25, _____, _____, _____, _____, _____, _____, _____

6.   An Olympic swimming pool is 25 metres **wide**:

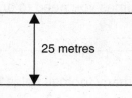

25 metres

a)   If you swim 3 widths, how many metres will you swim in total?

b)   If you swim 5 widths, how many metres will you swim?

7.   Count by 50s: 50, _____, _____, _____, _____, _____, _____, _____, _____, _____

8.   An Olympic swimming pool is 50 metres **long**:

50 metres

a)   If you swim 3 lengths, how many metres will you swim in total?

b)   If you swim 4 lengths, how many metres will you swim?

c)   How many lengths would you need to swim to travel 100 metres?

d)   How many lengths would you need to swim to travel 500 metres?

9.   A small city block is about 100 m long.
     Write the name of a place you can walk to from your home (a store, a park, your school).
     Approximately how many metres away from your home is the place you named?

ME3-9: Kilometres

A **kilometre** (km) is a unit of measurement for **length** equal to 1000 metres.

1. a) Skip count by 100s to find out how many times you need to add 100 to make 1000.

   _____

   b) A football field is about 100 m long. How many football fields long is a kilometre?

   _____

2. Count by 10s to find the number of times you need to add 10 to make each number.

   a) 100 = _____ tens   b) 200 = _____ tens   c) 300 = _____ tens

   d) 400 = _____ tens   e) 500 = _____ tens   f) 600 = _____ tens

3. Using the pattern in Question 3, how many times would you need to add 10 to make 1000?

4. A school bus is about 10 m long. How many school buses, line up end to end, would be:

   a) close to a kilometre long?   b) close to 2 km long?

   _____   _____

5. Continue the pattern to find out how many times you need to add 2 to make 1000.

   a) 100 = _50_ twos   b) 200 = _100_ twos   c) 300 = _150_ twos   d) 400 = _200_ twos

   e) 500 = _____ twos   f) 600 = _____ twos   g) 700 = _____ twos   h) 800 = _____ twos

   i) 900 = _____ twos   j) 1000 = _____ twos

6. A bike is about 2 m long.
   How many bikes, lined up, would make a kilometre?

   _____

7. If you lined up the following objects would their length be:

   • close to 1 km,   • less than 1 km, or   • more than 1 km?

   Explain your answer.
   HINT: First decide if the length of each object is close to a metre, less than a metre or more than a metre.

   a) 1000 paper clips   b) 1000 bikes   c) 1000 JUMP books   d) 1000 baseball bats

James uses a map to plan a trip to Nova Scotia and New Brunswick.

The numbers on the map are the lengths of the roads between the cities (in kilometres).

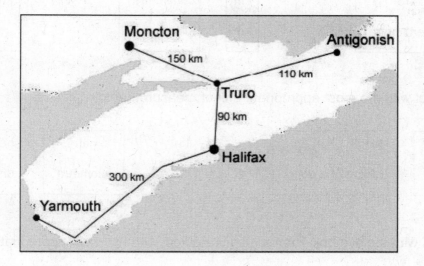

----

8. Fill in the blanks.

   a) Moncton and Truro are _____ km apart.

   b) Yarmouth and Halifax are _____ km apart.

   c) Truro and Antigonish are _____ km apart.

   d) Halifax and Truro are _____ km apart.

9. How far would you travel if you made the following trips?

   a) Start in Moncton. Drive through Truro to Antigonish – you would travel _____ km.

   b) Start in Yarmouth. Drive through Halifax to Truro – you would travel _____ km.

   c) Start in Halifax. Drive through Truro to Antigonish – you would travel _____ km.

   d) Start in Antigonish. Drive through Truro and Halifax to Yarmouth – you would travel _____ km.

   BONUS
10. Look at the kilometre scale on a map of Canada.

    Estimate the distance between two cities.

    Explain how you made your estimate.

    Ask your parent to check the actual distance in kilometres.

ME3-10: Ordering and Assigning Appropriate Units

1. Match the word with the symbol.

a)
cm		metre
m		centimetre

b)
cm		centimetre
km		kilometre

c)
km		kilometre
m		metre

2. Match the object with the most appropriate unit of measurement.

a)
metre		length of an ant
centimetre		height of a door

b)
metre		height of an adult
kilometre		distance to the moon

3. Match the word with the symbol. Then match the object with the most appropriate unit of measurement.

a)
cm		kilometre		thickness of a book
m		centimetre		distance across an ocean
km		metre		height of a room

b)
km		metre		height of a door
cm		kilometre		distance to Rome
m		centimetre		length of a pencil

4. Order the following objects from shortest (1), to next shortest (2), to longest (3).

a) _____ Length of an ant

_____ Distance an airplane flies

_____ Height of an adult

b) _____ Length of a carrot

_____ Length of a bus

_____ Distance from Toronto, ON, to Victoria, BC

5. Order the following items from shortest to longest (1 = shortest, 2 = next shortest, 3 = longest). What unit would you use to measure each?

cm	m	km

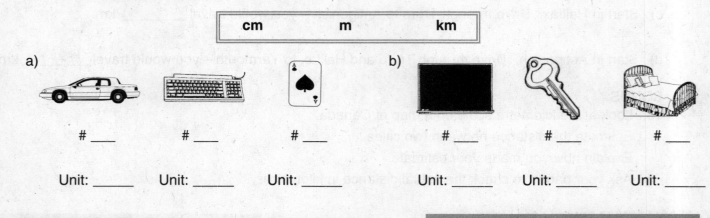

a)

___   # ___   # ___

Unit: _____   Unit: _____   Unit: _____

b)

___   # ___   # ___

Unit: _____   Unit: _____   Unit: _____

No unauthorized copying   **Measurement 1**

6. How many centimetres are in a metre? _____

7. Change the following measurements into centimetres.

   a) 3 m = _____ cm   b) 5 m = _____ cm   c) _____ cm = 2 m

8. Circle the larger amount.
   HINT: Change the measurement in metres (m) to centimetres (cm). Show your work in the box provided.

   a) 3 m   or   5 cm   b) 5 m   or   45 cm   c) 780 cm   or   6 m

   [cm   ]   [cm   ]   [cm   ]

9. Mark the measurements on the number line. (First change all measurements to cm.)

   A.   50 cm

   B.   1 m

   C.   2 m

   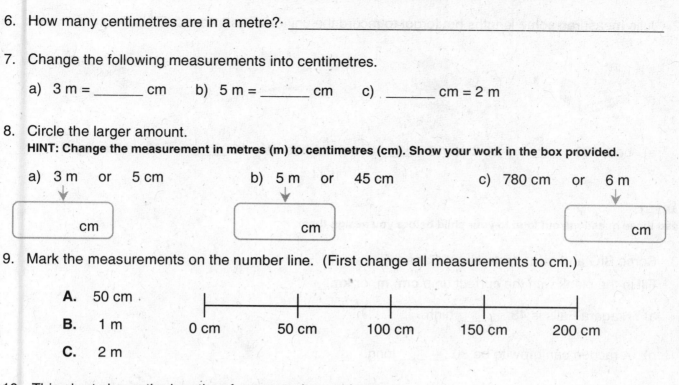

   0 cm   50 cm   100 cm   150 cm   200 cm

10. This chart shows the lengths of some snakes at the zoo.

Snake	Length
Garter Snake - **G**	150 cm
Coral Snake - **C**	50 cm
Fox Snake - **F**	100 cm
Boa Snake - **B**	2 m

Mark the lengths of **G**, **C**, **F** and **B** on the number line.

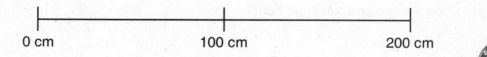

0 cm   100 cm   200 cm

11. Order the animals from lowest flier (1) to highest flier (5).

Animal	Greatest Height of Flight
Bat	50 m
Eagle	5 000 m
Blue Jay	2 000 m
Butterfly	25 m
Small insect	150 m

1. _____

2. _____

3. _____

4. _____

5. _____

12. Julie measured some lengths but forgot to record the unit of measurement. Fill in the correct units.

a) bed: 180 _____   b) bus: 10 _____   c) toothbrush: 16 _____   d) driveway: 10 _____

PARENT:
Read these questions out loud to your child before you assign them.

13. Some BIG and SMALL facts about Canada!

Fill in the blank with the correct unit: **cm**, **m,** or **km**.

a) Niagara Falls is 48 _____ high.

b) A racoon can grow to be 80 _____ long.

c) The St. Lawrence River is 3058 _____ long.

d) A black bear is 2 _____ long.

e) The width of maple leaf is approximately 16 _____.

f) The Mackenzie River in the Northwest Territories is 4241 _____ long.

14. A horse can run 50 kilometres in an hour.

a)   How far can you run in an hour?

b)   Name a city or town about 50 kilometres from where you live.

15. What would you use to measure the following distances – metres or kilometres?
Explain one of your answers.
HINT: You can walk a kilometre in about 15 minutes (taking about 2000 steps).

a) From your class to the gym.   b) From your home to school.

c) Between Toronto and Ottawa.   d) Around the school yard.

Carlo makes a figure using toothpicks.

He counts the number of toothpicks around the outside of the figure:

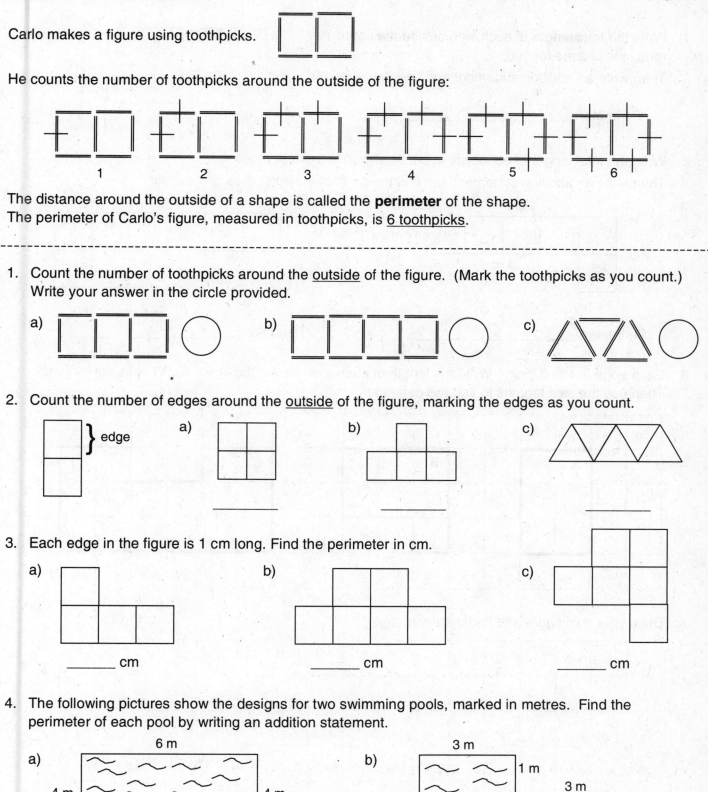

The distance around the outside of a shape is called the **perimeter** of the shape.
The perimeter of Carlo's figure, measured in toothpicks, is <u>6 toothpicks</u>.

----

1. Count the number of toothpicks around the <u>outside</u> of the figure. (Mark the toothpicks as you count.)
   Write your answer in the circle provided.

   a)   b)   c)

2. Count the number of edges around the <u>outside</u> of the figure, marking the edges as you count.

   edge   a)   b)   c)

3. Each edge in the figure is 1 cm long. Find the perimeter in cm.

   a)   b)   c)

   _____ cm   _____ cm   _____ cm

4. The following pictures show the designs for two swimming pools, marked in metres. Find the
   perimeter of each pool by writing an addition statement.

   a)   b)
        6 m   3 m
   4 m   4 m   1 m
        6 m   3 m   3 m
                                                       2 m
                                             6 m

   _____   _____

ME3-12: Exploring Perimeter

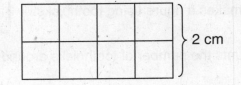

1. Write the total length of each side beside the figure
   (one side is·done for you).

   Then write an addition statement and find the perimeter.

   Perimeter: _____

2. Write the total length of each side in cm as shown in the first figure.

   Then write an addition statement and find the perimeter. Don't miss any edges!

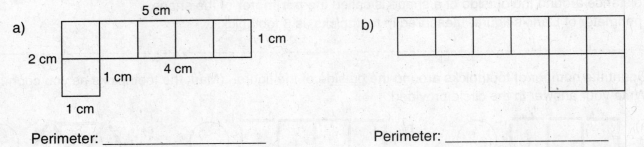

   a)

   5 cm

   2 cm   1 cm

   1 cm   4 cm

   1 cm

   b)

   Perimeter: _____   Perimeter: _____

3. Each edge is 1 unit long. Write the length of each side beside the figure (don't miss any edges!).
   Then use the side lengths to find the perimeter.

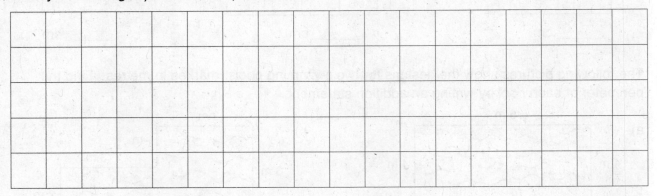

   A   B   C

4. Draw your own figure and find the perimeter.

5. On grid paper, draw your own figures and find their perimeters. Try making letters or other shapes!
    **PARENT: Children really enjoy this activity. Let your child spend some time inventing shapes and then
    finding their perimeter.**

1. Estimate the perimeter of each shape in centimetres. (Use your finger on another object.)
   Then measure the perimeter with a ruler.

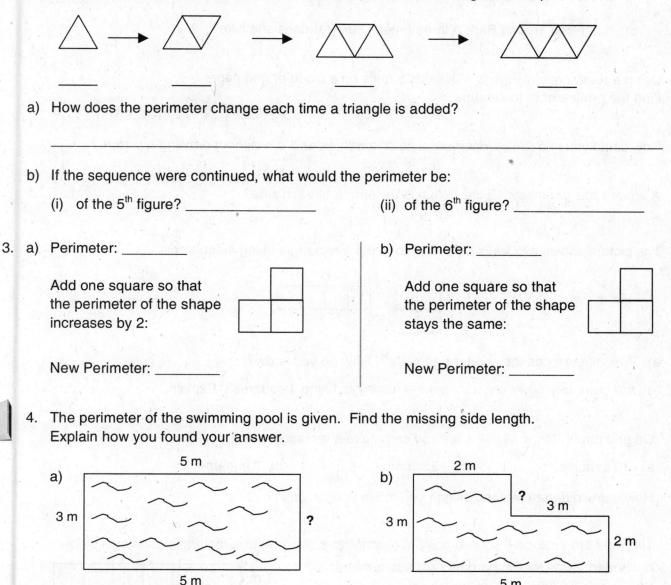

   a)

   Estimate = _____

   Perimeter = _____

   b)

   Estimate = _____

   Perimeter = _____

   c)

   Estimate = _____

   Perimeter = _____

2. Write the perimeter of each figure in the sequence (assume each edge is 1 unit).

   a) How does the perimeter change each time a triangle is added?

   _____

   b) If the sequence were continued, what would the perimeter be:

   (i) of the 5th figure? _____   (ii) of the 6th figure? _____

3. a) Perimeter: _____

   Add one square so that
   the perimeter of the shape
   increases by 2:

   New Perimeter: _____

   b) Perimeter: _____

   Add one square so that
   the perimeter of the shape
   stays the same:

   New Perimeter: _____

4. The perimeter of the swimming pool is given. Find the missing side length.
   Explain how you found your answer.

   a)
   5 m
   3 m   ?
   5 m
   Perimeter = 16 m

   b)
   2 m
   ?
   3 m
   3 m   2 m
   5 m
   Perimeter = 16 m

Answer the following questions in your notebook.

5. **Park A:**

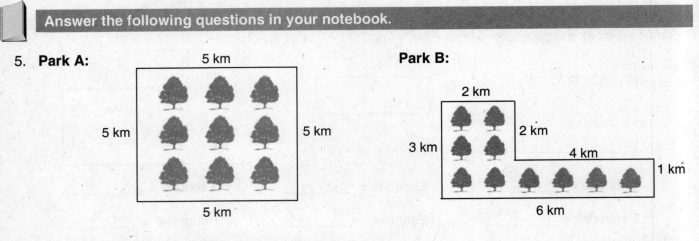

Park B:

a) Kim hikes around the perimeter of Park A.
   Leslie hikes around Park B. Who hikes the farthest?

b) Kim hikes around Park A three times. How far does she hike?

6. Using a ruler, draw a square with sides 3 units on a piece of grid paper.
   Find the perimeter of the square.

7. How could you find the perimeter of a square with sides 5 cm without drawing a picture?

8. A square has perimeter 12 cm. What is the length of each side?

9. The picture shows two ways (A and B) to make a rectangle using 4 squares:

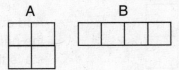

a) Which figure has the shorter perimeter? How do you know?

b) Are there any other ways to make a rectangle using 4 squares? Explain.

10. On grid paper, show all the ways you can make a rectangle using:

   a) 10 squares   b) 12 squares   c) 7 squares

   How many different rectangles can you make in each case?

11. Tim wants to arrange 6 square posters (each with sides 1 m) in a rectangle as shown below:
   A wooden frame for the border costs 25¢ a metre.
   How much will the border cost?

PARENT:
Review the meaning of the terms "less than," "greater than," "odd," "even," "multiples of 2," and "multiples of 3."

REMEMBER:
Zero is an even number and is also a multiple of any number.

1. Write the numbers from 0 to 9 in order.

2. Write all the numbers from 0 to 9 that are.

    a) greater than 7

    b) greater than 6

    c) greater than 5

    d) less than 4

    e) less than 5

    f) less than 2

    g) greater than 8

    h) less than 8

    i) greater than 4

    j) odd numbers

    k) even numbers

    l) multiples of 2

    m) multiples of 3

    n) multiples of 4

    o) multiples of 5

3. Make two lists (and circle the numbers that appear on both lists) to find the numbers from 0 to 9 that are.

    a) **odd numbers greater than 5**

        i) odd numbers: 1, 3, 5, (7), (9)

        ii) numbers greater than 5: 6, (7), 8, (9)

        Answer: 7, 9

    b) **even numbers greater than 5**

        i) even numbers:

        ii) numbers greater than 5:

        Answer:

Logic and Systematic Search

c) **odd numbers less than 3**

    i) odd numbers:

    ii) numbers less than 3:

    Answer:

d) **even numbers less than 6**

    i) even numbers:

    ii) numbers less than 6:

    Answer:

e) **odd numbers less than 5**

    i) odd numbers:

    ii) numbers less than 5:

    Answer:

f) **even numbers greater than 5**

    i) even numbers:

    ii) numbers greater than 5:

    Answer:

g) **numbers greater than 4 and less than 7**

    i) numbers greater than 4:

    ii) numbers less than 7:

    Answer:

h) **numbers greater than 3 and less than 5**

    i) numbers greater than 3:

    ii) numbers less than 5:

    Answer:

i) **even numbers that are multiples of 3**

    i) even numbers:

    ii) multiples of 3:

    Answer:

j) **odd numbers that are multiples of 3**

    i) odd numbers:

    ii) multiples of 3:

    Answer:

4. Write the numbers from 0 to 9 in order:

a) Circle the number that is greater than 8.

b) Underline the number that is less than 1.

c) Cross out the number that is less than 8 and greater than 6.

Many problems in mathematics and science have more than one solution.

If a problem involves two quantities, you can be sure you have not missed any possible solutions if you list the values of one of the quantities in increasing order.

For instance, to find all the ways you can make 35¢ with dimes and nickels, start by assuming you have no dimes, then 1 dime, and so on up to 3 dimes (4 would be too many).

In each case, count on by 5s to 35 to find out how many nickels you need to make 35¢:

Step 1:

dimes	nickels
0	
1	
2	
3	

Step 2:

dimes	nickels
0	7
1	5
2	3
3	1

---

1. Fill in the amount of pennies or nickels you need to …

a) … make 15¢

dimes	nickels
0	
1	

b) … make 25¢

dimes	nickels
0	
1	
2	

c) … make 12¢

nickels	pennies
0	
1	
2	

d) … make 18¢

nickels	pennies
0	
1	
2	
3	

e) … make 65¢

quarters	nickels
0	
1	
2	

f) … make 85¢

quarters	nickels
0	
1	
2	
3	

2.

dimes	nickels
0	
1	
2	

Sharon wants to find all the ways she can make 25¢ using dimes and nickels. Why did she stop at 2 dimes?

_____

_____

3. Fill in the amount of pennies, nickels, dimes, or quarters you need to make:

   HINT: You may not need to use all of the rows.

   a) 13¢

dimes	pennies

   b) 35¢

dimes	nickels

   c) 80¢

quarters	nickels

PARENT:

Give your child practice with questions like the one above before you allow him or her to continue.

4. Birds have 2 legs, cats have 4 legs, and ants have 6 legs. Complete the charts to find out how many legs each combination of 2 animals has.

   a)

birds	cats	total number of legs
0	2	
1	1	
2	0	

   b)

birds	ants	total number of legs
0	2	
1	1	
2	0	

5. Fill in the charts to find the solution to each problem.

   a)

birds	dogs	total number of legs

   2 pets have a total of 6 legs.
   Each pet is either a bird or a dog.
   How many birds and dogs?

   b)

birds	cats	total number of legs

   3 pets have a total of 8 legs.
   Each pet is either a bird or cat.
   How many birds and cats?

Logic and Systematic Search

LSS3-3: Charts

1. Clare can choose from these activities at camp:

    Morning – painting or music

    Afternoon – drama, pottery or dance

    She makes a chart to show all of her choices.

    She starts by writing each of her morning choices 3 times.

    a) Why did Clare write each of her choices for the morning 3 times?

morning	afternoon
painting	
painting	
painting	
music	
music	
music	

    b) Complete the chart to show all of Clare's choices.

2. Make a chart to show all the choices.

    a) A restaurant offers these choices for a sandwich:

    Bread – pita or bagel   **Filling** – cheese, hummus, or peanut butter

    b) A camp offers these activities:

    Morning – drama or music   **Afternoon** – painting, drawing or poetry

3. Make a chart to show all the scores you could get by throwing two darts.

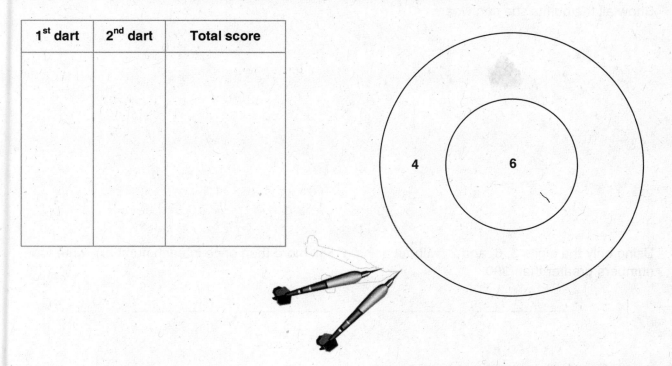

1st dart	2nd dart	Total score

Logic and Systematic Search

1. Show all the ways you can stack one scoop each of vanilla (V), chocolate (C) and strawberry (S) ice cream on a cone.

Using the picture here as a guide, draw all the possibilities.

2. Drawing pictures of flags (like the one here), show all the ways you can colour the flag using <u>two</u> of the following <u>three</u> colours: red (R), blue (B), and green (G).

3. Nandita has:

   ♣ a long-sleeved shirt,

   ♣ and a short-sleeved shirt.

   Show all the outfits she can wear.

   She also has:

   ♣ a pair of pants,

   ♣ and a skirt.

4. Using only the digits 3, 6, and 2 (without using a digit more than once in each number), write four numbers greater than 300.

   _____   _____   _____   _____

Logic and Systematic Search

LSS3-5: Arrangements and Combinations (Advanced)

1. Using the digits 7, 5, and 6 show how many numbers you can make that are greater than 600.
NOTE: Don't use a digit more than once in each number.

2. Using the digits 9, 5, and 8 (without using a digit more than once in each number):
   a) show how many even numbers you can make that are greater than 800:

   b) show how many odd numbers you can make that are greater than 800:

   c) show how many numbers divisible by 5 you can make that are greater than 800:

3. The picture below shows all of the ways you can make a rectangular array of 6 dots.

Show all of the rectangular arrays you can make with:

a) 4 dots b) 8 dots c) 10 dots d) 5 dots

1. Place the numbers 1, 2, 3 and 4 in the circles so that, if you add any pair of numbers joined by a straight line, you get the same sum.

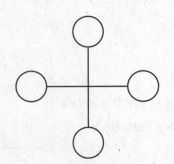

2. Place the numbers 1, 2, 3, 4 and 5 in the circles so that, if you add any three numbers joine by a straight line, you get the same sum.

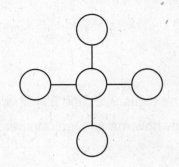

3. Place the numbers 1, 2, 3, 4, 5 and 6 in the circles so that ...

a) ... if you add any pair of numbers joined by a straight line, you get the same sum.

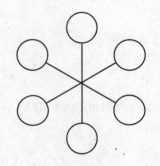

b) ... if you add any three numbers on an edge of the triangle, you get the same sum.

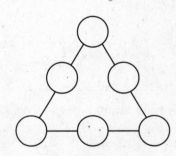

4. Pat and Anna want to share their coins so they each have the same amount of money. Show how they can do this.

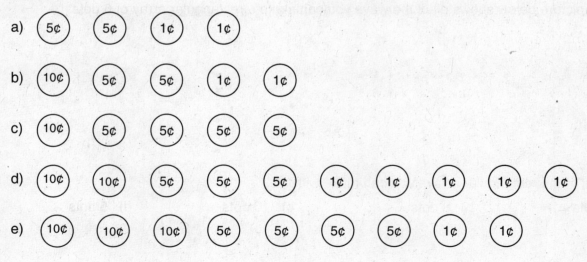

a) (5¢) (5¢) (1¢) (1¢)

b) (10¢) (5¢) (5¢) (1¢) (1¢)

c) (10¢) (5¢) (5¢) (5¢) (5¢)

d) (10¢) (10¢) (5¢) (5¢) (5¢) (1¢) (1¢) (1¢) (1¢) (1¢)

e) (10¢) (10¢) (10¢) (5¢) (5¢) (5¢) (5¢) (1¢) (1¢)

Logic and Systematic Search

For the exercises on this page, you will need to know:

The Days of the Week: **Sunday, Monday, Tuesday, Wednesday, Thursday, Friday, Saturday**

The Months of the Year: **January, February, March, April, May, June, July, August, September, October, November, December**

---

1. Andrew starts working on Monday morning.

   He paints 3 houses each day.

   How many houses has he painted by Thursday evening?

Day	Total Number of Painted Houses
Monday	3

2. Zaki saves $10 in July.

   He saves $5 each month after that.

   How much has he saved by the end of October?

Month	Amount of Money Saved
July	

3. The snow is 2 cm deep at 6 pm.

   Every hour, 3 cm of snow falls.

   How deep is the snow at 9 pm?

Time	Depth of Snow
6 pm	2 cm

4. Sandra's maple sapling is 2 cm high in May.

   It grows 7 cm each month after that.

   How high is the sapling by the end of August?

Month	Height of Sapling

5. A candle is 20 cm high at 7 pm. At 8 pm, the candle is 18 cm high. At 9 pm, it is 16 cm high.

a) How many cm does the candle burn down every hour?

   Write your answers (with a minus sign) in the circles provided.

b) How high is the candle at 11 pm?

Time	Height of the Candle	
7 pm	20 cm	
8 pm	18 cm	-2
9 pm	16 cm	◯
10 pm		◯
11 pm		◯

6. John has $27 in his savings account at the end of April.

   He spends $5 each month.

   How much does he have in his account at the end of July?

Month	Savings	
April	$27	◯
		◯
		◯

7. Tashi has $18 in her savings account at the end of March.

   She spends $4 each month.

   How much does she have at the end of June?

Month	Savings	
March	$18	◯
		◯
		◯

8. Rosie collects 11 stamps in February.
   She collects 6 stamps every month after that.
   How many stamps has she collected by the end of May?

Month	Number of Stamps	
February	11	◯
		◯
		◯

9. Rick starts working on Tuesday morning.
   He rakes 6 lawns each day.
   How many lawns has he raked by Friday evening?

Day	Number of Lawns	
Tuesday	6	◯
		◯
		◯

PA3-18: Number Lines

Tom Thomson is famous for the landscapes he painted in Algonquin Park.

On Monday morning, Karen's campsite is 20 km away from Tea Lake.

She plans to hike 6 km each day.

She uses a number line to find out how far from the lake she will be by Wednesday evening.

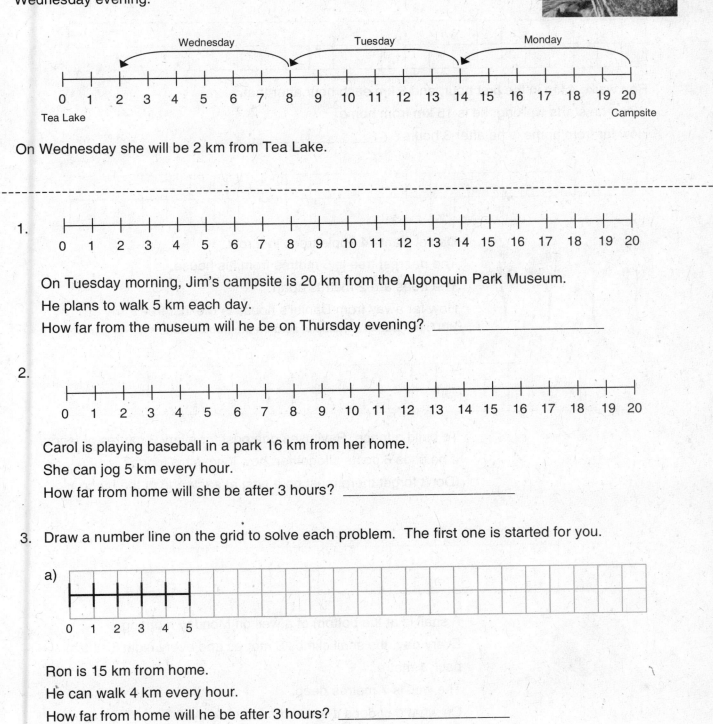

On Wednesday she will be 2 km from Tea Lake.

1.

On Tuesday morning, Jim's campsite is 20 km from the Algonquin Park Museum.

He plans to walk 5 km each day.

How far from the museum will he be on Thursday evening? _____

2.

Carol is playing baseball in a park 16 km from her home.

She can jog 5 km every hour.

How far from home will she be after 3 hours? _____

3. Draw a number line on the grid to solve each problem. The first one is started for you.

a)

```
0  1  2  3  4  5
```

Ron is 15 km from home.

He can walk 4 km every hour.

How far from home will he be after 3 hours? _____

b)

Keiko is 12 blocks from home.

She can walk 2 blocks in a minute.

How many minutes will it take her to walk home? _____

c)

Ron walks 4 km in the first hour, and 3 km each hour after that.

When he starts walking, he is 15 km from home.

How far from home is he after 3 hours? _____

4.

Daniel plants 4 apple trees in a row.

The nearest tree is 5 metres from his house.

The trees are 2 metres apart.

How far away from Daniel's house is the last tree?

HINT: Put Daniel's house at zero on the number line.

5.

To build a fence, Ravi uses one post for every 3 metres of fence.

If he uses 6 posts altogether, how long is his fence?

(Don't forget there must be a post at each end of the fence.)

6.

A snail is at the bottom of a well on Monday morning.

Every day, the snail climbs 3 metres and every night it slides back 1 metre.

The well is 7 metres deep.

On what day does it reach the top of the well?

Patterns & Algebra 2

PA3-18: Number Lines (continued)

7. Amber is riding an elevator in her building.

    Draw arrows between the floors to show what floor she ends up on.

    The first one has been started for you.

a)

10
9
8
7
6
5
4
3
2
1
Ground

From the 2ⁿᵈ floor,
Amber goes
up 8 floors,
then **down** 3 floors.

What floor does she end
up on?

b)

10
9
8
7
6
5
4
3
2
1
Ground

From the 5ᵗʰ floor,
Amber goes
up 4 floors,
then **down** 7 floors.

What floor does she end
up on?

c)

10
9
8
7
6
5
4
3
2
1
Ground

From the 10ᵗʰ floor,
Amber goes
down 6 floors,
then **up** 4 floors.

What floor does she end
up on?

d)

10
9
8
7
6
5
4
3
2
1
Ground

From the 8ᵗʰ floor,
Amber goes
up 2 floors,
then **down** 5 floors.

What floor does she end
up on?

Draw a number line on grid paper.

e) Amber is on the 3ʳᵈ floor. She goes up to the 9ᵗʰ floor.
    How many floors did she go up?

f) Amber pushes the button to go to the 10ᵗʰ floor.
    She travels up 4 floors before getting off.
    What floor did she start on?

PA3-19: Mixed Patterns

Repeating Patterns:

1. Circle the core of the following patterns. Then continue the pattern.

a)

b) A B C C A B C C A ___ ___ ___ ___

c) 1 2 5 9 1 2 5 9 1 2 ___ ___ ___

d) 5 7 3 5 7 3 ___ ___ ___

e)

f)

g)

h)

i)

j) J K Q 2 J K Q 2 J K ___ ___ ___

2. Circle the core of the following patterns. Then continue the pattern.

a) A B A A B A ___ ___ ___ ___ ___

b) A B B A A B B A ___ ___ ___ ___

c)

d) C B C C C B C C ___ ___ ___ ___

e) A B C A A B C A ___ ___ ___ ___

f) 1 3 5 1 1 3 5 1 1 ___ ___ ___

g) 7 6 7 7 6 7 7 ___ ___ ___

Patterns & Algebra 2

PA3-19: Mixed Patterns (continued)

Periodic Patterns:

3. Continue the patterns.

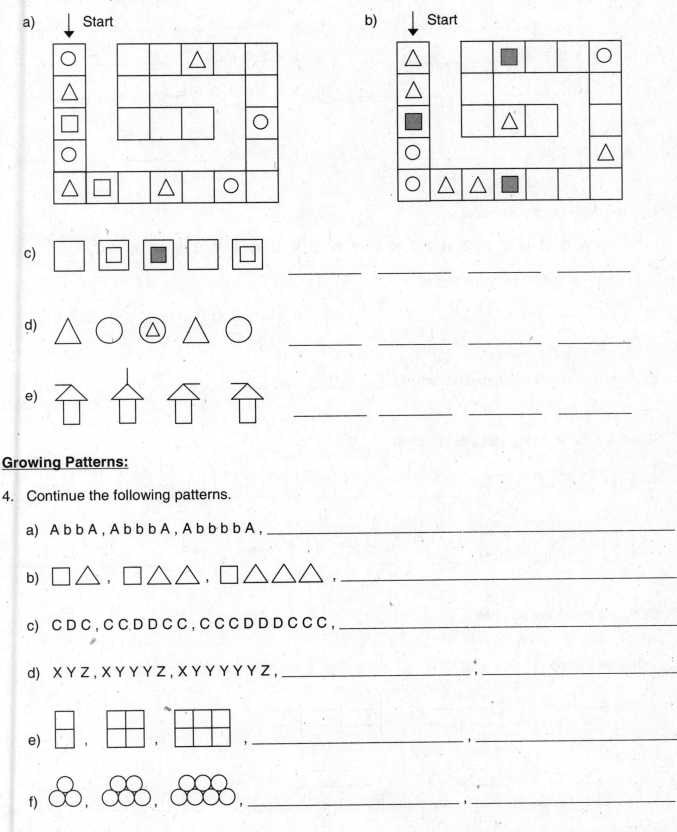

Growing Patterns:

4. Continue the following patterns.

a) A b b A , A b b b A , A b b b b A , _____

b) ▢△ , ▢△△ , ▢△△△ , _____

c) C D C , C C D D C C , C C C D D D C C C , _____

d) X Y Z , X Y Y Y Z , X Y Y Y Y Y Z , _____ , _____

e) _____

f) _____

Patterns & Algebra 2

Mixed Patterns:

5. Continue the following patterns (numbers).

a) 1, 5, 1, 5, _____, _____, _____, _____   b) 20, 30, 40, 50, _____, _____, _____, _____

c) 3, 0, 7, 3, 0, 7, 3, _____, _____, _____   d) 1, 1, 2, 2, 3, 3, _____, _____, _____, _____

e) 1, 10, 100, _____, _____   f) 1, 3, 5, 9, 1, 3, 5, 9, 1, _____, _____, _____

BONUS

g) 8, 8, 8, 9, 9, 9, _____, _____, _____, _____   h) 1, 2, 2, 3, 3, 3, _____, _____, _____, _____

6. Use the letters of the alphabet…

A B C D E F G H I J K L M N O P Q R S T U V W X Y Z

… to continue the following patterns.

a) A , C , E , G , _____ , _____   b) A , D , G , J , _____ , _____

c) Z , X , V , T , _____ , _____   d) Z , W , T , Q , _____ , _____

e) Create your own alphabet pattern: _____, _____, _____, _____, _____, _____

7. Continue the following patterns (shapes).

a) 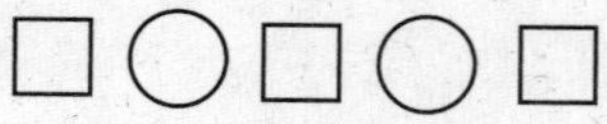 □ ◯ □ ◯ □ ___ ___ ___   b) 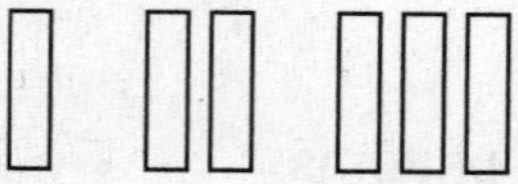 | || ||| _____ _____

c) 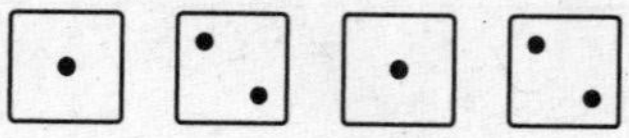 [·] [·.] [·] [·.] ___ ___   d)  ↑ → ↓ ← ___ ___ ___ ___

8. Complete the following chart.

Original Figure	Step 1:	Step 2:	Step 3:
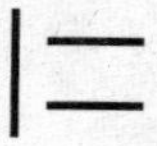 ⊨	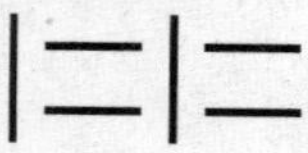 ⊨⊨	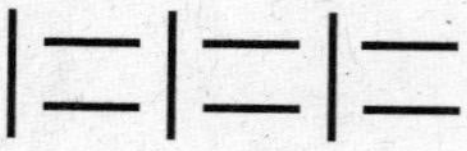 ⊨⊨⊨	
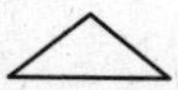 △	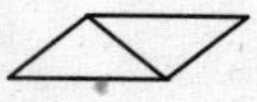 ◁▷	 ◁▽▷	

PA3-20: Describing and Creating Patterns

In the sequence below, each number is greater than the one before it. The sequence is always **increasing**:   7   8   10   15   21

In the sequence below, each number is less than the one before it. The sequence is always **decreasing**:   25   23   18   11   8

----

1. Write a **+** sign in the circle to show where the sequence <u>increases</u>.
    Write a **−** sign to show where it <u>decreases</u>. The first question is done for you.

a) 7 (+) , 9 (−) , 8 (+) , 10   b) 2 ◯ , 5 ◯ , 8 ◯ , 3   c) 10 ◯ , 8 ◯ , 7 ◯ , 9

d) 2 ◯ , 6 ◯ , 3 ◯ , 9   e) 6 ◯ , 4 ◯ , 8 ◯ , 7   f) 4 ◯ , 6 ◯ , 7 ◯ , 8

g) 1 ◯ , 8 ◯ , 3 ◯ , 11   h) 12 ◯ , 13 ◯ , 17 ◯ , 16   i) 19 ◯ , 15 ◯ , 14 ◯ , 21

j) 27 ◯ , 37 ◯ , 47 ◯ , 57   k) 27 ◯ , 32 ◯ , 19 ◯ , 81   l) 57 ◯ , 63 ◯ , 86 ◯ , 99

2. Write a **+** sign in the circle to show where the sequence <u>increases</u>.
    Write a **−** sign to show where it <u>decreases</u>. Then write...

    ... an A beside the sequence if it always **increases**
    ... a B beside the sequence if it always **decreases**
    ... a C beside the sequence if it **increases** and **decreases**.

a) 4 (+) 8 (−) 3 (+) 7   ___C___   b) 6 ◯ 5 ◯ 4 ◯ 3   _____

    2 ◯ 5 ◯ 8 ◯ 10   _____   9 ◯ 7 ◯ 4 ◯ 8   _____

    9 ◯ 7 ◯ 5 ◯ 2   _____   2 ◯ 5 ◯ 6 ◯ 10   _____

c) 3 ◯ 5 ◯ 7 ◯ 9   _____   d) 17 , 15 ◯ , 13 ◯ , 11 ◯   _____

    8 ◯ 5 ◯ 3 ◯ 6   _____   21 , 23 ◯ , 19 ◯ , 25 ◯   _____

    7 ◯ 6 ◯ 2 ◯ 1   _____   20 , 27 ◯ , 32 ◯ , 41 ◯   _____

3. Find the <u>amount</u> by which the sequence <u>increases</u> or <u>decreases</u>.
(Write a number with a **+** sign if the sequence increases, or a **–** sign if it decreases.)

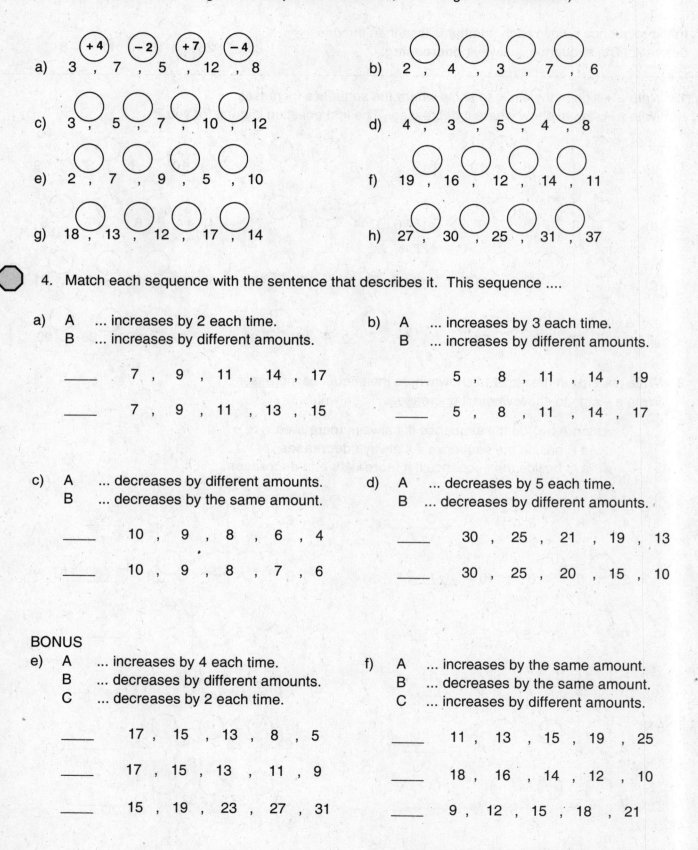

a) 3 , 7 , 5 , 12 , 8　（+4）（–2）（+7）（–4）

b) 2 , 4 , 3 , 7 , 6

c) 3 , 5 , 7 , 10 , 12

d) 4 , 3 , 5 , 4 , 8

e) 2 , 7 , 9 , 5 , 10

f) 19 , 16 , 12 , 14 , 11

g) 18 , 13 , 12 , 17 , 14

h) 27 , 30 , 25 , 31 , 37

4. Match each sequence with the sentence that describes it.　This sequence ....

a) A　... increases by 2 each time.
B　... increases by different amounts.

_____　7 , 9 , 11 , 14 , 17

_____　7 , 9 , 11 , 13 , 15

b) A　... increases by 3 each time.
B　... increases by different amounts.

_____　5 , 8 , 11 , 14 , 19

_____　5 , 8 , 11 , 14 , 17

c) A　... decreases by different amounts.
B　... decreases by the same amount.

_____　10 , 9 , 8 , 6 , 4

_____　10 , 9 , 8 , 7 , 6

d) A　... decreases by 5 each time.
B　... decreases by different amounts.

_____　30 , 25 , 21 , 19 , 13

_____　30 , 25 , 20 , 15 , 10

BONUS
e) A　... increases by 4 each time.
B　... decreases by different amounts.
C　... decreases by 2 each time.

_____　17 , 15 , 13 , 8 , 5

_____　17 , 15 , 13 , 11 , 9

_____　15 , 19 , 23 , 27 , 31

f) A　... increases by the same amount.
B　... decreases by the same amount.
C　... increases by different amounts.

_____　11 , 13 , 15 , 19 , 25

_____　18 , 16 , 14 , 12 , 10

_____　9 , 12 , 15 , 18 , 21

PA3-20: Describing and Creating Patterns (continued)

5. Write a rule for each pattern (use the words <u>add</u> or <u>subtract</u>, and say what number the pattern starts with).

a) 3 (+4) , 7 (+4) , 11 (+4) , 15   Start at 3, add 4

b) 2 , 5 , 8 , 11   _____

c) 19 , 17 , 15 , 13   _____

d) 31 , 28 , 25 , 22   _____

6. Write a rule for each pattern.

   NOTE: One sequence doesn't have a rule – see if you can find it.

a) 7 , 10 , 13 , 16   _____

b) 12 , 9 , 6 , 3   _____

c) 22 , 20 , 18 , 15 , 10   _____

d) 62 , 66 , 70 , 74   _____

7. Describe each pattern as <u>increasing</u>, <u>decreasing</u> or <u>repeating</u>.

a) 1 , 3 , 5 , 7 , 9 , 11 _____   b) 2 , 1 , 3 , 2 , 1 , 3 _____

c) 8 , 7 , 6 , 5 , 4 , 3 _____   d) 2 , 4 , 6 , 8 , 10 , 12 _____

e) 1 , 5 , 1 , 5 , 1 , 5 _____   f) 19 , 14 , 10 , 7 , 5 , 4 _____

8. Write the first 5 numbers in the pattern.

a) Start at 5, add 4   b) Start at 16, subtract 3

9. Create an increasing number pattern. Give the rule for your pattern.

10. Create a repeating pattern using: a) letters   b) shapes   c) numbers

11. Create a pattern and ask a parent or a friend to find the rule for your pattern.

               Patterns & Algebra 2

PA3-21: 2-Dimensional Patterns

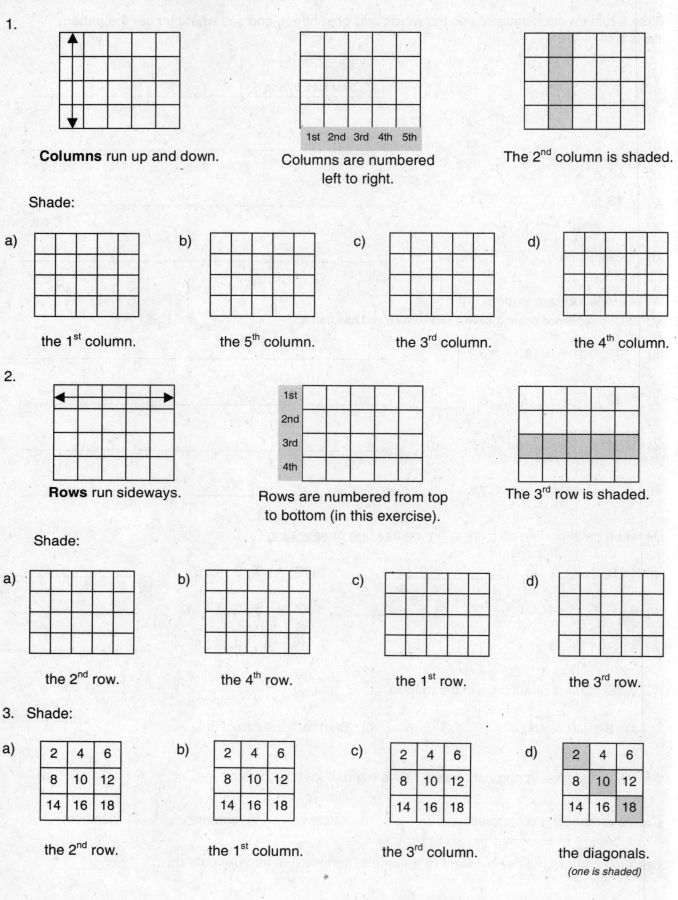

1.

Columns run up and down.

Columns are numbered left to right.

1st 2nd 3rd 4th 5th

The 2nd column is shaded.

Shade:

a) the 1st column.

b) the 5th column.

c) the 3rd column.

d) the 4th column.

2.

Rows run sideways.

1st 2nd 3rd 4th

Rows are numbered from top to bottom (in this exercise).

The 3rd row is shaded.

Shade:

a) the 2nd row.

b) the 4th row.

c) the 1st row.

d) the 3rd row.

3. Shade:

a)
2	4	6
8	10	12
14	16	18

the 2nd row.

b)
2	4	6
8	10	12
14	16	18

the 1st column.

c)
2	4	6
8	10	12
14	16	18

the 3rd column.

d)
2	4	6
8	10	12
14	16	18

the diagonals.
(one is shaded)

4. Describe the patterns you see in this chart. You should use the words "rows," "columns," and "diagonals" in your answer.

1	3	5
3	5	7
5	7	9

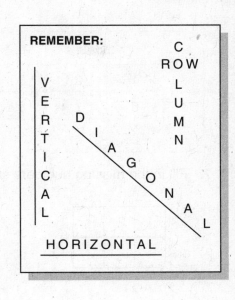

REMEMBER:

5. Complete the addition chart. Describe the patterns you see in the rows, columns, and diagonals of the chart.

+	1	2	3	4	5
1	2	3			
2		4			
3		5			
4					
5					

6.

×	1	2	3	4	5	6
1						
2	2	4	6	8	10	12
3						
4	4	8	12	16	20	24
5						
6						

a) Fill in the missing numbers in the multiplication chart.

b) Describe any patterns you see in the chart.

c) The numbers in row 4 are double those in row 2.

Can you see any other relations between rows?

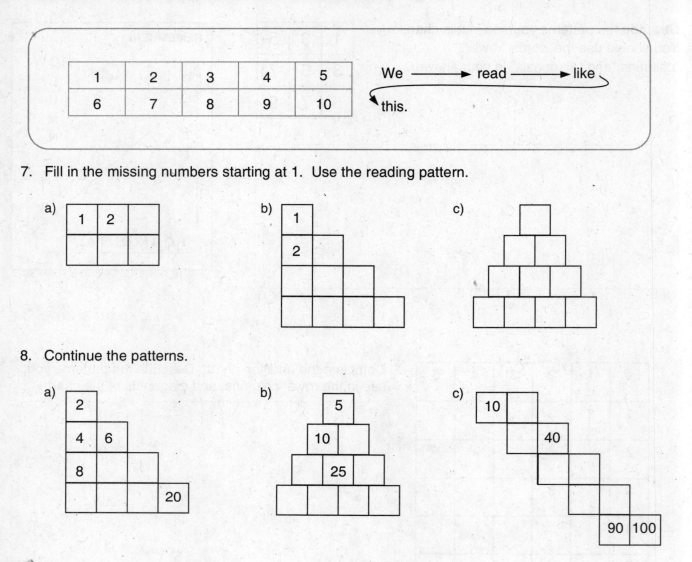

1	2	3	4	5
6	7	8	9	10

We ⟶ read ⟶ like this.

7. Fill in the missing numbers starting at 1. Use the reading pattern.

a)

1	2	

b)

1	
2	

c)

8. Continue the patterns.

a)

2	
4	6
8	
	20

b)

| 5 |
| 10 |
| 25 |

c)

10	
	40
90	100

> **PARENT:**
> For the following exercises your child will need one copy of the hundreds charts from page xxxvi.

9. a) Shade any column of a hundreds chart.
    b) What do you notice about the <u>ones</u> digits of all the numbers in the column?
    c) What pattern do you see in the <u>tens</u> digits of the numbers you shaded?

10. a) Shade any number in the first row of a hundreds chart.
    b) Add 10 to the number. Shade the result.
        Repeat these steps until you reach the bottom of the chart.
        What do you notice about the positions of the numbers you shaded?

11. a) Shade any number in the first row of a hundreds chart.
    b) Add 5 to the number. Shade the result.
        Repeat these steps until you reach the bottom of the chart.
        What do you notice about the positions of the numbers you shaded?

1. Use addition to complete the following charts.

a)

Quarters	Cents
1	25
2	
3	
4	
5	

b)

Years	Months
1	12
2	
3	
4	
5	

c)

Year	Weeks
1	52
2	
3	
4	
5	

Use T-tables to solve the following problems in your notebook.

2. There are 24 hours in a day.
   How many hours are there in 4 days?

3. A sparrow can fly 45 km each hour.
   How far can a sparrow fly in 3 hours?

4. A piano has 88 keys.
   How many keys would 3 pianos have?

5. Lisa earns $23 on Monday.
   She earns $20 each day after that.
   How much will she earn by Friday evening?

6. Use a calculator to work out the first few examples. Find a pattern.
   Use the pattern to complete the exercise.

   a) 9 × 22 = _____

   9 × 33 = _____

   9 × 44 = _____

   9 × 55 = _____

   9 × 66 = _____

   b) 9 × 222 = _____

   9 × 333 = _____

   9 × 444 = _____

   9 × 555 = _____

   9 × 666 = _____

BONUS
7. Using a calculator, can you discover any patterns like the ones in Question 6?

Show your work for the questions below in your notebook.

1. How many triangles will be needed for the 6th figure?

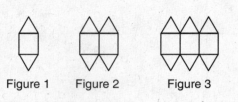

Figure 1   Figure 2   Figure 3

2. Anna saves $12 in August.

She saves $5 every month after that.

How much has she saved by the end of November?

3. Helen has already biked 20 km from her home. She cycles 5 km every hour.

How far will she be from home after cycling 3 more hours?

4. Ravi wants to plant tomato seedlings in his garden, in the pattern shown.

He has 20 seedlings.

Does he have enough seedlings to plant 5 rows?

How did you solve this problem?

Did you use a T-table? A picture? A model?

Row 3	I I I I I
Row 2	I I I
Row 1	I

5. Wendy has to climb 5 walls in an obstacle course.

The 1st wall is 100 metres from the start.

After that, each wall is 50 metres farther than the last.

How far from the start is the 3rd wall?

6. Alan saves $15 in August.

He saves $3 each month after that.

Nora saves $12 in August.

She saves $4 each month after that.

Who has saved the most money by the end of December?

7. What strategy would you use to find the 17ᵗʰ shape in the following pattern? What is the shape?

☐ ◯ ◯ ☐ ◯ ◯

8. Find the mystery number.

   a) I am greater than 15 and less than 20. I am a multiple of 3. What am I?

   b) I am greater than 13 and less than 17. I am a multiple of 4. What am I?

   c) I am less than 15. I am a multiple of 3 <u>and</u> a multiple of 4. What am I?

9. Bill and Linda run up 12 steps with muddy shoes.

   a) Bill steps on every 2ⁿᵈ step and Linda steps on every 3ʳᵈ step.
      Which steps have both of their footprints on them?

   b) If Bill's right foot lands on the 2ⁿᵈ step, on which steps does his left foot land?

10. The chart below shows the life cycle of a butterfly.

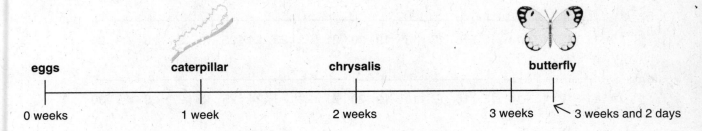

eggs	caterpillar	chrysalis	butterfly
0 weeks	1 week	2 weeks	3 weeks 3 weeks and 2 days

If an egg is laid on Monday, June 1ˢᵗ:

   a) On what day of the week will the chrysalis become a butterfly?

   b) How many days will it take the caterpillar to turn into a butterfly?

Patterns & Algebra 2

1. Draw an arrow to the 0 or 10 to show whether the circled number is closer to **0** or **10**.

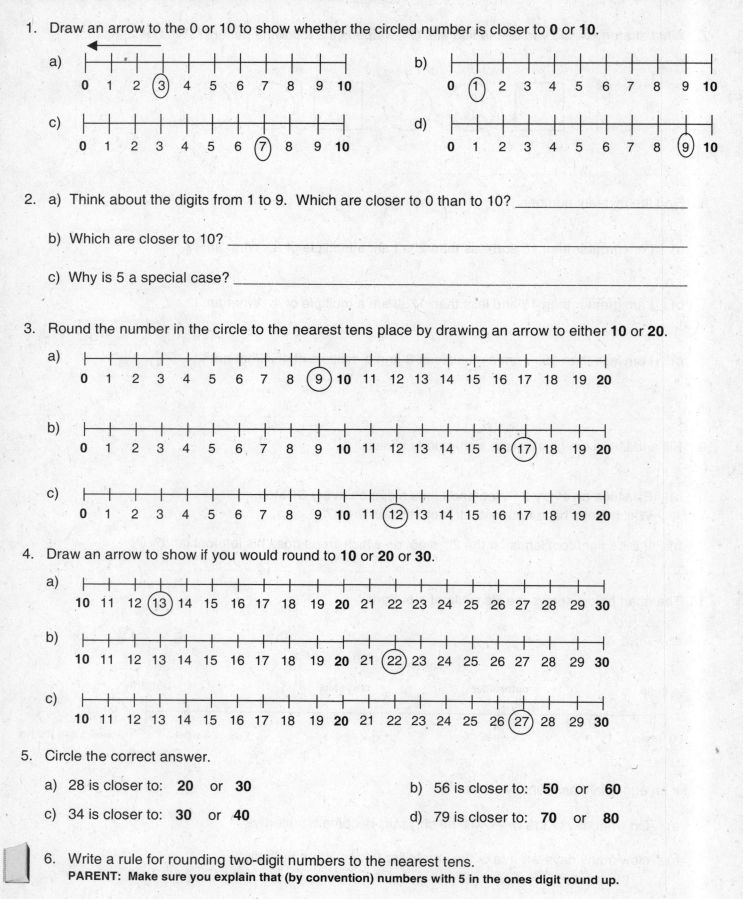

a)

| 0 1 2 ③ 4 5 6 7 8 9 10 |

b)

| 0 ① 2 3 4 5 6 7 8 9 10 |

c)

| 0 1 2 3 4 5 6 ⑦ 8 9 10 |

d)

| 0 1 2 3 4 5 6 7 8 ⑨ 10 |

2. a) Think about the digits from 1 to 9. Which are closer to 0 than to 10? _____

   b) Which are closer to 10? _____

   c) Why is 5 a special case? _____

3. Round the number in the circle to the nearest tens place by drawing an arrow to either **10** or **20**.

   a)

   | 0 1 2 3 4 5 6 7 8 ⑨ 10 11 12 13 14 15 16 17 18 19 20 |

   b)

   | 0 1 2 3 4 5 6 7 8 9 10 11 12 13 14 15 16 ⑰ 18 19 20 |

   c)

   | 0 1 2 3 4 5 6 7 8 9 10 11 ⑫ 13 14 15 16 17 18 19 20 |

4. Draw an arrow to show if you would round to **10** or **20** or **30**.

   a)

   | 10 11 12 ⑬ 14 15 16 17 18 19 20 21 22 23 24 25 26 27 28 29 30 |

   b)

   | 10 11 12 13 14 15 16 17 18 19 20 21 ㉒ 23 24 25 26 27 28 29 30 |

   c)

   | 10 11 12 13 14 15 16 17 18 19 20 21 22 23 24 25 26 ㉗ 28 29 30 |

5. Circle the correct answer.

   a) 28 is closer to: **20** or **30**

   b) 56 is closer to: **50** or **60**

   c) 34 is closer to: **30** or **40**

   d) 79 is closer to: **70** or **80**

6. Write a rule for rounding two-digit numbers to the nearest tens.
   PARENT: Make sure you explain that (by convention) numbers with 5 in the ones digit round up.

7. Draw an arrow to show which multiple of ten the number in the circle is closest to.

Example: Is the given number 124 closer to **120** or **130**?

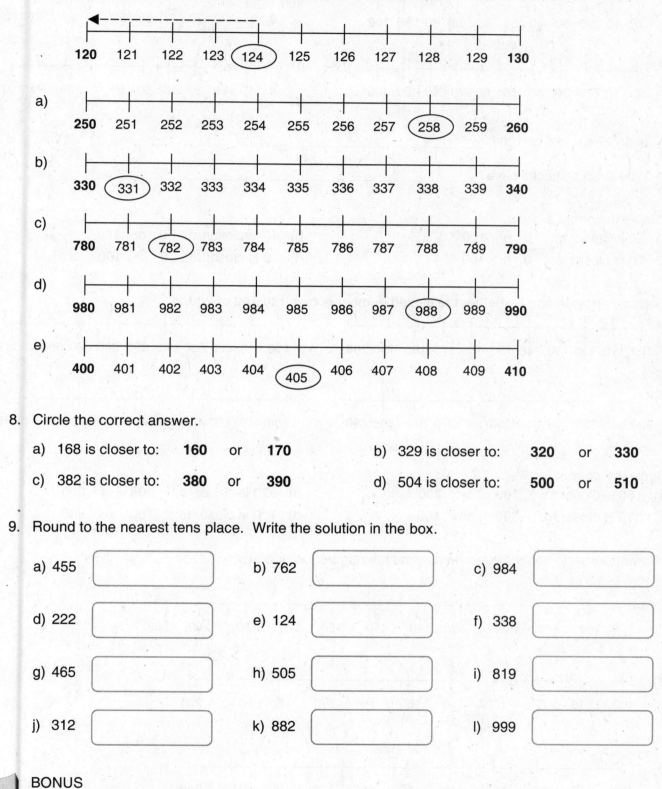

8. Circle the correct answer.

a) 168 is closer to: **160**   or   **170**   b) 329 is closer to: **320**   or   **330**

c) 382 is closer to: **380**   or   **390**   d) 504 is closer to: **500**   or   **510**

9. Round to the nearest tens place. Write the solution in the box.

a) 455   b) 762   c) 984

d) 222   e) 124   f) 338

g) 465   h) 505   i) 819

j) 312   k) 882   l) 999

BONUS

10. Explain why rounding 999 to the nearest tens is a special case.

NS3-46: Round to the Nearest Hundreds

1. Draw an arrow to show whether the circled number is closer to **0** or **100**.

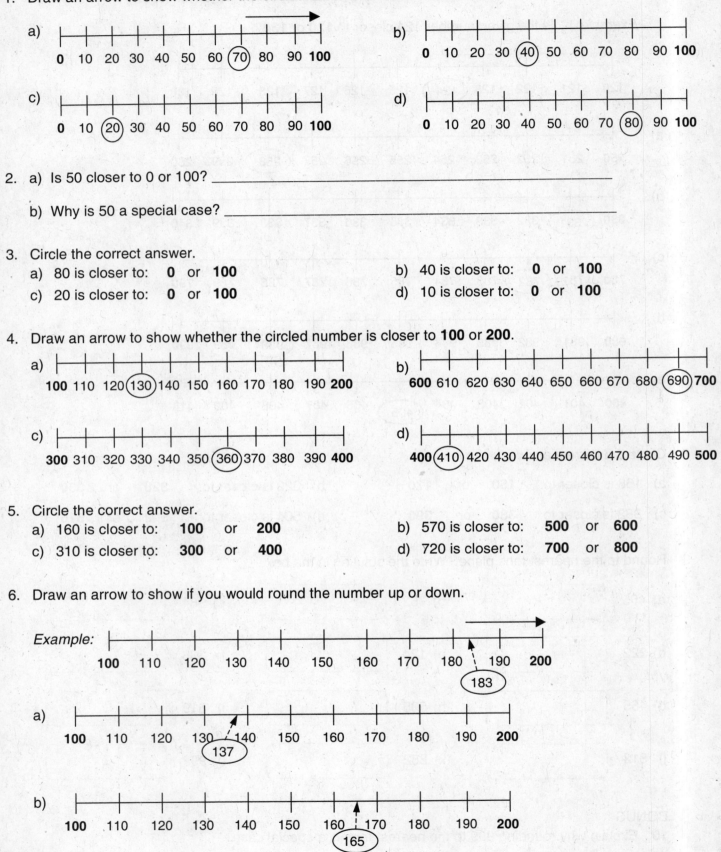

a) 0 10 20 30 40 50 60 (70) 80 90 **100**

b) 0 10 20 30 (40) 50 60 70 80 90 **100**

c) 0 10 (20) 30 40 50 60 70 80 90 **100**

d) 0 10 20 30 40 50 60 70 (80) 90 **100**

2. a) Is 50 closer to 0 or 100? _____

   b) Why is 50 a special case? _____

3. Circle the correct answer.

   a) 80 is closer to: **0** or **100**   b) 40 is closer to: **0** or **100**

   c) 20 is closer to: **0** or **100**   d) 10 is closer to: **0** or **100**

4. Draw an arrow to show whether the circled number is closer to **100** or **200**.

   a) **100** 110 120 (130) 140 150 160 170 180 190 **200**

   b) **600** 610 620 630 640 650 660 670 680 (690) **700**

   c) **300** 310 320 330 340 350 (360) 370 380 390 **400**

   d) **400** (410) 420 430 440 450 460 470 480 490 **500**

5. Circle the correct answer.

   a) 160 is closer to: **100** or **200**   b) 570 is closer to: **500** or **600**

   c) 310 is closer to: **300** or **400**   d) 720 is closer to: **700** or **800**

6. Draw an arrow to show if you would round the number up or down.

   Example:
   100 110 120 130 140 150 160 170 180 190 **200**
   (183)

   a) **100** 110 120 130 140 150 160 170 180 190 **200**
   (137)

   b) **100** 110 120 130 140 150 160 170 180 190 **200**
   (165)

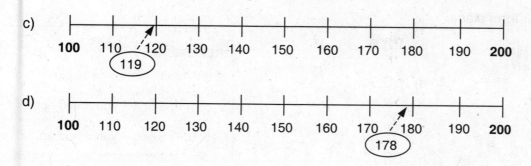

c)

d)

7. Draw an arrow to show if you would round up or down to the nearest hundred.

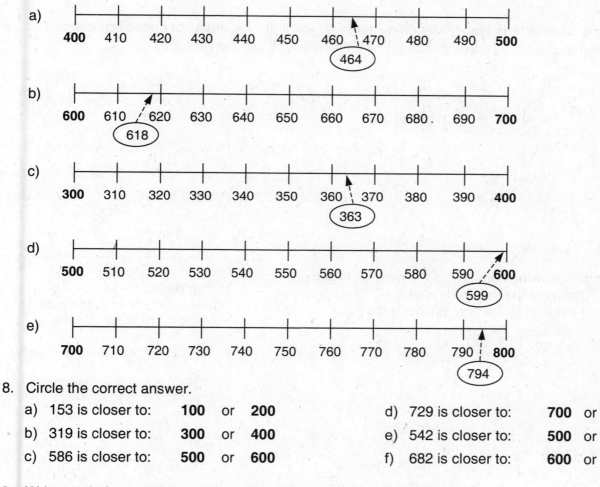

a)

b)

c)

d)

e)

8. Circle the correct answer.

a) 153 is closer to: **100** or **200**

b) 319 is closer to: **300** or **400**

c) 586 is closer to: **500** or **600**

d) 729 is closer to: **700** or **800**

e) 542 is closer to: **500** or **600**

f) 682 is closer to: **600** or **700**

9. Write a rule for rounding a three-digit number to the nearest hundreds.

NS3-47: Rounding

1. Round to the nearest **tens** place.

   a) 14 ☐   b) 23 ☐

   c) 72 ☐   d) 66 ☐

   e) 81 ☐   f) 93 ☐

   g) 11 ☐   h) 53 ☐

   i) 68 ☐   j) 37 ☐   k) 82 ☐

   > **REMEMBER:**
   >
   > If the number in the ones digit is:
   >
   > 0, 1, 2, 3 or 4 – you round <u>down</u>
   >
   > 5, 6, 7, 8 or 9 – you round <u>up</u>

2. Round to the nearest **tens** place. Underline the tens digit first. Then put your pencil on the digit to the right (the ones digit). This digit tells you whether to round up or down.

   a) 1<u>4</u>5 → 150   b) 172 ☐   c) 323 ☐

   d) 255 ☐   e) 794 ☐   f) 667 ☐

   g) 441 ☐   h) 939 ☐   i) 318 ☐

   j) 528 ☐   k) 985 ☐   l) 834 ☐

   m) 758 ☐   n) 545 ☐   o) 293 ☐

3. Round the following numbers to the nearest **hundreds** place. Underline the hundreds digit first. Then put your pencil on the digit to the right (the tens digit).

   > **REMEMBER:**   3<u>4</u>5
   > To round to the nearest hundreds, look at the tens digit.
   >
   > 0, 1, 2, 3 or 4 – you round <u>down</u>
   >
   > 5, 6, 7, 8 or 9 – you round <u>up</u>

   a) <u>3</u>40 → 300   b) 870 ☐

   c) 650 ☐   d) 190 ☐

   e) 240 ☐   f) 630 ☐   g) 710 ☐

   h) 720 ☐   i) 580 ☐   j) 930 ☐

   k) 650 ☐   l) 940 ☐   m) 490 ☐

   o) 148 ☐   p) 218 ☐   q) 321 ☐

   r) 678 ☐   s) 543 ☐   t) 292 ☐

   u) 374 ☐   v) 867 ☐   w) 547 ☐

   x) 525 ☐   y) 484 ☐   z) 832 ☐

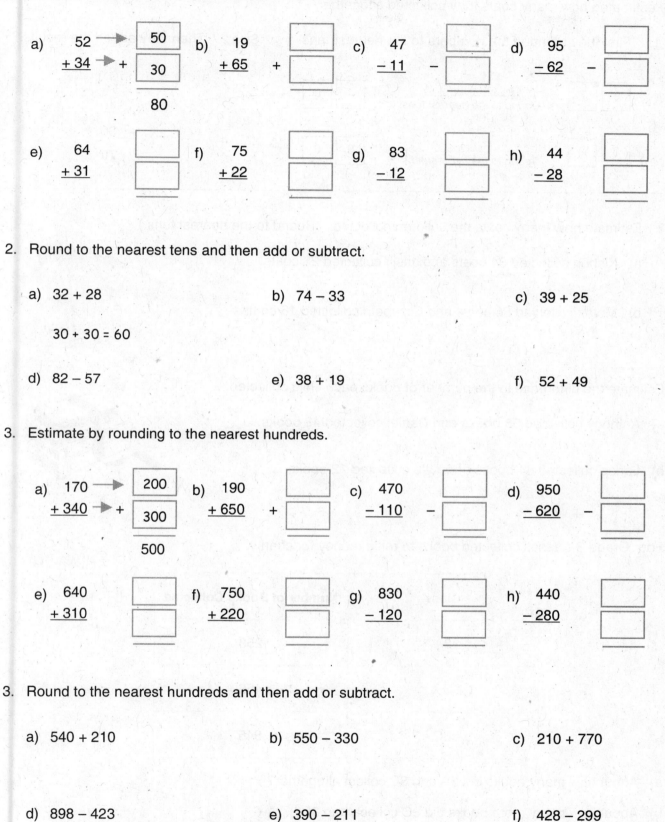

1. Estimate by rounding to the nearest tens (as in the example).

a) 52 → [50]
   + 34 → + [30]
   _____
   80

b) 19 [ ]
   + 65 + [ ]

c) 47 [ ]
   − 11 − [ ]

d) 95 [ ]
   − 62 − [ ]

e) 64 [ ]
   + 31 [ ]

f) 75 [ ]
   + 22 [ ]

g) 83 [ ]
   − 12 [ ]

h) 44 [ ]
   − 28 [ ]

2. Round to the nearest tens and then add or subtract.

a) 32 + 28

   30 + 30 = 60

b) 74 − 33

c) 39 + 25

d) 82 − 57

e) 38 + 19

f) 52 + 49

3. Estimate by rounding to the nearest hundreds.

a) 170 → [200]
   + 340 → + [300]
   _____
   500

b) 190 [ ]
   + 650 + [ ]

c) 470 [ ]
   − 110 − [ ]

d) 950 [ ]
   − 620 − [ ]

e) 640 [ ]
   + 310 [ ]

f) 750 [ ]
   + 220 [ ]

g) 830 [ ]
   − 120 [ ]

h) 440 [ ]
   − 280 [ ]

3. Round to the nearest hundreds and then add or subtract.

a) 540 + 210

b) 550 − 330

c) 210 + 770

d) 898 − 423

e) 390 − 211

f) 428 − 299

Teshika collected 37 coats for charity and Kiril collected 32.
They estimated how many coats they collected altogether.

Step 1:   First they rounded the numbers to the nearest tens.   Step 2:   Then they added the results.

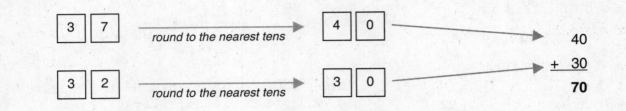

```
    40
  + 30
    70
```

----

1.   Estimate how many coats the children collected. (Round to the nearest tens.)

    a)   Kishon collected 34 coats and Jasjit collected 23 coats.

    b)   Motaz collected 86 coats and Elizabeth collected 18 coats.

2.   Estimate the difference in the number of books each child collected.

    a)   Anthony collected 58 books and Daniel collected 43 books.

    b)   Lance collected 84 books and Kyle collected 72 books.

3.   Four Grade 3 classes collected books to raise money for charity.

Class	Number of Books Collected
3A	258
3B	456
3C	645

    a)   About how many books did 3A and 3B collect altogether?

    b)   About how many more books did 3C collect than 3B?

    c)   About how many books did all the Grade 3s (3A, 3B, 3C) collect altogether?

4.

How many basketballs are on the rack? _____

Round to the nearest tens: _____

a) About how many basketballs would be on 2 racks? _____

b) About how many basketballs would be on 3 racks? _____

c) About how many basketballs would be on 5 racks? _____

5.

How many golf balls in the bucket? _____

Round to the nearest tens: _____

About how many golf balls would be in:

a) 2 buckets? _____

b) 4 buckets? _____

c) 5 buckets? _____

6. Aziz is eating a piece of watermelon and he notices the piece has 18 seeds. Approximately how many seeds would:

a) 2 pieces have? _____

b) 4 pieces have? _____

c) 7 pieces have? _____

7. Kevin counted 237 words on a page. Approximately how many words would be on:

a) 2 pages? _____   b) 3 pages? _____

Explain how you found your answers.

8.

Box 1

a) To the nearest tens, estimate how many dots are in Box 1.

_____

b) How many dots would be in four boxes?

_____

Number Sense 2

NS3-50: Mental Math and Estimation

1. Count by 2s.

   __2__   __4__   __6__   _____   _____

   _____   _____   _____   _____   _____

2. Trisha multiplies by two by counting on her fingers by 2s.

   6 × 2 ← Count by 2s until you have raised 6 fingers   7 × 2 ← Count by 2s until you have raised 7 fingers

   Multiply.

   a) 5 × 2 = _____   b) 3 × 2 = _____   c) 6 × 2 = _____   d) 7 × 2 = _____

   e) 8 × 2 = _____   f) 4 × 2 = _____   g) 9 × 2 = _____   h) 10 × 2 = _____

3. Double each number by multiplying by 2.

	5	7	9	8	4	6	3	10
Double								

4. Double each number by doubling the ones and tens digits separately.

	23	11	31	41	24	13	14	32	53
Double	46								

5. The numbers 8 and 6 differ by 2 (8 − 6 = 2).
   Claude adds numbers that differ by 2 by doubling the number in between.

   Claude's Strategy

   8 + 6
   −1   +1

   7 + 7 = 14

   Claude finds the number between 8 and 6 and doubles it.

   Add by doubling the number in between.

   a)   7 + 5   b)   9 + 7

   −1 ↓   ↓ +1   -1 ↓   ↓ +1

   ☐ + ☐ = ☐   ☐ + ☐ = ☐

6. Explain Eva's doubling strategy for adding numbers that differ by 1.

   6 + 7   7 + 8

   = 6 + ☐6☐ + ☐1☐   = 7 + ☐7☐ + ☐1☐

   = 12 + 1   = 14 + 1

   = 13   = 15

   Eva's Strategy

   Use Eva's strategy to add 8 + 9 and 5 + 6.

7.   Find the answer mentally by doubling.

a)   One eraser costs 42¢.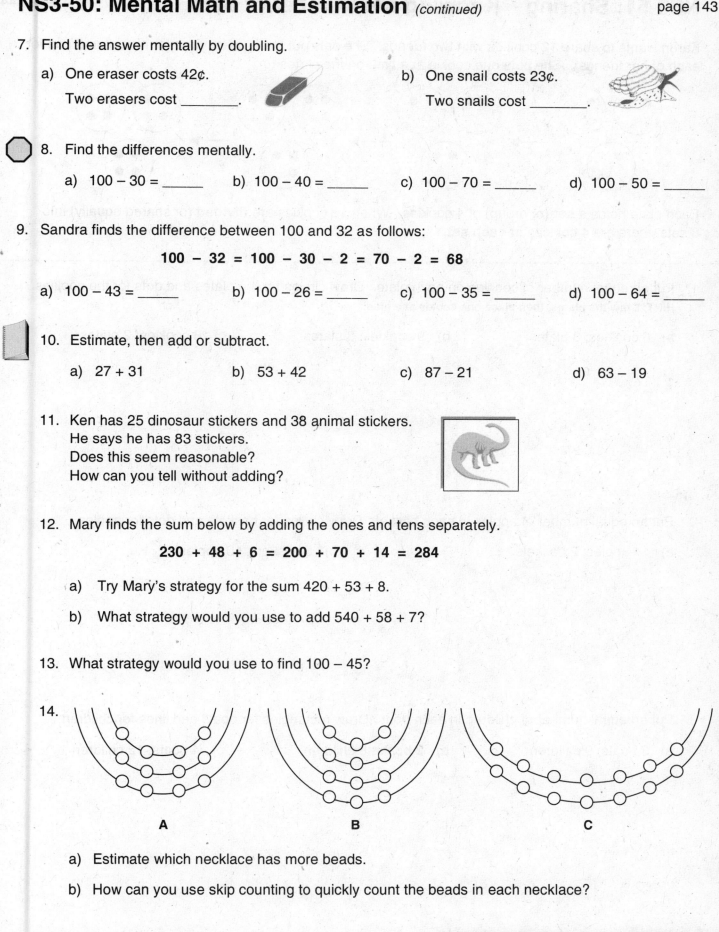

     Two erasers cost _____.

b)   One snail costs 23¢.

     Two snails cost _____.

8.   Find the differences mentally.

a)   100 – 30 = _____   b)   100 – 40 = _____   c)   100 – 70 = _____   d)   100 – 50 = _____

9.   Sandra finds the difference between 100 and 32 as follows:

100 – 32 = 100 – 30 – 2 = 70 – 2 = 68

a)   100 – 43 = _____   b)   100 – 26 = _____   c)   100 – 35 = _____   d)   100 – 64 = _____

10. Estimate, then add or subtract.

a)   27 + 31   b)   53 + 42   c)   87 – 21   d)   63 – 19

11. Ken has 25 dinosaur stickers and 38 animal stickers.
     He says he has 83 stickers.
     Does this seem reasonable?
     How can you tell without adding?

12. Mary finds the sum below by adding the ones and tens separately.

230 + 48 + 6 = 200 + 70 + 14 = 284

a)   Try Mary's strategy for the sum 420 + 53 + 8.

b)   What strategy would you use to add 540 + 58 + 7?

13. What strategy would you use to find 100 – 45?

14.

A   B   C

a)   Estimate which necklace has more beads.

b)   How can you use skip counting to quickly count the beads in each necklace?

Karen wants to share 12 cookies with two friends. She sets out three plates (one for herself and one for each of her friends). She puts one cookie at a time on the plates.

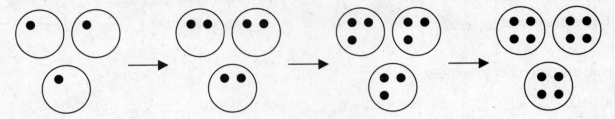

Each plate holds a **set** (or group) of 4 cookies. When 12 cookies are **divided** (or shared equally) into 3 sets, there are 4 cookies **in each set**.

----

1. Put an equal number of cookies on each plate. Draw circles for the plates and dots for the cookies.

    HINT: Draw the plates, then place one cookie at a time.

    a) 6 cookies; 3 plates

    b) 9 cookies; 3 plates

    c) 8 cookies; 2 plates

2. Put an equal number of apples in each basket. Draw circles for baskets and dots for apples.

    a) 14 apples; 2 baskets

    b) 5 baskets; 10 apples

3. Put an equal number of children in each boat. Draw rectangles for boats and lines for children.

    a) 3 boats; 9 children

    b) 2 boats; 8 children

    c) 4 boats; 12 children

4. Draw dots for the things being shared or divided equally. Draw circles for the sets.

a) 3 wagons; 9 kids
    How many kids in each wagon?

b) 15 stamps; 3 pages
    How many stamps on each page?

c) 16 fleas; 4 dogs
    How many fleas on each dog?

d) 2 boxes; 10 pens
    How many pens in each box?

e) 4 boats; 12 kids
    How many kids on each boat?

f) 10 grapes; 5 plates
    How many grapes on each plate?

Draw a picture or make a model to solve the problem.

5. 4 friends share 8 tickets.
    How many tickets does each friend get?

6. 12 chairs are placed in 3 rows.
    How many chairs in each row?

7. 10 trees are planted in 5 rows.
    How many trees in each row?

8. 24 flowers are planted in 6 rows.
    How many flowers in each row?

9. Roger earned 20 loonies for his work. He worked 5 hours.
    How much did he earn each hour?
    HINT: Draw dots for loonies and circles for hours.

10. Kate earned 15 loonies for her work. She worked 3 hours.
    How much did she earn each hour?

NS3-52: Sharing – Knowing How Many in Each Set

Nick has 20 apples. He wants to give 5 apples to each of his friends.

To find out how many friends he can give apples to, he starts by counting out 5 apples.

He then keeps counting out **sets** of 5 apples until he has used all 20 apples.

He can give apples to 4 friends. When 20 apples are divided into sets of 5 apples, there are 4 sets.

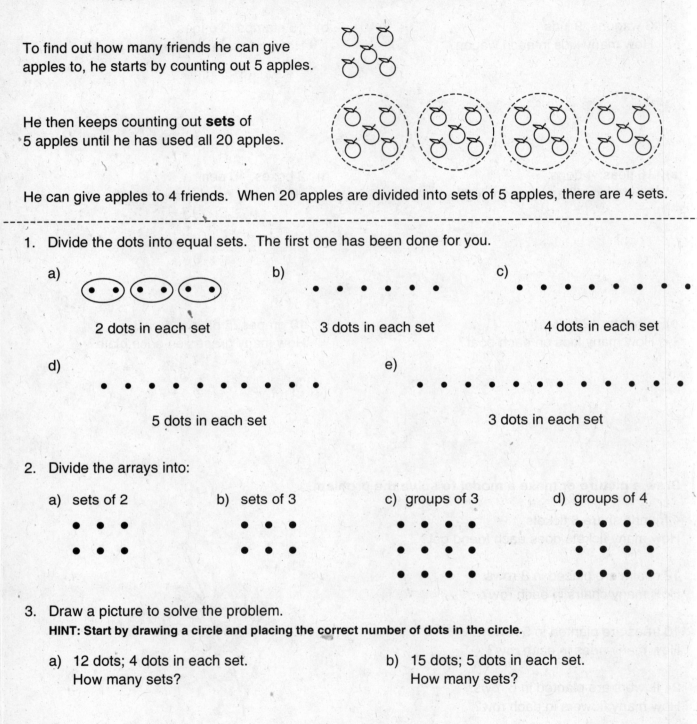

1. Divide the dots into equal sets. The first one has been done for you.

a)

2 dots in each set

b)

3 dots in each set

c)

4 dots in each set

d)

5 dots in each set

e)

3 dots in each set

2. Divide the arrays into:

a) sets of 2   b) sets of 3   c) groups of 3   d) groups of 4

3. Draw a picture to solve the problem.

   HINT: Start by drawing a circle and placing the correct number of dots in the circle.

a) 12 dots; 4 dots in each set.
   How many sets?

b) 15 dots; 5 dots in each set.
   How many sets?

_____ sets

_____ sets

4. Draw dots (or lines) for the things being shared or divided equally. Draw circles (or rectangles) for the sets.

   a) 10 kids; 5 kids in each wagon
      How many wagons?

      _____ wagons

   b) 12 stamps; 4 stamps on each page
      How many pages?

      _____ pages

   c) 20 books; 4 books on each shelf
      How many shelves?

      _____ shelves

   d) 15 fish; 5 fish in each tank
      How many tanks?

      _____ tanks

Use counters or pictures to model the problems.

5. Sam has 10 oranges.
   He wants to give 2 oranges to each friend.
   How many friends can he give them to?

6.  Carol has 12 books.
   She wants to lend 3 books to each friend.
   How many friends can she give them to?

7. Ali has 15 stamps.
   He wants to put 5 stamps on each page of his stamp book.
   How many pages will he need?

8.  A canoe can hold 3 kids.
   There are 12 kids.
   How many canoes will the kids need?

9. Jane earned 6 loonies for each hour of work.
   She earned 18 loonies in total.
   How many hours did she work?
   HINT: Use circles for hours and dots for loonies.

12 kids go canoeing. A canoe holds 3 kids.

There are 4 canoes.

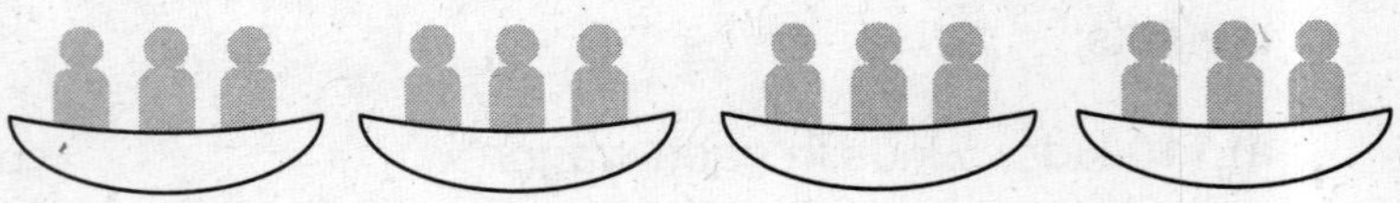

What has been shared or divided into sets?   (Kids.)

How many sets are there?   (There are 4 sets of kids.)

How many of the things being divided are in each set?   (There are 3 kids in each set.)

---

1. a)

What has been shared or divided into sets?

_____

How many sets? _____

How many in each set? _____

b)

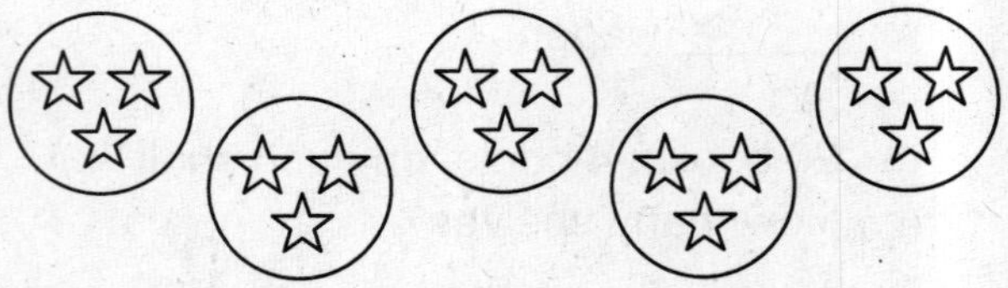

What has been shared or divided into sets?

_____

How many sets? _____

How many in each set? _____

2. Using circles for <u>sets</u> and dots for <u>things</u>, draw a picture to show:

a) 3 sets;
    4 things in each set

b) 4 groups;
    5 things in each group

c) 2 sets;
    3 things in each set

d) 3 groups;
    4 things in each group

3.

	What has been shared or divided into sets?	How many sets?	How many in each set?
a) 15 kids 3 kids in each boat 5 boats	Kids	5	3
b) 5 friends 20 cookies 4 cookies for each friend			
c) 18 oranges 6 boxes 3 oranges in each box			
d) 4 dogs 20 spots 5 spots on each dog			
e) 5 stamps on each page 35 stamps 7 pages			
f) 3 playgrounds 12 swings 4 swings at each playground			
g) 5 people in each house 10 people 2 houses			

BONUS

4. Draw a picture for Question 3, parts a), b), and c), using circles for sets and dots for the things being divided.

NS3-54: Two Ways of Sharing

Sarah has 12 beads. There are two ways she can share or **divide** her beads equally:

I ☐ She can decide how many **sets** (or **groups**) of beads she wants to make.

For example:
Sarah wants to make 3 sets of beads. She draws 3 circles.

She then puts one bead at a time into the circles until she has placed all 12 beads.

II ☐ She can decide how many beads she wants to put **in each set**.

For example:
Sarah wants to put 3 beads in each set. She counts out 3 beads.

She keeps counting out sets of 3 beads until she has placed all 12 beads in sets.

---

1. Share **12** dots equally. How many dots are in each set?
   HINT: Place one dot at a time.

   a)

   3 sets:

   There are _____ dots in each set.

   b)

   4 sets:

   There are _____ dots in each set.

2. Share **15** dots equally. How many dots are in each set?

   a)

   3 sets:

   There are _____ dots in each set.

   b)

   5 sets:

   There are _____ dots in each set.

3. Share the triangles equally among the sets.
   HINT: Count the triangles first.

   a)

   b)

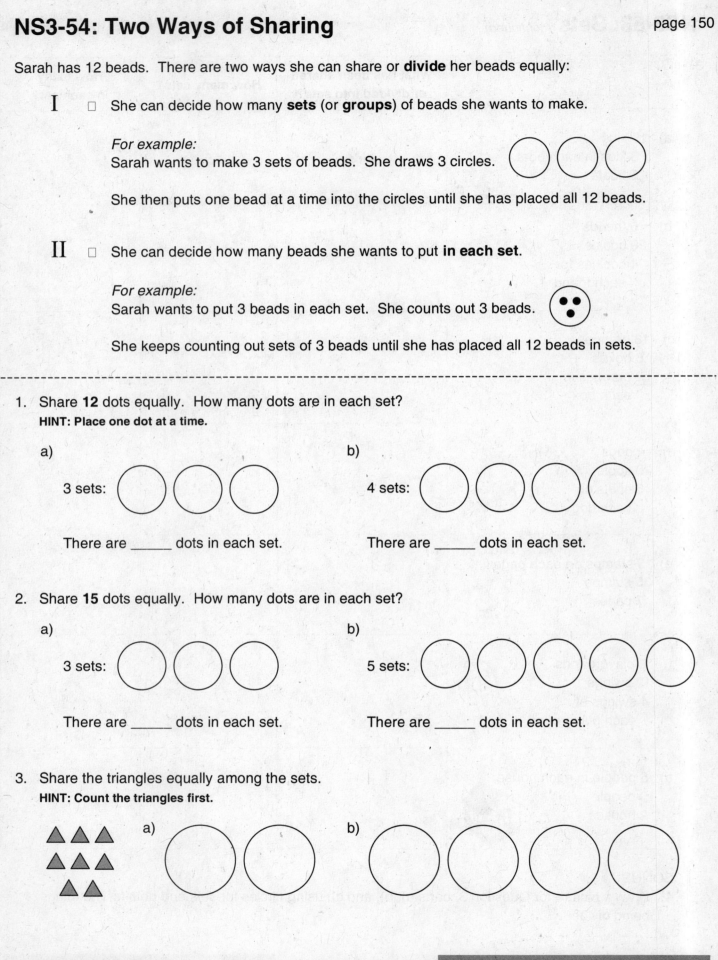

Number Sense 2

NS3-54: Two Ways of Sharing *(continued)*

4. Share the squares equally among the sets.

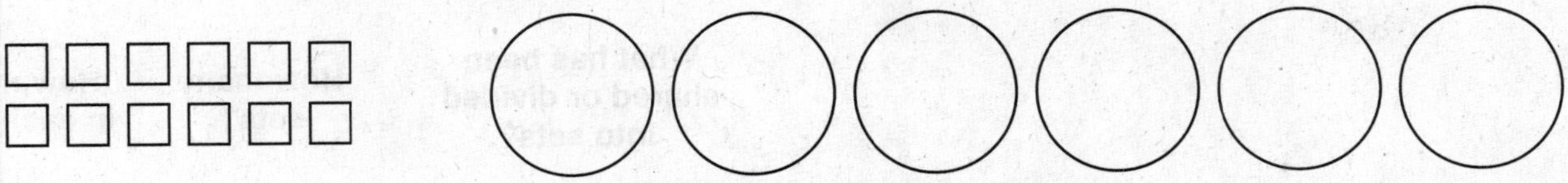

5. Group **12** dots so that…

a) … there are 3 dots in each set.

b) … there are 6 dots in each set.

6. Show how you could put **10** apples in baskets so that…

a) … there are 5 apples in each basket.

b) … there are 2 apples in each basket.

7. Divide the dots into sets.

REMEMBER: If you know the number of sets, start by drawing circles for sets. If you know the number of dots in each set, fill one circle at a time with the correct number of dots.

a) 10 dots; 5 sets

_____ dots in each set

b) 6 dots; 3 dots in each set

_____ sets

c) 15 dots; 5 dots in each set

_____ sets

d) 8 dots; 4 sets

_____ dots in each set

8. In each question, fill in what you know. Write a question mark for what you don't know.

	What has been shared or divided into sets?	How many sets?	How many in each set?
a) Jake has 15 stamps. He puts 5 stamps on each page of his book.	15 stamps	?	5
b) 20 kids go canoeing in 10 canoes.	20 kids	10	?
c) Dan has 15 pens. He puts them into 3 boxes.			
d) 4 friends share 20 apples.			
e) Carol has 10 cookies. She puts them on 5 plates.			
f) 16 kids go sailing in 4 boats.			

9. Draw dots for things, animals or people (or parts of animals or people) and circles for sets.

   a) 12 kids go sailing on 3 boats.
      How many kids in each boat?

   b) Aziz has 20 stamps.
      He wants to put 5 stamps on each page of his album.
      How many pages will he need?

   c) Paul counts 16 legs at a kennel.
      How many dogs are in the kennel?

10. Make up a division problem of your own and solve it.

NS3-55: Division

When 12 things are divided into 3 sets, there are 4 things in each set.

We write: **12 ÷ 3 = 4**

We could also describe the picture as follows: When 12 things are divided into sets of size 4, there are 3 sets (**12 ÷ 4 = 3**).

PARENT:
Division statements are ambiguous: 6 ÷ 2 = 3 can be read as "6 divided into sets of size 2 gives 3 sets" or "6 divided into 2 sets gives 3 things in each set." In the exercises in lessons NS3-55 to 57, your child will become familiar with both readings.

----

1. Fill in the blanks. Then write two division statements.

    a)

    _____ lines _____ sets

    _____ lines in each set

    b)

    _____ lines _____ sets

    _____ lines in each set

    c)

    _____ lines _____ sets

    _____ lines in each set

2. Fill in the blanks. Then write two division statements.
    HINT: To write a division statement, count the individual figures first (e.g. the dots, the triangles or the stars).

    a)

    _____ sets

    _____ dots in each set

    b)

    _____ sets

    _____ triangles in each set

    c)

    _____ sets

    _____ stars in each set

3. Solve the problem by drawing a picture. Then write a division statement for your answer.

    a) 8 dots; 2 dots in each set

    b) 12 triangles; 4 sets

    How many sets? _____

    How many triangles in each set? _____

NS3-56: Dividing by Skip Counting

Every **division** statement implies an **addition** statement.

Example: The statement "12 divided into sets of size 3 gives 4 sets" can also be written:

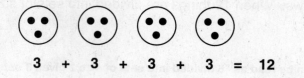

3 + 3 + 3 + 3 = 12

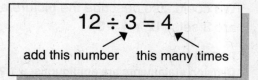

$$12 \div 3 = 4$$
add this number   this many times

Hence the division statement $12 \div 3 = 4$ can be read as: "If you add three 4 times, you get 12."

----

1. Draw a picture and write an **addition** statement for each **division** statement. The first one has been done for you.

a) $6 \div 2 = 3$

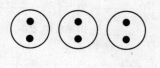

   $2 + 2 + 2 = 6$

b) $8 \div 4 = 2$

   _____

c) $15 \div 5 = 3$

   _____

d) $9 \div 3 = 3$

   _____

2. Draw a picture and write a **division** statement for each **addition** statement.

a) $4 + 4 + 4 = 12$

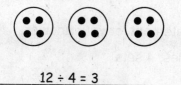

   $12 \div 4 = 3$

b) $3 + 3 + 3 + 3 + 3 = 15$

   _____

c) $2 + 2 + 2 = 6$

   _____

d) $6 + 6 + 6 = 18$

   _____

NS3-56: Dividing by Skip Counting (continued)

3. You can solve the division problem **12 ÷ 3 = ?** by skip counting on the number line.

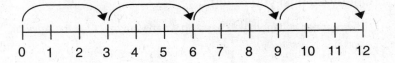

The number line shows that it takes 4 skips of size 3 to get 12:

3 + 3 + 3 + 3 = 12, so ...   **12 ÷ 3 = 4**

Use the number lines provided to find the answer to the following division questions.

a)

6 ÷ 2 = ___3___

b)

6 ÷ 3 = _____

4. Use the number line to find the answer to the division statement.
   HINT: Be sure to draw arrows to show your skip counting.

a)

8 ÷ 4 = _____

b)

16 ÷ 4 = _____

c)

15 ÷ 5 = _____

d)

8 ÷ 2 = _____

5. What division statement does the picture represent?

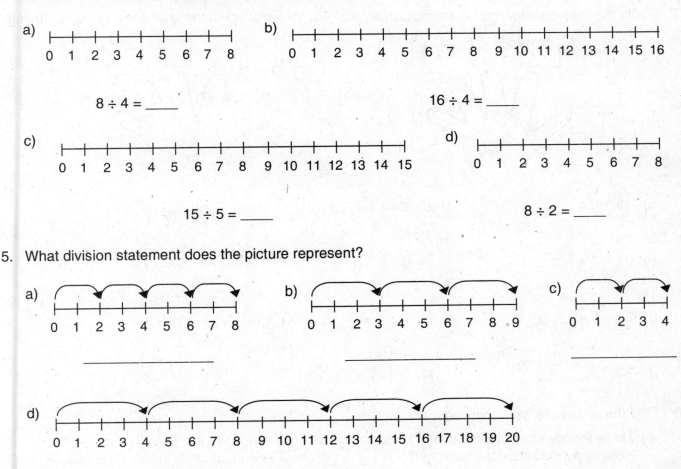

a)

_____

b)

_____

c)

_____

d)

_____

         Number Sense 2

6. You can also find the answer to a division question by skip counting on your fingers.

To find **6 ÷ 2**, count by 2s until you reach 6.

The number of fingers you have up when you say "6" is the answer.

So 6 ÷ 2 = **3**

Find the answers by skip counting on your fingers.

a) 10 ÷ 2 = _____   b) 8 ÷ 2 = _____   c) 4 ÷ 2 = _____   d) 9 ÷ 3 = _____   e) 10 ÷ 5 = _____

f) 15 ÷ 5 = _____   g) 25 ÷ 5 = _____   h) 20 ÷ 5 = _____   i) 12 ÷ 3 = _____   j) 6 ÷ 3 = _____

k) 12 ÷ 2 = _____   l) 5 ÷ 5 = _____   m) 2 ÷ 2 = _____   n) 30 ÷ 5 = _____   o) 15 ÷ 3 = _____

p) 25 ÷ 5 = _____   q) 2 ÷ 2 = _____   r) 6 ÷ 3 = _____   s) 20 ÷ 5 = _____   t) 12 ÷ 3 = _____

7. Fill in the missing numbers on the hands below. Find the answers to the questions by skip counting.

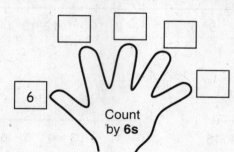

Count by **6s**

Count by **7s**

a) 18 ÷ 6 = _____   b) 24 ÷ 6 = _____   c) 12 ÷ 6 = _____

d) 21 ÷ 7 = _____   e) 35 ÷ 7 = _____   f) 28 ÷ 7 = _____

g) 30 ÷ 6 = _____   h) 6 ÷ 6 = _____   i) 14 ÷ 7 = _____

j) 7 ÷ 7 = _____   k) 21 ÷ 7 = _____   l) 24 ÷ 6 = _____

8. Find the answer by skip counting.

a) Three friends share 12 stickers.
How many stickers does each get?

b) Twenty four kids sit at 6 tables.
How many kids are at each table?

_____   _____

Sam wants to put his collection of seashells into a display case.

Sam has 12 shells. The display case has 3 shelves. How many shells go on each shelf?

Sam counts by 3's on his fingers until he reaches 12:

Each time Sam counts he imagines placing 3 shells, <u>one on each shelf</u>. He raises 4 fingers so he will have to place 3 shells (one per shelf) 4 times.

He puts 4 shells on each shelf.

- -

9. Draw circles to divide the objects in the number of equal sets given.

HINT: Count the objects. Then divide the number of objects by the number of sets to find the number of objects in each set.

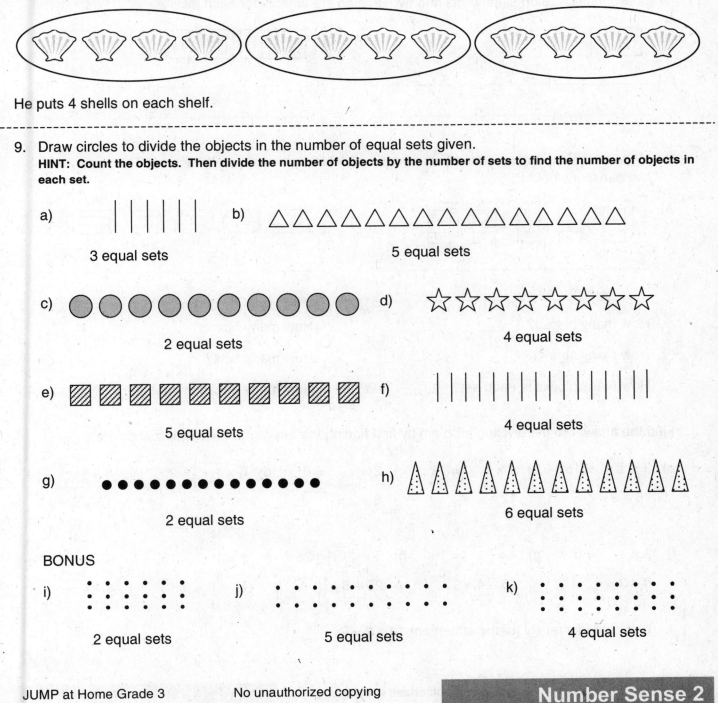

a) 3 equal sets

b) 5 equal sets

c) 2 equal sets

d) 4 equal sets

e) 5 equal sets

f) 4 equal sets

g) 2 equal sets

h) 6 equal sets

BONUS

i) 2 equal sets

j) 5 equal sets

k) 4 equal sets

To say: "8 divided into sets of size 2 gives 4 sets" (or **8 ÷ 2 = 4**) is the same as saying:

"8 divided into 4 sets give sets of size 2" (or **8 ÷ 4 = 2**).

But these two division statements imply the statement:

"4 sets of size 2 equals 8" (**4 × 2 = 8** or **2 × 4 = 8**)

The equations **8 ÷ 2 = 4, 8 ÷ 4 = 2, 4 × 2 = 8** and **2 × 4 = 8** are all part of the same fact family.

---

1. Write two multiplication statements and two division statements for each picture.

   a) _____   b) _____

   _____   _____

2. Write two multiplication statements and two division statements each picture. Then answer the questions below.

   a) _____   b) _____

   _____   _____

   How many blocks? _____   How many blocks? _____

   How many sets? _____   How many sets? _____

   How many blocks in each set? _____   How many blocks in each set? _____

3. Find the answer to the division problem by first finding the answer to the multiplication statement.

   a) 3 × 5 = 15   b) 4 × ☐ = 12   c) 2 × ☐ = 8   d) 5 × ☐ = 20   e) 6 × ☐ = 18

   15 ÷ 3 = 5   12 ÷ 4 = ☐   8 ÷ 2 = ☐   20 ÷ 5 = ☐   18 ÷ 6 = ☐

   f) 3 × ☐ = 6   g) 4 × ☐ = 16   h) 5 × ☐ = 25   i) 6 × ☐ = 12   j) 4 × ☐ = 8

   6 ÷ 3 = ☐   16 ÷ 4 = ☐   25 ÷ 5 = ☐   12 ÷ 6 = ☐   8 ÷ 4 = ☐

4. Write the fact family for the statement **14 ÷ 2 = 7**.

Ori wants to share 7 pears with 2 friends.
He sets out 3 plates, one for himself and one for each of his friends.
He puts one cookie at a time on a plate.

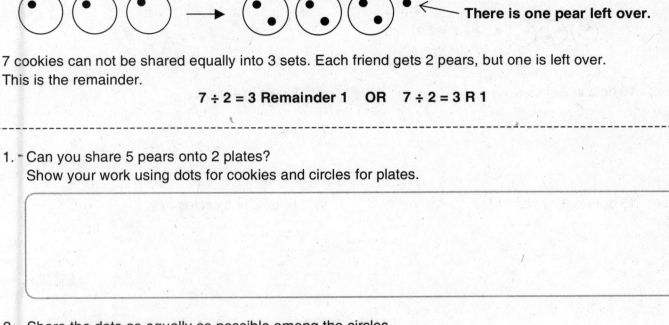

There is one pear left over.

7 cookies can not be shared equally into 3 sets. Each friend gets 2 pears, but one is left over.
This is the remainder.

7 ÷ 2 = 3 Remainder 1   OR   7 ÷ 2 = 3 R 1

---

1. Can you share 5 pears onto 2 plates?
   Show your work using dots for cookies and circles for plates.

2. Share the dots as equally as possible among the circles.
   IMPORTANT: In one question, the dots <u>can</u> be shared equally.

   a) 7 dots in 2 circles

   b) 10 dots in 4 circles

   _____ dots in each circle; _____ dots remaining   _____ dots in each circle; _____ dots remaining

   c) 10 dots in 5 circles

   d) 15 dots in 4 circles

   _____ dots in each circle; _____ dots remaining   _____ dots in each circle; _____ dots remaining

   e) 9 dots in 4 circles

   f) 10 dots in 3 circles

   _____ dots in each circle; _____ dots remaining   _____ dots in each circle; _____ dots remaining

3. Share the dots as equally as possible among the circles.
   Draw a picture and write a division statement for your picture.

   a) 7 dots in 3 circles

   b) 11 dots in 4 circles

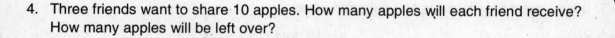 7 ÷ 3 = 2 R1

   c) 10 dots in 6 circles

   d) 9 dots in 4 circles

   e) 15 dots in 3 circles

   f) 14 dots in 3 circles

4. Three friends want to share 10 apples. How many apples will each friend receive?
   How many apples will be left over?

5. Find two different ways to share 7 cookies into equal groups so that one cookie is left over.

BONUS

6. Fred, George and Paul altogether have less than 10 oranges and more than 3 oranges.
   They share the oranges evenly. How many oranges do they have?
   (Is there more than one answer?)

Answer the following questions in your notebook.

1. What is the fact family for the equation $3 \times 5 = 15$?

2. Find the mystery numbers.
   a) I am a multiple of 2.
      I am greater than 10 and less than 13.
   b) I am a multiple of 3.
      I am between 13 and 20.
      I am an even number.

3. Apple trees in an orchard are planted in 7 rows.
   There are 4 trees in each row.
   How many trees are in the orchard?
   How did you find your answer: mental math?
   Skip counting? A picture?

4. A hummingbird feeds 6 times each hour.
   How many times does it feed in 7 hours?

5. Find two different ways to share 11 apples
   in equal groups so there is one apple left over.

6. Find two numbers that give the same
   remainder when divided by 3.

7. Name 2 numbers less than 20 that give
   a remainder of 1 when divided by:

   a) 2   b) 3   c) 4   d) 6

8. Four starfish have 20 arms.
   How many arms will 6 starfish have?
   What strategy did you use to solve the problem?

9. Each day, a woolly mammoth grazed for 20 hours and ate 225 kg of food.
   a) How many hours would a mammoth graze in 3 days?
   b) How many kg of food would it eat?
   c) Is your answer to part b) reasonable?
      How could you check your answer with
      a calculator?

10. 6 is twice as much as (or double) 3. Is 6×5 twice as much as 3×5? Use an array to decide.

NS3-60: Multiplication and Division (Review)

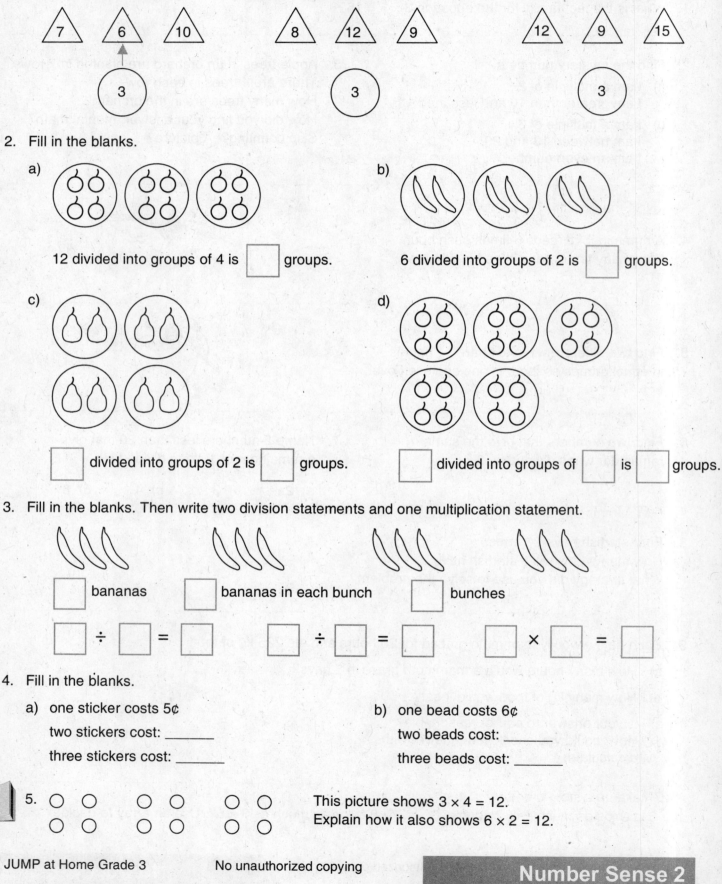

1. Draw an arrow to the number that is:

   a) two times as big as 3.

   7   6   10

   3

   b) three times as big as 3.

   8   12   9

   3

   c) four times as big as 3.

   12   9   15

   3

2. Fill in the blanks.

   a)

   12 divided into groups of 4 is [ ] groups.

   b)

   6 divided into groups of 2 is [ ] groups.

   c)

   [ ] divided into groups of 2 is [ ] groups.

   d)

   [ ] divided into groups of [ ] is [ ] groups.

3. Fill in the blanks. Then write two division statements and one multiplication statement.

   [ ] bananas   [ ] bananas in each bunch   [ ] bunches

   [ ] ÷ [ ] = [ ]   [ ] ÷ [ ] = [ ]   [ ] × [ ] = [ ]

4. Fill in the blanks.

   a) one sticker costs 5¢

   two stickers cost: _____

   three stickers cost: _____

   b) one bead costs 6¢

   two beads cost: _____

   three beads cost: _____

5. This picture shows 3 × 4 = 12.
   Explain how it also shows 6 × 2 = 12.

6. Write as many multiplication and division statements as you can for each array.

a) × × × × ×
    × × × × ×
    × × × × ×

b)

7. A hawks nest holds at least 3 eggs and at most 5 eggs.

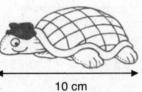

   a) What is the <u>least</u> number of eggs 3 nests would hold?

   b) What is the <u>greatest</u> number of eggs 3 nests would hold?

   c) Show two different ways to put 13 eggs in 3 nests (with at least one egg in each nest).

8. A shelf is 40 cm long.
   How many stuffed animals of each type would fit end to end? Explain.

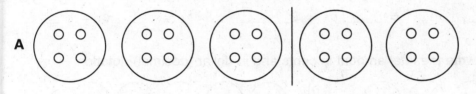

   a)   b)   c)

   5 cm   4 cm   10 cm

9. Picture A shows that:
   Five sets of 4 equals three sets of 4 plus two sets of 4.

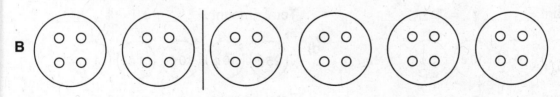

A

   What does picture B show?

B

10. Fill in the blanks with the numbers 2, 3, and 4 to make each statement true.

   a) ☐ × ☐ + ☐ = 11   b) ☐ ÷ ☐ + ☐ = 5

11. Clare divided two numbers and got the number 3.
    What might the numbers have been?

12. Make up a story problem for each expression.

   a) 5 × 4 = 20   b) 12 ÷ 3 = 4

NS3-61: Dollar and Cent Notation

The charts show how to represent money in cent notation and in dollar notation.

	Cent Notation	Dollar (Decimal) Notation			Cent Notation	Dollar (Decimal) Notation
Sixty-five cents	65¢	$0.65 dimes pennies		Seven cents	7¢	$0.07 dimes pennies

A dime is a <u>tenth</u> of a dollar. A penny is a <u>hundredth</u> of a dollar.

---

1. For the given number of dimes and pennies in the T-tables, write the total amount of money in cents and in dollar (decimal) notation.

a)
dimes	pennies
2	5

= __25__ ¢ = $ __0.25__

b)
dimes	pennies
7	5

= _____ ¢ = $ _____

c)
dimes	pennies
3	1

= _____ ¢ = $ _____

d)
dimes	pennies
8	3

= _____ ¢ = $ _____

e)
dimes	pennies
4	9

= _____ ¢ = $ _____

f)
dimes	pennies
0	4

= _____ ¢ = $ _____

2. Count the given coins and write the total amount in cents and in dollar (decimal) notation.

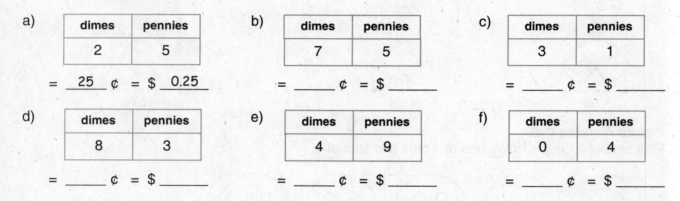

a) 10¢ 10¢ 5¢ 5¢ 1¢ 1¢

Total amount = _____ ¢ = $ _____

b) 25¢ 25¢ 25¢ 10¢ 1¢

Total amount = _____ ¢ = $ _____

c) 25¢ 25¢ 10¢ 10¢ 5¢

Total amount = _____ ¢ = $ _____

d) 25¢ 10¢ 10¢ 1¢ 1¢

Total amount = _____ ¢ = $ _____

e) 25¢ 10¢ 10¢ 10¢ 10¢ 5¢ 1¢

Total amount = _____ ¢ = $ _____

f) 25¢ 10¢ 10¢ 5¢ 5¢ 1¢ 1¢

Total amount = _____ ¢ = $ _____

BONUS

g) 25¢ 25¢ 10¢ 10¢ 10¢ 5¢ 1¢ 1¢

Total amount = _____ ¢ = $ _____

No unauthorized copying

Number Sense 2

3. There are 100 cents in a dollar. We write the same money amount in two different ways,
   for example:

   100¢ as $1.00   200¢ as $2.00   214¢ as $2.14   etc.

   Complete the chart.

	Amount in ¢	Dollars	Dimes	Pennies	Amount in $
a)	152¢	1	5	2	$ 1.52
b)	219¢				
c)	425¢				
d)	554¢				
e)	816¢				
f)	6¢				
g)	747¢				
h)	45¢				
i)	8¢				
j)	999¢				

dollars
↓
100 ¢ = $ 1.00
↑ ↖
dimes   pennies

dollars
↓
214 ¢ = $ 2.14
↑ ↖
dimes   pennies

4. Count the given coins and write the total amount in decimal notation. The first one is done for you.

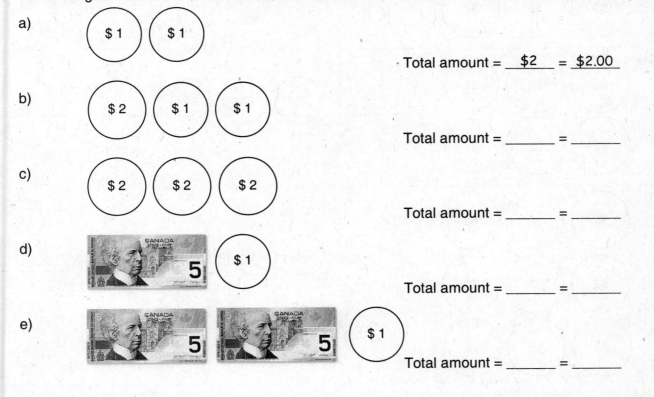

a) $1 $1   Total amount = __$2__ = __$2.00__

b) $2 $1 $1   Total amount = _____ = _____

c) $2 $2 $2   Total amount = _____ = _____

d) [5] $1   Total amount = _____ = _____

e) [5] [5] $1   Total amount = _____ = _____

NS3-62: Counting and Changing Units

1. Complete the chart as shown in a).

Dollar Amount	Cent Amount	Total
a) $2 $2 = ___$4___	25¢ 10¢ = ___35¢___	___$4.35___
b) $2 $2 $1 = _____	5¢ 5¢ 1¢ = _____	_____
c) $1 $1 = _____	10¢ 10¢ 10¢ = _____	_____
d) $2 $2 $2 = _____	25¢ 25¢ 5¢ = _____	_____
e) $2 = _____	5¢ 1¢ 1¢ = _____	_____
f) $2 $2 $2 / $2 $2 $2 = _____	5¢ 5¢ 1¢ = _____	_____
g) $2 $2 $1 / $2 $2 $1 = _____	25¢ 25¢ 5¢ = _____	_____
h) $2 $2 $2 / $2 $2 $2 / $2 $2 $2 = _____	5¢ 1¢ 1¢ = _____	_____

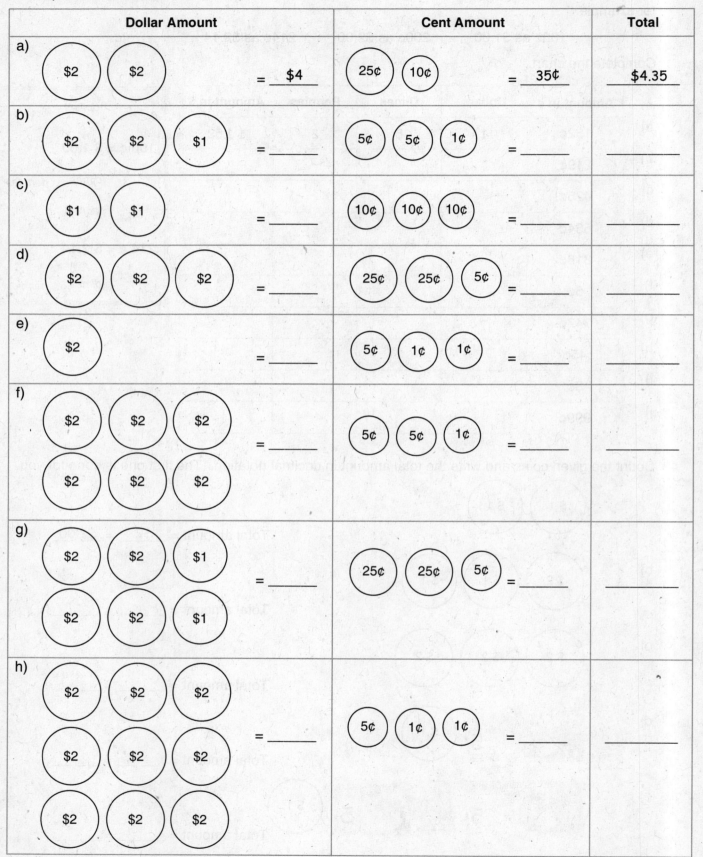

Number Sense 2

NS3-62: Counting and Changing Units (continued)

2. Count the given coins. Write the total amount in cents and in dollars (decimals).

Coins						Cent Notation	Dollar Notation
a)	25¢ 25¢ 25¢ 25¢ 10¢					110¢	$1.10
b)	25¢ 25¢ 25¢ 10¢ 10¢ 1¢					_____	_____
c)	25¢ 25¢ 25¢ 25¢ 1¢ 1¢					_____	_____
d)	25¢ 25¢ 25¢ 25¢ 25¢					_____	_____
e)	25¢ 25¢ 25¢ 10¢ 10¢ 10¢					_____	_____
f)	25¢ 25¢ 25¢ 25¢ 1¢					_____	_____
g)	25¢ 25¢ 25¢ 25¢ 10¢ 5¢					_____	_____
h)	25¢ 25¢ 25¢ 25¢ 10¢ 1¢					_____	_____
i)	25¢ 25¢ 25¢ 25¢ 5¢ 5¢					_____	_____
j)	25¢ 25¢ 25¢ 25¢ 5¢					_____	_____

3. Andy used 2 coins to buy a pen for $0.30.
   Which coins did he use?

4. Chris used 4 coins to buy a notebook for $0.70.
   Which coins did he use?

5. Draw a picture and add up each amount.

   a) 3 quarters, 2 dimes   b) 3 loonies, 2 quarters, 3 dimes   c) 4 loonies, 3 quarters, 2 nickels

6. Trade coins to make the amount with fewer coins.

   a) $1 $1 25¢   b) $1 $1 5¢ 5¢   c) $1 $1 $1 5¢ 5¢

Number Sense 2

Dollar notation and **cent notation** are related in the following way:

$1.00 = 100¢ $0.50 = 50¢ $0.05 = 5¢ $3.82 = 382¢

----

1. Write each amount in <u>cent notation</u>. The first is done for you.

   a) $3.00 = __300¢__   b) $4.00 = _____   c) $5.00 = _____   d) $1.00 = _____

   e) $7.00 = _____   f) $12.00 = _____   g) $15.00 = _____   h) $14.00 = _____

   i) $1.99 = _____   j) $1.11 = _____   k) $1.51 = _____   l) $0.04 = _____

   m) $0.82 = _____   n) $4.06 = _____   o) $0.30 = _____   p) $0.09 = _____

2. Write each amount in <u>dollar notation</u>. The first is done for you.

   a) 200¢ = __$2.00__   b)   7¢ = _____   c)   8¢ = _____   d)   50¢ = _____

   e) 150¢ = _____   f) 101¢ = _____   g) 116¢ = _____   h) 175¢ = _____

   i) 144¢ = _____   j) 250¢ = _____   k) 288¢ = _____   l) 468¢ = _____

   m) 45¢ = _____   n) 99¢ = _____   o)   3¢ = _____   p)   9¢ = _____

   q) 28¢ = _____   r)   1¢ = _____   s) 53¢ = _____   t)   7¢ = _____

3. Change the amount in dollar notation to cent notation. Then circle the greater amount.

   a)   78¢   or $1.78   b) $1.00   or   99¢   c) $5.00   or   6¢

   d) $4.98   or   497¢   e) 655¢   or $6.05   f) $0.88   or   187¢

4. Write the dollar amounts in <u>dollar notation</u>.

   a) eighty five cents = _____   b) four cents = _____

   c) eight dollars and five cents = _____   d) nine dollars and sixty four cents = _____

   e) six dollars and fifty two cents = _____   f) seven dollars and three cents = _____

NS3-64: Adding Money

1. Add.

a)
```
      6  3
  +   3  3
```

b)
```
      8  1
  +      3
```

c)
```
      5  4
  +   3  2
```

d)
```
      9  0
  +      9
```

e)
```
      8  2
  +   1  6
```

2. Vanessa spent $3.42 on breakfast and $4.55 on lunch. To find out how much she spent, she added the amounts using the following steps.

$	3.	4	2
+ $	4.	5	5

Step 1:
She lined up the numerals: she put dollars above dollars, dimes above dimes and pennies above pennies.

$	3.	4	2
+ $	4.	5	5
	7	9	7

Step 2:
She added the numerals, starting with the ones digits (the pennies).

$	3.	4	2
+ $	4.	5	5
	7.	9	7

Step 3:
She added a decimal to show the amount in dollars.

Find the total by adding.

a) $2.45 + $3.23

$	2.	4	5
+ $	3.	2	3
	.		

b) $4.81 + $2.07

$	.		
+ $	.		
	.		

c) $3.52 + $1.34

$	.		
+ $	.		

d) $7.23 + $1.64

$	.		
+ $	.		

3. In order to add the amounts below, you will have to regroup. The first one has been done for you.

a)
```
    1   1
  $ 4.  4   7
+ $ 2.  7   6
  7.    2   3
```

b)
```
  $ 3.  5   6
+ $ 6.  2   6
```

c)
```
  $ 5.  3   7
+ $ 3.  8   1
```

d)
```
  $ 7.  4   8
+ $ 1.  6   3
```

e)
```
  $ 3.  4   2
+ $ 3.  7   8
```

f)
```
  $ 6.  5   7
+ $ 1.  9   0
```

Number Sense 2

NS3-64: Adding Money (continued)

Answer the following questions in your notebook.

4. Add.

a) $2.18 + $3.45

b) $6.05 + $4.26

c) $5.63 + $2.82

d) $8.23 + $1.61

e) $5.25 + $4.29

5. How much did each child spend?

a) Shelly paid 50¢ for a muffin and 35¢ for an apple.

b) Anne bought a pencil for 23¢ and a pen for 65¢.

c) Amy bought a pair of socks for $1.25 and a pair of gloves for $4.14.

d) Josh bought a toy car for $4.24 and a notebook for $3.55.

6. ☐ Samuel paid for a plant with 2 toonies, 2 loonies and 1 quarter.

☐ Vinnie paid with 3 loonies, 2 quarters and 3 pennies.

☐ Krista paid with 2 toonies, 3 dimes and 4 pennies.

☐ Tim paid with 2 toonies, 1 loonie, 3 dimes and 2 nickels.

Match each child's name with the plant they bought.

| Plant A | Plant B | Plant C | Plant D | Plant E |
| $ 5.50 | $ 2.65 | $ 4.34 | $ 6.25 | $ 3.53 |

7. Mansa has $10.

a) If she buys a cap and a soccer ball, will she have enough money to buy a book?

b) Does Mansa have enough money to buy the tennis rackets and a cap?

$5.50

$3.29

$2.42

$7.65

NS3-65: Subtracting Money

1. Find the amount remaining by subtracting.

a)
	8	4
−	3	1

b)
	2	6
−		5

c)
	6	7
−	2	5

d)
	7	6
−	4	3

e)
	7	4
−	3	4

2. Answer the following word problems. Show your work.

a) Karim has 75¢. He lends 45¢ to his friend. How much money does he have left?

	7	5 ¢
−	4	5 ¢

b) Abi lost 42¢ from her pocket. She had 84¢. How much money does she have left?

		¢
−		¢

3. Subtract the given money amounts by regrouping once or twice.

An example has been done for you.

Step 1:

	5	10	
$	6.	0	0
− $	3.	4	1
		.	

Step 2:
9

	5	10	10
$	6.	0	0
− $	3.	4	1
$	2.	5	9

a)
$	5.	0	0
− $	4.	2	5

b)
$	9.	0	0
− $	4.	3	5

c)
$	7.	0	0
− $	3.	4	5

d)
$	3.	0	0
− $	1.	2	1

e)
$	5.	4	0
− $	2.	4	5

f)
$	9.	0	0
− $	5.	4	6

4. Amon has $5.27. Joan has $6.79. How much more money does Joan have?

5. Daniel buys a hat for $5.28. He pays $6.00. What change should he get back?

6. Anita bought a sandwich for $3.59. She paid $5.00 and received $1.31 change. Did she receive the correct change?

Number Sense 2

NS3-66: Equal Parts

Fractions name equal parts of a whole.

The pie is cut into 4 equal parts. 3 parts out of 4 are shaded.

$\frac{3}{4}$ of a pie is shaded.

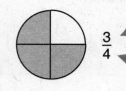

$\frac{3}{4}$

The **numerator** (3) tells you how many parts are counted.

The **denominator** (4) tells you how many parts are in the whole.

----

1. Name the fraction shown by the shaded part of each image.

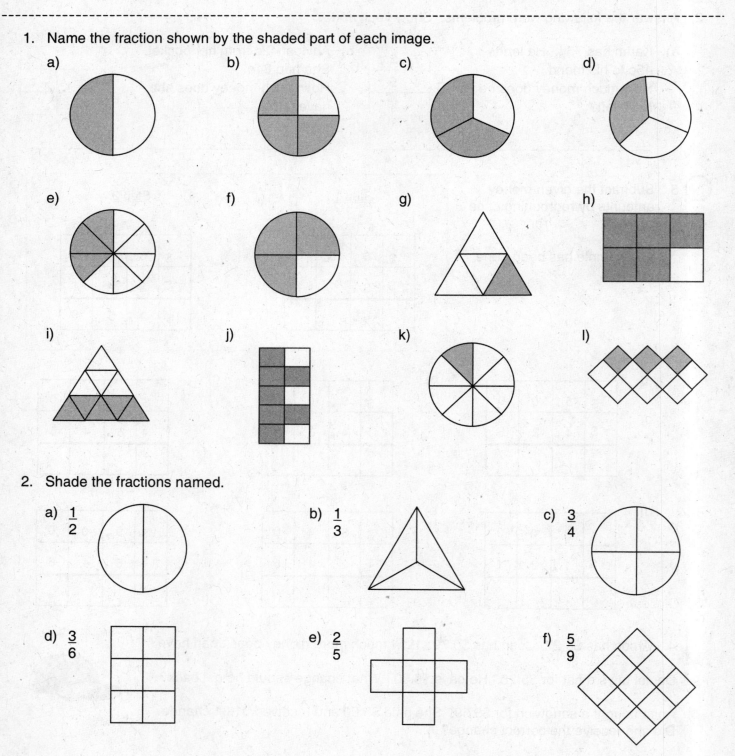

2. Shade the fractions named.

a) $\frac{1}{2}$

b) $\frac{1}{3}$

c) $\frac{3}{4}$

d) $\frac{3}{6}$

e) $\frac{2}{5}$

f) $\frac{5}{9}$

Number Sense 2

NS3-67: Models of Fractions

1. Name these shaded fractions.

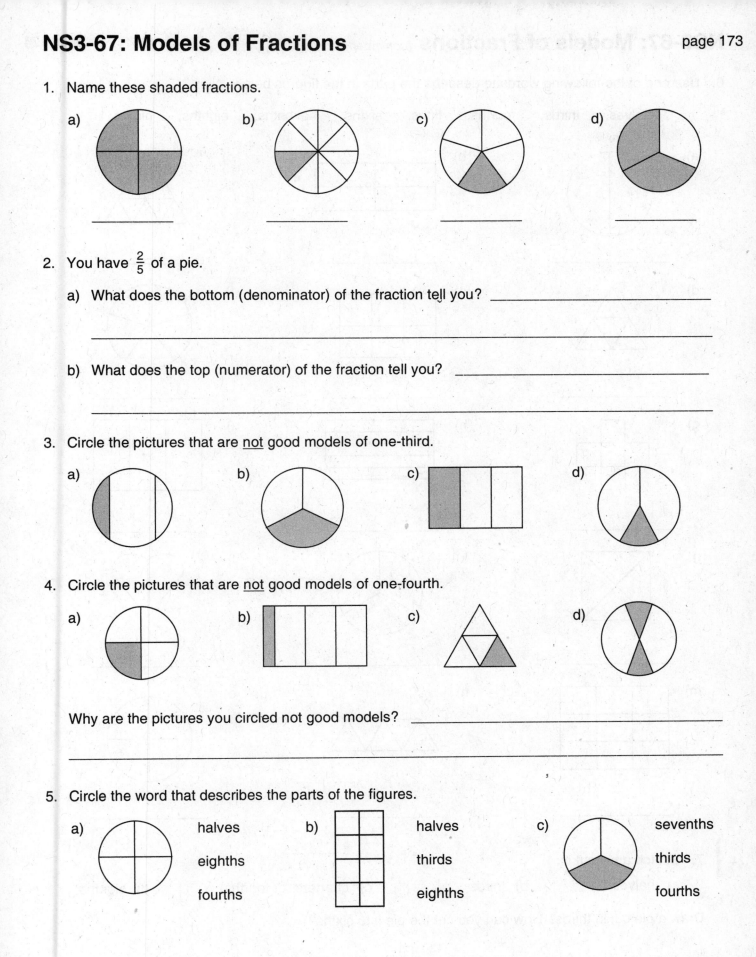

   a)   b)   c)   d)

   _____   _____   _____   _____

2. You have $\frac{2}{5}$ of a pie.

   a) What does the bottom (denominator) of the fraction tell you? _____

   _____

   b) What does the top (numerator) of the fraction tell you? _____

   _____

3. Circle the pictures that are <u>not</u> good models of one-third.

   a)   b)   c)   d)

4. Circle the pictures that are <u>not</u> good models of one-fourth.

   a)   b)   c)   d)

   Why are the pictures you circled not good models? _____

   _____

5. Circle the word that describes the parts of the figures.

   a)   halves   b)   halves   c)   sevenths

               eighths   thirds   thirds

               fourths   eighths   fourths

6. Use one of the following words to describe the parts in the figures below.

halves,   thirds,   fourths,   fifths,   sixths,   sevenths,   eighths,   ninths

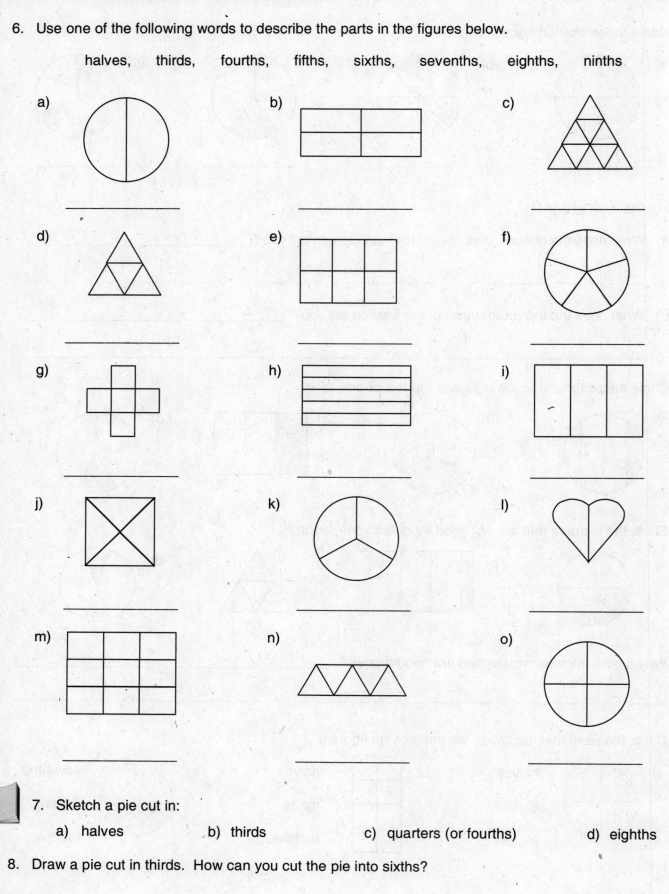

a)

b)

c)

d)

e)

f)

g)

h)

i)

j)

k)

l)

m)

n)

o)

7. Sketch a pie cut in:

   a) halves   b) thirds   c) quarters (or fourths)   d) eighths

8. Draw a pie cut in thirds. How can you cut the pie into sixths?

NS3-68: Fractions of a Region or a Length

1. Use a ruler to divide each line into:

    a) 4 equal parts:

    b) 2 equal parts:

    c) 3 equal parts:

    _____

    4 cm

    _____

    2 cm

    _____

    3 cm

2. Use a ruler to divide each box into:

    a) 3 equal parts:

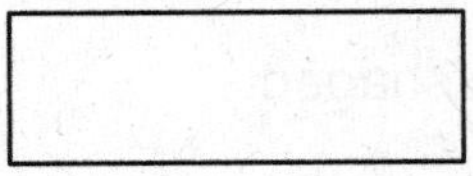

    b) 5 equal parts:

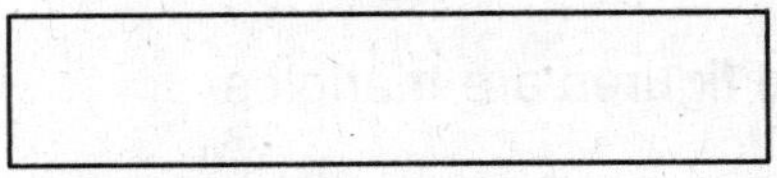

3. Using a ruler, find what fraction of each of the following boxes is shaded.

    a)

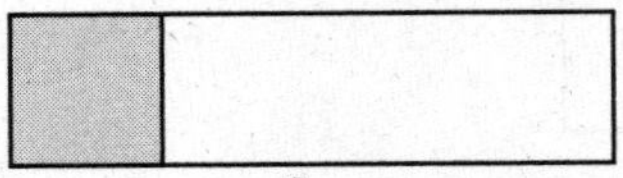

    _____ is shaded

    b)

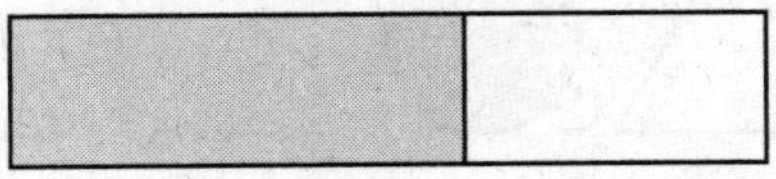

    _____ is shaded.

4. Using a ruler, complete the following figures to make a whole.

    a)

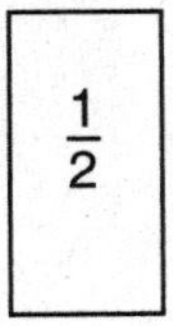

    $\frac{1}{2}$

    b)

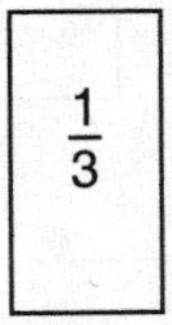

    $\frac{1}{3}$

    c)

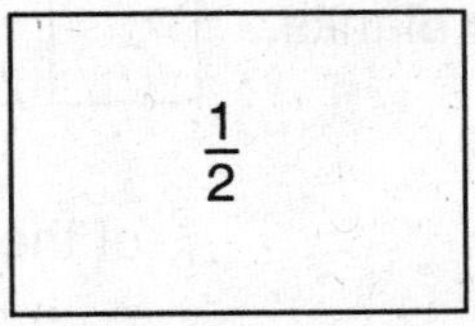

    $\frac{1}{2}$

5. Each of the lines below is $\frac{1}{3}$ of a whole line. Using a ruler, draw the rest to make a whole line.

    a) ———

    b) ————————

6. Draw 4 congruent rectangles on grid paper. Show 4 different ways to cut a rectangle in half.
    REMEMBER: "Congruent" means "the same shape and size."

7. On grid paper, draw a rectangle with width 2 boxes and length 4 boxes. Shade <u>half</u> of the boxes.
    How many boxes are in the whole rectangle?
    How many are in half?

NS3-69: Equal Parts of a Set

Fractions can name parts of a set: $\frac{2}{5}$ of the figures are circles, $\frac{2}{5}$ are triangles and $\frac{1}{5}$ are squares.

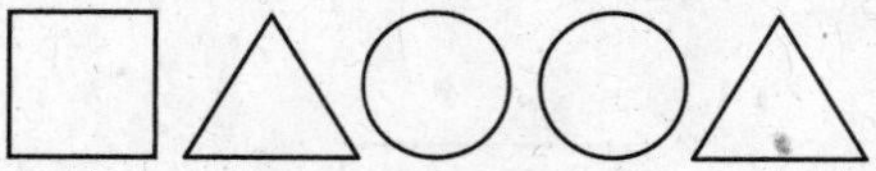

1. Fill in the blanks.

a)

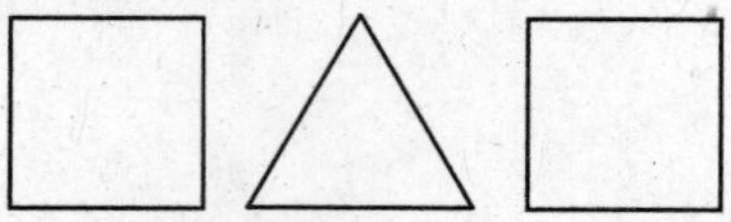

_____ of the figures are triangles.

_____ of the figures are squares.

b)

_____ of the figures are shaded.

_____ of the figures are unshaded.

c)

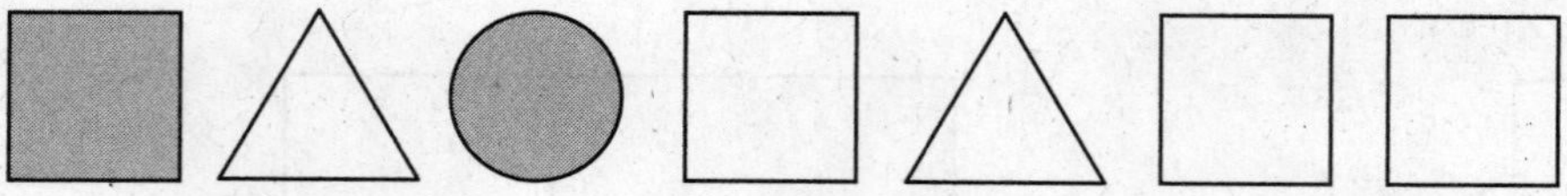

_____ of the figures are triangles.

_____ of the figures are squares.

_____ of the figures are shaded.

_____ of the figures are unshaded.

2. Fill in the blanks.

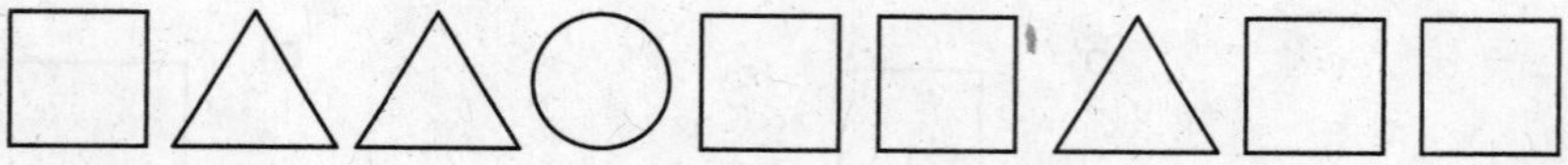

$\frac{5}{9}$ of the figures are _______________

$\frac{3}{9}$ of the figures are _______________

$\frac{1}{9}$ of the figures are _______________

3. Write at least 3 fraction statements for the picture:

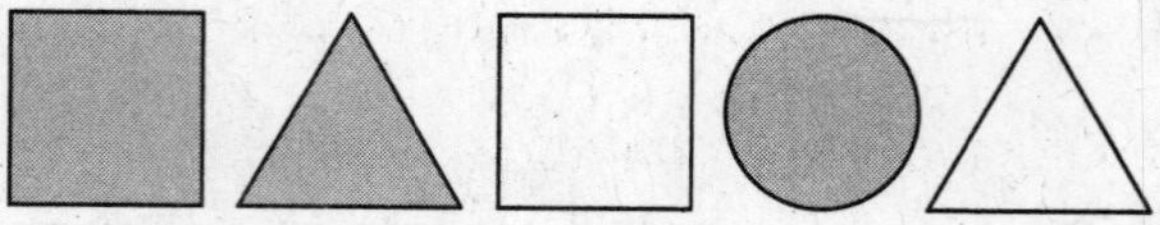

i) _______________

ii) _______________

iii) _______________

4. △◯△◉◯ Can you describe this picture in two different ways using the fraction $\frac{2}{5}$?

5. A baseball team wins 4 games and loses 2 games.

    a) How many games did the team play? _____

    b) What <u>fraction</u> of the games did the team win? _____

    c) Did the team win more than half its games? _____

6. A hockey team wins 6 games, loses 4 games and ties 1 game.
    What fractions of the games did the team:

    a) win? _____   b) lose? _____   c) tie? _____

7. Draw a picture to solve the puzzle.

    There are 5 triangles and squares.

    $\frac{2}{5}$ of the figures are shaded.

    $\frac{3}{5}$ of the figures are triangles, the rest are squares.

    One triangle is shaded.

8. There are 5 children: $\frac{2}{5}$ are boys and $\frac{3}{5}$ are girls.

    a) Draw a picture to show the girls and boys.

    b) Describe the picture. (How many boys are there and how many girls?)

9. Name a set of things in your home and describe some fraction of the set.

1. What fraction has a larger numerator, $\frac{1}{4}$ or $\frac{3}{4}$? _____

   Which fraction is larger? _____

   Explain your thinking: _____

   _____

2. Circle the larger fraction in each pair.

   a) $\frac{2}{11}$ or $\frac{5}{11}$?   b) $\frac{9}{11}$ or $\frac{2}{11}$?   c) $\frac{6}{7}$ or $\frac{3}{7}$?

3. Two fractions have the same **denominators** (bottoms) but different **numerators** (tops). How can you tell which fraction is larger?

   _____

   _____

   _____

4. a) Beside each pie, write the fraction that is shaded.

   Pie 1   **Pie 2**   **Pie 3**   **Pie 4**

   b) Which pie has the <u>greatest</u> number of pieces? _____

   c) Which pie has the <u>smallest</u> sized pieces? _____

   d) Which fraction has the <u>biggest</u> denominator: $\frac{1}{2}$, $\frac{1}{3}$, $\frac{1}{4}$ or $\frac{1}{8}$? _____

   e) Which fraction is the <u>smallest</u> size: $\frac{1}{2}$, $\frac{1}{3}$, $\frac{1}{4}$ or $\frac{1}{8}$? _____

5. Which fraction is larger, $\frac{1}{2}$ or $\frac{1}{100}$? _____

   Explain your thinking: _____

   _____

6. a) Cut the following square in half.

   What fraction of the square is each part? _____

   b) Next, cut each of these parts in half.

   What fraction of the square is each new part? _____

   c) As the denominator of the fraction <u>increases</u>, what happens to the size of each piece?

   _____

7. Circle the <u>larger</u> fraction in each pair.

   a) $\frac{1}{3}$ or $\frac{1}{7}$?

   b) $\frac{1}{11}$ or $\frac{1}{9}$?

   c) $\frac{1}{257}$ or $\frac{1}{242}$?

8. Fraction A and Fraction B have the same **numerators** (tops) but different **denominators** (bottoms). How can you tell which fraction is larger?

   _____

   _____

9. Circle the <u>larger</u> fraction in each pair.

   a) $\frac{1}{2}$ or $\frac{1}{7}$?

   b) $\frac{3}{12}$ or $\frac{7}{12}$?

   c) $\frac{2}{5}$ or $\frac{4}{5}$?

10. 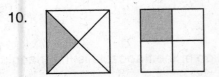 The two shaded pieces to the left have different shapes. But are they different sizes? Explain your thinking.

    _____

    _____

11. Is it possible for $\frac{1}{3}$ of a pie to be bigger than $\frac{1}{2}$ of another pie? Show your thinking with a picture.

12. What fraction is shaded? Show how you know.

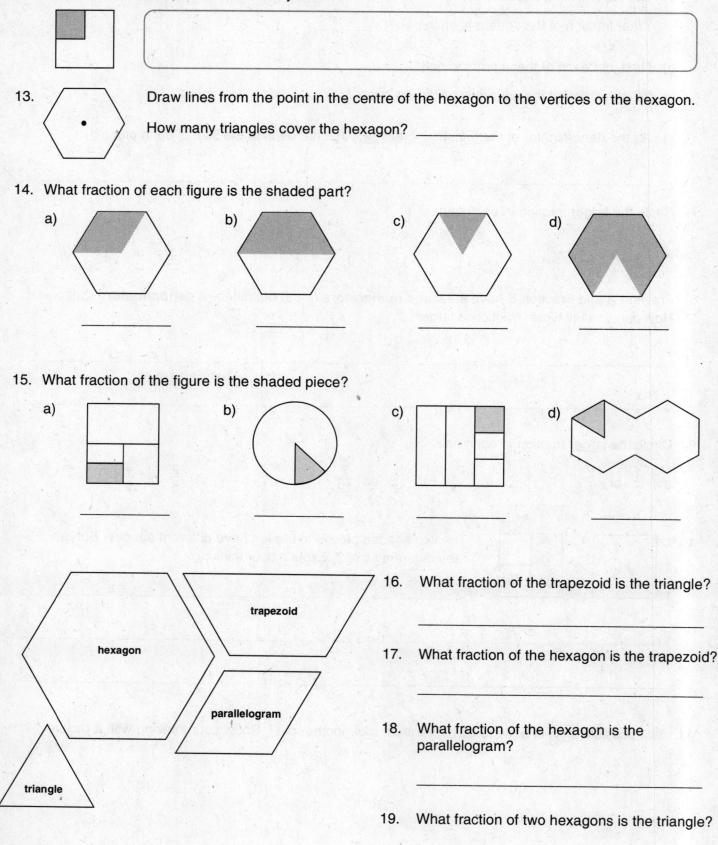

13. Draw lines from the point in the centre of the hexagon to the vertices of the hexagon.

How many triangles cover the hexagon? _____

14. What fraction of each figure is the shaded part?

a) _____ b) _____ c) _____ d) _____

15. What fraction of the figure is the shaded piece?

a) _____ b) _____ c) _____ d) _____

16. What fraction of the trapezoid is the triangle?

_____

17. What fraction of the hexagon is the trapezoid?

_____

18. What fraction of the hexagon is the parallelogram?

_____

19. What fraction of two hexagons is the triangle?

_____

NS3-71: Sharing and Fractions

Richard has 6 cookies. He wants to give $\frac{1}{3}$ of his cookies to a friend.

To do so, he shares the cookies equally onto 3 plates.

There are 3 equal groups, so each group is $\frac{1}{3}$ of 6. There are 2 cookies in each group, so $\frac{1}{3}$ of 6 is 2.

----

1. How many plates should Richard use to divide his cookies if he wants to give away:

a) $\frac{1}{2}$ of his cookies.

b) $\frac{1}{4}$ of his cookies.

c) $\frac{1}{5}$ of his cookies.

_____ plates

_____ plates

_____ plates

2. Find the fraction of the whole amount by sharing the cookies equally. The first one is started for you.
   HINT: Draw the correct number of plates then place the cookies one at a time.

a) Find $\frac{1}{4}$ of 8 cookies.

$\frac{1}{4}$ of 8 is _____

b) Find $\frac{1}{2}$ of 10 cookies.

$\frac{1}{2}$ of 10 is _____

c) Find $\frac{1}{2}$ of 4 cookies.

$\frac{1}{2}$ of 4 is _____

d) Find $\frac{1}{3}$ of 9 cookies.

$\frac{1}{3}$ of 9 is _____

3. By drawing circles and dots, find:

a) $\frac{1}{3}$ of 12

$\frac{1}{3}$ of 12 is _____

b) $\frac{1}{2}$ of 8

$\frac{1}{2}$ of 8 is _____

c) $\frac{1}{2}$ of 6

$\frac{1}{2}$ of 6 is _____

d) $\frac{1}{4}$ of 12

$\frac{1}{4}$ of 12 is _____

 Number Sense 2

4. Kevin finds $\frac{1}{2}$ of 6 by dividing: 6 divided into 2 groups gives 3 in each group ($6 \div 2 = 3$).

   Write a division statement to find the amount.

   a) $\frac{1}{2}$ of 8   b) $\frac{1}{2}$ of 10   c) $\frac{1}{2}$ of 16   d) $\frac{1}{2}$ of 20

   _____ $8 \div 2 = 4$ _____   _____   _____   _____

   e) $\frac{1}{2}$ of 6   f) $\frac{1}{2}$ of 14   g) $\frac{1}{2}$ of 18   h) $\frac{1}{2}$ of 4

   _____   _____   _____   _____

5. Circle $\frac{1}{2}$ of each set of lines.

   HINT: Count the lines and divide by 2.

   a) | | | | | b) | | | | | | | | | c) | | | |

   d) | | | | | | | | e) | | | | | | | | | | |

6. Fill in the missing number to make a fraction that is <u>equal to</u> $\frac{1}{2}$.

   a) $\frac{\square}{10}$ b) $\frac{\square}{6}$ c) $\frac{\square}{4}$ d) $\frac{\square}{8}$ e) $\frac{\square}{20}$

   f) $\frac{\square}{12}$ g) $\frac{\square}{14}$ h) $\frac{\square}{18}$ i) $\frac{4}{\square}$ j) $\frac{3}{\square}$

7. Complete each statement by writing "more than half," "half," or "less than half."

   HINT: Start by finding half of the larger number by skip counting by 2s.

   a) 4 is _____ more than half _____ of 6   b) 4 is _____ of 8

   c) 7 is _____ of 12   d) 3 is _____ of 10

8. Circle the fractions that are **greater than** $\frac{1}{2}$.

   HINT: Start by finding half of the denominator.

   a) $\frac{7}{10}$ b) $\frac{3}{10}$ c) $\frac{5}{8}$ d) $\frac{2}{6}$ e) $\frac{2}{4}$

9. Circle $\frac{1}{4}$ of each set of triangles.

   HINT: Count the triangles and divide by 4.

   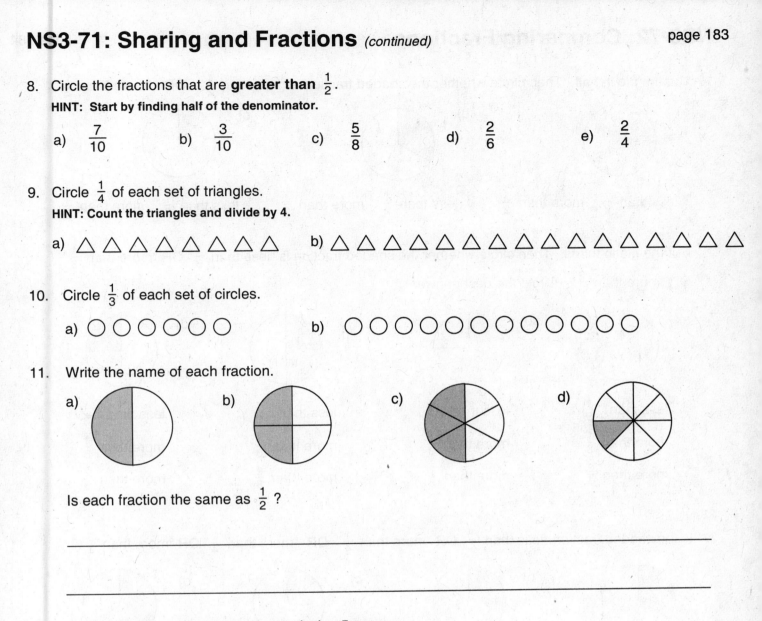

10. Circle $\frac{1}{3}$ of each set of circles.

11. Write the name of each fraction.

    a)   b)   c)   d)

    Is each fraction the same as $\frac{1}{2}$?

    _____

    _____

12. A hockey team plays 12 games and wins 5 games.
    Did they win more than half their games?
    Explain.

    _____

    _____

13. Beth is making a black and white patchwork quilt. Half the quilt has been completed.

    a) How many black squares will be in the finished quilt?

    b) How did you find your answer? (Did you use a calculation, a picture, a model, a list?)

    c) Is your answer reasonable? How could you check it?

NS3-72: Comparing Fractions

1. Cut the pie in half. Then circle whether the shaded fraction is "less than $\frac{1}{2}$" **OR** "more than $\frac{1}{2}$".

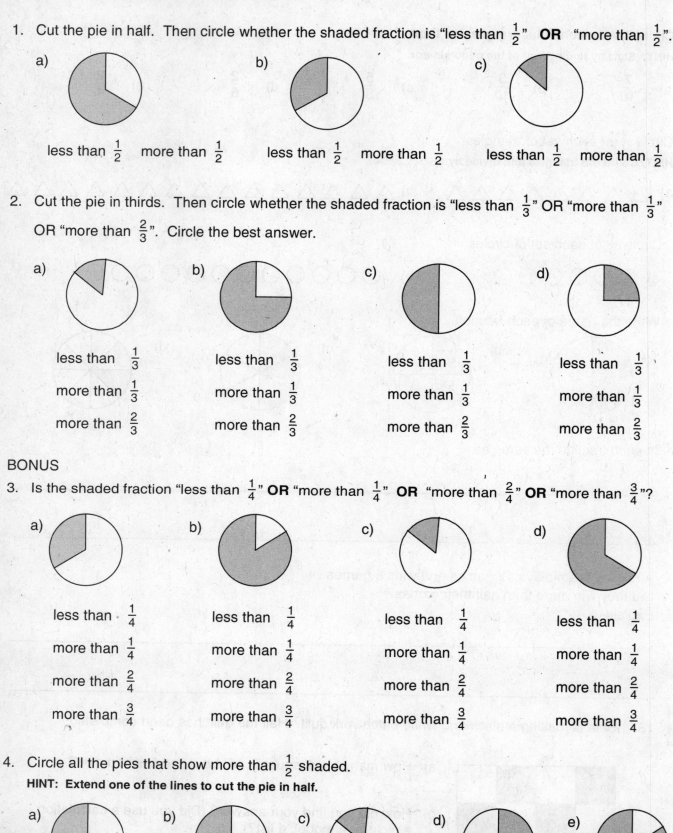

   a)

   less than $\frac{1}{2}$ more than $\frac{1}{2}$

   b)

   less than $\frac{1}{2}$ more than $\frac{1}{2}$

   c)

   less than $\frac{1}{2}$ more than $\frac{1}{2}$

2. Cut the pie in thirds. Then circle whether the shaded fraction is "less than $\frac{1}{3}$" OR "more than $\frac{1}{3}$" OR "more than $\frac{2}{3}$". Circle the best answer.

   a)

   less than $\frac{1}{3}$

   more than $\frac{1}{3}$

   more than $\frac{2}{3}$

   b)

   less than $\frac{1}{3}$

   more than $\frac{1}{3}$

   more than $\frac{2}{3}$

   c)

   less than $\frac{1}{3}$

   more than $\frac{1}{3}$

   more than $\frac{2}{3}$

   d)

   less than $\frac{1}{3}$

   more than $\frac{1}{3}$

   more than $\frac{2}{3}$

BONUS

3. Is the shaded fraction "less than $\frac{1}{4}$" **OR** "more than $\frac{1}{4}$" **OR** "more than $\frac{2}{4}$" **OR** "more than $\frac{3}{4}$"?

   a)

   less than $\frac{1}{4}$

   more than $\frac{1}{4}$

   more than $\frac{2}{4}$

   more than $\frac{3}{4}$

   b)

   less than $\frac{1}{4}$

   more than $\frac{1}{4}$

   more than $\frac{2}{4}$

   more than $\frac{3}{4}$

   c)

   less than $\frac{1}{4}$

   more than $\frac{1}{4}$

   more than $\frac{2}{4}$

   more than $\frac{3}{4}$

   d)

   less than $\frac{1}{4}$

   more than $\frac{1}{4}$

   more than $\frac{2}{4}$

   more than $\frac{3}{4}$

4. Circle all the pies that show more than $\frac{1}{2}$ shaded.

   HINT: Extend one of the lines to cut the pie in half.

   a)   b)   c)   d)   e)

NS3-72: Comparing Fractions (continued)

5. Circle the pies that show exactly $\frac{1}{4}$ shaded.

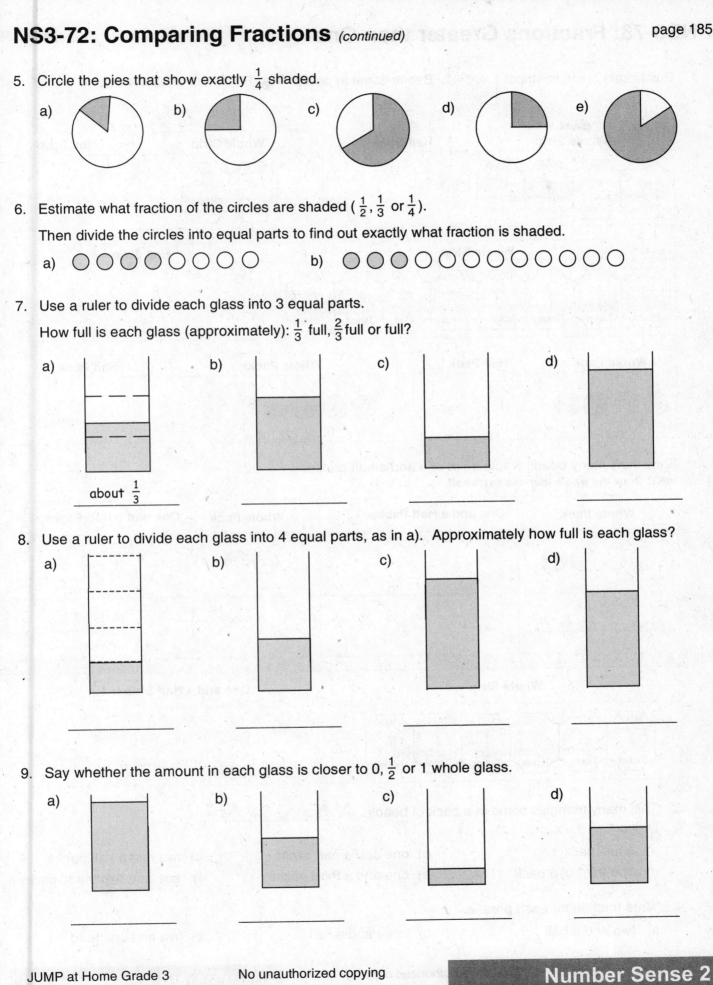

a)   b)   c)   d)   e)

6. Estimate what fraction of the circles are shaded ($\frac{1}{2}$, $\frac{1}{3}$ or $\frac{1}{4}$).

    Then divide the circles into equal parts to find out exactly what fraction is shaded.

    a)   b)

7. Use a ruler to divide each glass into 3 equal parts.

    How full is each glass (approximately): $\frac{1}{3}$ full, $\frac{2}{3}$ full or full?

    a)   b)   c)   d)

    about $\frac{1}{3}$

8. Use a ruler to divide each glass into 4 equal parts, as in a). Approximately how full is each glass?

    a)   b)   c)   d)

9. Say whether the amount in each glass is closer to 0, $\frac{1}{2}$ or 1 whole glass.

    a)   b)   c)   d)

No unauthorized copying   **Number Sense 2**

1. Bus tickets come in strips: . Beads come in packs: 🌀🌀. Show half of each amount.

Whole Strip	Half Strip
BUS Ticket BUS Ticket BUS Ticket BUS Ticket	

Whole Strip	Half Strip
BUS Ticket BUS Ticket	

Whole Strip	Half Strip
BUS Ticket BUS Ticket BUS Ticket BUS Ticket BUS Ticket BUS Ticket BUS Ticket BUS Ticket	

Whole Pack	Half Pack
⬤⬤⬤⬤	

Whole Pack	Half Pack
⬤⬤⬤⬤⬤⬤	

2. Show how many beads would be in one and a half packs.
   HINT: Draw the whole then the extra half.

Whole Pack	One and a Half Packs: $1\frac{1}{2}$
⬤⬤⬤⬤	
△△△△△△	

Whole Pack	One and a Half Packs: $1\frac{1}{2}$
⬤⬤	
◇◇◇◇	

Whole Strip	One and a Half Strips: $1\frac{1}{2}$
BUS Ticket BUS Ticket BUS Ticket BUS Ticket BUS Ticket BUS Ticket	

3. This many triangles come in a pack of beads: △△△△△△.
   Draw:

   a) a half pack
   b) one and a half packs
   c) two and a half packs
   d) one third of a pack
   e) one and a third packs
   f) one and two thirds packs

4. Write fraction for each phrase.

   a) two and a half
   b) three and a half
   c) five and one third

Number Sense 2

1. Two half squares △△ make a whole square ◹. How many squares are in each picture?

   a)

   b)

   c)

2. There are 10 berries on a strawberry plant.
   Bill eats half.
   How many are left?

3. There are 9 grapes in a bunch.
   Jamil eats one-third of the grapes.
   How many are left in the bunch?

4. Jane eats $\frac{4}{5}$ of a pie.

   What fraction of the pie is left over?

   Explain your answer with a picture.

5. Which fraction is larger, $\frac{1}{2}$ or $\frac{1}{8}$?

   Explain.

6. What fraction of a pie must you add to $\frac{1}{4}$ of a pie to make a whole pie?

7. Carl says $\frac{1}{2}$ of a pie is the same as $\frac{2}{4}$ of a pie.
   Is he right?

8. a) How many whole squares are there altogether?

   b) How many whole squares are shaded?
       What fraction of the figure is shaded?

9. a) How many whole squares are there altogether?

   b) How many whole squares are shaded?

   c) What fraction of the figure is shaded?

10. What would happen if 2 friends tried to share 5 cookies?

    If the friends broke one of the cookies in half,

    how many cookies would each friend get?

    Draw a picture to show your answer.

11. Jodi must walk 8 blocks to school.

    She has walked 3 blocks so far.

    What fraction of the distance is left to walk?

Number Sense 2

1. Rachel is going bug watching! This is what she sees. (Try to do the sums in your head.)

    a) 16 spotted butterflies
       12 plain butterflies

       How many altogether? ___

    b) 24 ladybugs in the air
       13 ladybugs on the ground

       How many in all? ___

    c) 36 brown ants
       22 black flies

       How many altogether? ___

2. James went bug watching. The bugs got scared! (Try to do the subtraction in your head.)

    a) 25 butterflies
       13 flew away

       How many are left? ___

    b) 57 ants
       46 marched away

       How many are left? ___

    c) 37 hornets
       33 flew to their nest

       How many are left? ___

3. a) A dragonfly has 4 wings.

       How many wings do…

       …2 dragonflies have? ____

       …3 dragonflies have? ____

       …4 dragonflies have? ____

    b) A bumblebee has 3 stripes.

       How many stripes on…

       …3 bumblebees? ____

       …4 bumblebees? ____

       …5 bumblebees? ____

    c) A butterfly has 2 antenna.

       How many antenna on…

       …2 butterflies? ____

       …4 butterflies? ____

       …6 butterflies? ____

    d) A ladybug has 6 legs.

       How many legs on…

       …2 ladybugs? ____

       …3 ladybugs? ____

       …5 ladybugs? ____

4. You are at the grocery store. Multiply or divide.

    Example   16 apples. 4 boxes. How many apples in each box?

                    _____Divide_____

    | Read the problem. |
    | Look for clue words. |
    | Decide what to do. |

    a) 20 boxes.
       5 shelves.

       How many boxes on
       each shelf?

       _____

    b) 5 boxes.
       4 bagels in each box.

       How many bagels
       altogether?

       _____

    c) 7 bags.
       3 apples in each bag.

       How many apples
       altogether?

       _____

Answer the word problems below in your notebook.

1. Use the following information to decide where you need to add or subtract:

   Information:
   - Π Jason collected 32 cards
   - Π Robin collected 46 cards
   - Π Henry collected 28 cards
   - Π Kathy collected 15 cards
   - Π Kayla collected 27 cards

   a) How many cards did Henry and Robin collect together?

   b) How many cards did Kathy and Kayla collect together?

   c) How many MORE cards did Robin have than Jason?

   d) How many MORE cards did Jason have than Kathy?

   BONUS

   e) Which pair of children had more cards, Henry and Kayla *or* Robin and Kathy?

   f) How many <u>more</u> cards did this pair of children collect?

2. The chart shows the price of tickets for a play.

   Fill in the missing numbers.

Tickets	1	2		4	
Price	$5	$10			$25

3. Without counting, estimate how many dots are in the first box.

   About how many dots would be in all 4 boxes?

   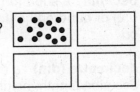

   How do you know?

4. A store sells 3 kinds of fruit: apples, bananas and oranges.
   One day, they sold 300 pieces of fruit.
   If they sold 152 apples and 75 bananas, how many oranges did they sell?

5. Which two numbers have a <u>sum</u> of 12 and a <u>difference</u> of 4?

6. Andy bought 5 packs of gum for 79¢ each.
   How much change did he receive from $5.00?

   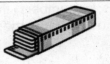

Glossary

add to find the total when combining two or more numbers together

area the amount of space occupied by the face or surface of an object

array an arrangement of things (for example, objects, symbols, or numbers) in rows and columns

base-10 materials materials used to represent ones (ones squares or cubes), tens (tens strips or rods), hundreds (hundreds squares or flats), and thousands (thousands cubes)

centimetre (cm) a unit of measurement used to describe length, height, or thickness

cent notation a way to express an amount of money (for example, 40¢)

column things (for example, objects, symbols, numbers) that run up and down

consecutive numbers numbers that occur one after the other on a number line

coordinate system a grid with labelled rows and columns, used to describe the location of a dot or object, for example the dot is at (A,3)

core the part of a pattern that repeats

decimal a short form for tenths (for example, 0.2) or hundredths (for example, 0.02), and so on

decimetre (dm) a unit of measurement used to describe length, height, or thickness; equal to 10 cm

decreasing sequence a sequence where each number is less than the one before it

denominator the number on the bottom portion of a fraction; tells you how many parts are in a whole

diagonal things (for example, objects, symbols, or numbers) that are in a line from one corner to another corner

difference the "gap" between two numbers; the remainder left after subtraction

divide to find how many times one number contains another number

divisible by containing a number a specific number of times without having a remainder (for example, 15 is divisible by 5 and 3)

divisor in a division problem, the number that is divided into another number

dollar notation a way to express an amount of money (for example, $4.50)

equivalent fractions fractions that represent the same amount, but have different denominators (for example,
$$\frac{2}{3} = \frac{4}{6})$$

estimate a guess or calculation of an approximate number

even number the numbers you say when counting by 2s (starting at 0)

expanded form a way to write a number that shows the place value of each digit (for example, 27 in expanded form can be written as 2 tens + 7 ones, or 20 + 7)

fraction a number used to name a part of a set or a region

greater than a term used to describe a number that is higher in value than another number

growing pattern a pattern in which each term is greater than the previous term

improper fraction a fraction that has a numerator that is larger than the denominator; this represents more than a whole

Glossary

increasing sequence a sequence where each number is greater than the one before it

kilometre (km) a unit of measurement for length; equal to 1000 cm

less than a term used to describe a number that is lower in value than another number

metre (m) a unit of measurement used to describe length, height, or thickness; equal to 100 cm

millimetre (mm) a unit of measurement used to describe length, height, or thickness; equal to 0.1 cm

mixed fraction a mixture of a whole number and a fraction

model a physical representation (for example, using base-10 materials to represent a number)

more than a term used to describe a number that is higher in value than another number

multiple of a number that is the result of multiplying one number by another specific number (for example, the multiples of 5 are 0, 5, 10, 15, and so on)

multiply to find the total of a number times another number

number line a line with numbers marked at intervals, used to help with skip counting

numerator the number on the top portion of a fraction; tells you how many parts are counted

odd number the numbers you say when counting by 2s (starting at 1); numbers that are not even

pattern (repeating pattern) the same repeating group of objects, numbers, or attributes

perimeter the distance around the outside of a shape

period the part of a pattern that repeats; the core of the pattern

product the result from multiplying two or more numbers together

quotient the result from dividing one number by another number

rectangle a quadrilateral with four right angles

rectangular having a face that is a rectangle (for example, a prism with a four-sided base)

regroup to exchange one place value for another place value (for example, 10 ones squares for 1 tens strip)

remainder the number left over after dividing or subtracting (for example, $10 \div 3 = 3$ R1)

row things (for example, objects, symbols, or numbers) that run left to right

set a group of like objects

skip counting counting by a number (for example, 2s, 3s, 4s) by "skipping" over the numbers in between

square centimetre (cm^2) a unit of measurement used to describe area

subtract to take away one or more numbers from another number

sum the result from adding two or more numbers together

T-table a chart used to compare two sequences of numbers

About the Authors

JOHN MIGHTON is a mathematician, author, and playwright. He completed a Ph.D. in mathematics at the University of Toronto and is currently a fellow of the Fields Institute for Mathematical Research. The founder of JUMP Math (www.jumpmath.org), Mighton also gives lectures to student teachers at York University and the Ontario Institute for Studies in Education, and invited talks and training sessions for parents and educators. He is the author of the *JUMP at Home* workbooks and the national bestsellers *The Myth of Ability* and *The End of Ignorance*. He has won the Governor General's Literary Award and the Siminovitch Prize for his plays.

DR. ANNA KLEBANOV received her B.Sc., M.Sc., Ph.D., and teaching certificate from the Technion – Israel Institute of Technology. She is the recipient of three teaching awards for excellence. She began her career at JUMP Math as a curriculum writer in 2007, working with Dr. John Mighton and Dr. Sindi Sabourin on JUMP Math's broad range of publications.

DR. SINDI SABOURIN received her Ph.D. in mathematics from Queen's University, specializing in commutative algebra. She is the recipient of the Governor General's Gold Medal Award from Queen's University and a National Sciences and Research Council Postdoctoral Fellowship. Her career with JUMP Math began in 2003 as a volunteer doing in-class tutoring, one-on-one tutoring, as well as working on answer keys. In 2006, she became a curriculum writer working on JUMP Math's broad range of publications.